Who *Are* We?

Who *Are* We?

And How Will We Survive in the Age of Asia?

Hugo de Burgh

FIRST EDITION

ISBNs:
Paperback: 978-1-80541-455-1
eBook: 978-1-80541-456-8

In a world increasingly dominated by Asia, the need for deep economic reform in Britain is growing ever more urgent. This book charts the path to recovery.

> Larry Elliott, Economics Editor, *The Guardian* and author (with Dan Atkinson) of *Going South, Fantasy Island, The Gods that Failed* and *The Age of Insecurity*

de Burgh captures the spirit of the Somewhere revolt against the Anywhere domination of our economy and culture.

> David Goodhart, author of *Head Hand Heart: The Struggle for Dignity and Status in the 21st Century* and *The Road to Somewhere: The Populist Revolt and the Future of Politics*

Hugo de Burgh has provided a rightly scathing critique of a British polity unable to set out a properly radical, detailed programme for a rejuvenated country.

> John Lloyd, contributing editor at the *Financial Times* and former editor of *Time Out* and the *New Statesman*

In this smart book Hugo de Burgh allows Britain to see itself through Chinese eyes. Essential reading.

> Tony Sewell, founder and chair of Generating Genius and former chair of the Commission on Race and Ethnic Disparities

thinking

KEIR HARDIE

bonnie fechter

Contents

WISE in a World Turned Upside Down

....

A China Story

In 1792, the UK sent ambassadors to show China, the richest and most splendid of empires, why it was in China's interests to cooperate with the most rapidly developing nation. The offer was rejected by a Chinese government which had the answer to everything and did not wish to take note of what was happening far away. The Chinese Emperor could not see what was obvious to the British: Developments around the world were rendering redundant how he saw himself and China's identity. The Emperor had no clothes.

Irritated by Chinese obduracy, 50 years after being rejected, Britain used its greater power to force the door open. The seizure of Hong Kong inaugurated 150 years of chaos in China and the ruin of its civilisation. This is a story that every Chinese schoolchild learns as a terrible warning of the perils of ignorance and arrogance.

....

Are we, now, like that Emperor?

In this 21st century, Asian countries will come to predominate in world affairs unless mutual resentment of the superpowers leads to a global war which exterminates civilised life.

The Western share of the global economy will continue to shrink. The proportion of the world's population that is European is going down (from 22% in 1950) to 7%. Africa's, then 9%, is now 39%. Three of the world's most populous nations—China, India and Indonesia—are in Asia. In purchasing power parity (PPP) terms, China became the world's largest economy in 2014, although it had been a mere 10% of the size of the American economy in 1980.[1]

In measures such as life expectancy and educational attainment, some Asian countries are now ahead of most in the West.[2] Many in Indonesia, Malaysia and Vietnam are better off than Europeans. Central and West Asia are modernising rapidly.[3] Even Pakistan and Bangladesh, long the despair of economists, have burgeoning middle classes. The Indian economy, following vast institutional and

[1] Mahbubani, K. (2019) *Has the West Lost It?* London: Penguin, p43 For a careful assessment of the relative strengths and weaknesses of the USA and China, see Zakaria, F (2023) 'The self-doubting superpower: America shouldn't give up on the world it made' in *Foreign Affairs*, January/February 2024
[2] Ferguson (2012) *The Great Degeneration,* London: Alan Lane, p35
[3] The swift development of many Asian countries, and the connection between this development and their relationships with China, is very well described in Khanna, Parag (2019) *The Future is Asian*, New York: Simon and Schuster

infrastructure developments undertaken in recent years, is predicted to surge ahead over the next 25.[4] At present, Asia's epicentre is China: 'The biggest player in the history of man'.[5] No matter that, thanks to some dysfunctional political choices, Chinese growth will not be as startling as once predicted;[6] our lives, like those of almost everybody in the world, are every day affected by decisions made in China, the economy of which already accounts for close to 20% of world GDP.[7]

We need to see the world as it is, not as we wish it were. Today, we in WISE are particularly blinkered or misinformed about China[8] and the rise of Asia's other

---

[4] Nageswaran, V. Anantha and Kaur, Gurvinder (2023) Don't Bet Against India, *Foreign Affairs*, Feb 17th, 2023

[5] A phrase often attributed to Lee Kuan Yew. I put in 'At present' when reminded by Alastair Mellon of the challenges to China's continued progress. The population is ageing rapidly, and young women no longer want to have children.

[6] In 2007, the then PRC premier described China's economy as "unstable, unbalanced, uncoordinated, and unsustainable". It is in even worse trouble now, yet the long term future is not in doubt. For the negative view, see Evans Pritchard. Ambrose (2004) 'China's economy is unstable and unsustainable', in *The Daily Telegraph* 260124. Of the many bad political decisions, the worst was the one child policy, and not only because it has led to the demographic 'timebomb'.

[7] Zakaria (2023) 'The self-doubting superpower' p 50

[8] HEPI (Higher Education Policy Institute) Report 2022 (Understanding-China-The-study-of-China-and-Mandarin-in-UK-schools-and-universities.pdf (hepi.ac.uk) See also Brown, Kerry (2019) *The Future of UK-China Relations: The Search for a New Model* London: Agenda Publishing

vast communities and their associations with China. So confident are our politicians of our superiority and the protection of the USA that they appear to have no more processed the new situation than did China's leaders two centuries ago. China was the most long-lasting and successful human civilisation there had ever been, and yet it was on the verge of collapse.

This matters because the UK economy is de-developing: Our debts are overwhelming, society is fragmenting, and the future is bleak if a multitude of problems are not tackled. All our most thoughtful and public service-minded say this, from economists to philosophers and journalists,[9] from the brightest of our civil servants to leaders of industry and the professions. Some of them will be cited in this book.

---

[9] The journalists include, for example, Hutton, Will (2023) Let's stop kidding ourselves we're a rich nation and get real... the UK's gone bust, *The Observer*, 13/08/2023; Ashworth-Hayes, Sam (2023) Britain is quietly inching towards a fate worse than bankruptcy in *The Daily Telegraph* 26/10/2023; Heath, Allister (2023) A new financial crisis is upon us – and our political class can no longer lie, in *The Daily Telegraph* 4/10/2023; Frost, David (2023) The political class is in denial about the true crisis now afflicting Britain, in *The Daily Telegraph* 13/10/2023; Jacobs, Sherelle (2022) Liz Truss has just two months to save broken Britain from terminal decline, in *The Daily Telegraph* 5/09/2022. These warnings have been uttered for well over a decade. See the book by economics editor for *The Observer*, Inman, Philip (2012) *The Financial Crisis,* London: Guardian Shorts and the works of Larry Elliott and Dan Atkinson of *The Guardian,* (2007) *Fantasy Island,* (2009) *The Gods that Failed* and (2012) *Going South.*

The Offshore Islanders[10]

Once upon a time, a British naval commander, when asked to take note of a much larger enemy fleet ahead, put his telescope to his blind eye and declared, "I see no ships." We can be thrilled by Nelson's chutzpah because we know he won the Battle of Copenhagen, but our politicians are using the same gesture in battles they can never win.

When our politicians pour taxpayers' money into wars abroad, and when they pompously assert our moral superiority as they call out selected countries for human rights violations or the temerity to be different, they demonstrate that they have not yet understood that those who waged the Iraq and Afghan wars are not taken seriously either as proconsuls of a virtual empire, or moral missionaries. In other words, our politicians' conception of our identity is outdated: They are still imperialists, though the Empire has evaporated.

When the UK was in the EU, we could forget about the Empire. The EU, for the political classes at least, was about subsuming national identity into a new European identity. EU officials could say to resentful former colonial subjects wanting to hold Belgium or Germany to account for their atrocities, "Not I. That was a country of which we know nothing." Brexit, though, has brought the British

---

[10] As far as I can tell, this expression was invented by Paul Johnson, whose 1972 book *The Offshore Islanders* gave us a perpetually valuable exploration of the four nations.

Empire back into discussions about *our* identity. Among the political class, there are just two characterisations of the UK. We've just met the 'imperial' one.

The other is what I call the 'repudiating' identity. To its adherents, 'Britain' is a weird construction put together for the purposes of foreign aggression. The English were mainly responsible, since the Irish, Welsh, and Scots were the first colonies of that greedy race. Internationally, all white people,[11] by disrupting cultures or establishing dominions, are uniformly guilty and to be condemned by the vast numbers of 'victims', classified as 'black'.

Since the 'imperialist' identity is associated with conservatives, contrarians naturally opt for repudiation. Seemingly ignorant of how our ideas and institutions developed and how they are distinctive, contemptuous of politics,[12] and fantasising about a world without borders, repudiators identify with supposedly global identities based on race, gender or social origins. Thus, we get *identity politics*, a regime of truth by which power is exerted.[13]

---

[11] It is habitually forgotten that the Japanese were, though not white, among the most ruthless of imperialists and that, in preceding centuries, Turks, Arabs, Mongols and Africans created empires too.

[12] Specifically on young Britons' conception of politics, see https://www.ntu.ac.uk/research/groups-and-centres/projects/young-people-and-politics-britain, accessed 060523

[13] Foucault's term is apt. Foucault, M. (1991) *Discipline and Punish: The Birth of the Prison* London: Penguin. I say 'supposedly global identities' because Asians and Africans, for example, may see them as American.

Brexiteers tried to unite both factions with a slogan that would project us beyond imperial nostalgia or repudiation: *Global Britain*. We were to see ourselves as culturally diverse, globally connected, untrammelled by our past but bold free traders. However, that doesn't work, in a world in which globalisation is unravelling and other nations are more and more nationalistic.

Nobody has come up with a way of conceiving our identity that makes sense in the 21st century. That's what I want to do with this book.

The funny thing about the identity put forward here is that it is fashioned for us from outside of the offshore islands by those who rejected us 200 years ago and suffered for it. Now that they have finally begun to supersede us in many indicators of achievement, we might learn from them. This is why I introduce Chinese perspectives throughout this book.

How does Chinese experience relate to us today?

The Case of China

A great deal went wrong for China when rising Britain and declining China clashed in the early 1800s. China suffered a breakdown in governance, leading to invasion and civil war. Following the collapse of the monarchy, because of the innate strength of civil society and conscientious reformers, there were nevertheless many achievements in the 1920s through the 1940s, from the re-founding of the legal, educational and administrative systems to parliamentary elections. These were mainly swept away in 1949 following a conquest made possible by foreign weapons and justified by a foreign ideology.[14] The conquerors, almost immediately, initiated 30 years of assault on Chinese civilisation and its exponents, causing suffering unimaginable even to those who had recently been victims of Japanese aggression and Civil War.

All that might have been avoided if China's 19th-century leaders had successfully compromised, recalibrated their own traditions of governance and philosophy of life, and kept what was valuable about China while adapting to the new world.[15] At that time, Chinese thinkers hoped for a moderate, organic progression of China into modernity, such as Britain had achieved, yet the virus of Marxism-Leninism overwhelmed them.

What has this got to do with these islands today? Aren't we so obviously more advanced that we don't have to pay attention to anybody else? Aren't our politics mild and civilised compared to countries beyond the English Channel? We've got democracy, and the most powerful military on earth, that of the USA, will always save us. Everybody speaks English and wants to be like us or to immigrate to Anglo-American countries. Since 1997, 20% of the UK population may be new arrivals: we're globalised. Why do we need to think about our identity?

---

[14] The ideology was Marxism-Leninism, a secularised version of Abrahamic monotheism. The weapons were Russian.

[15] As, arguably, did the Japanese, with the Meiji Restoration.

We need to rethink it for these reasons. The two conceptions I described above are dysfunctional. The first makes us enemies all over the world (see Section 6). The second tears our country into hostile tribes and denies the amazing achievements of our four nations. Neither of them helps us find a justification for the renewal of our nations that is necessary if they are to continue to play a leading part in the development of humanity.

Why should we arrogate such a part to ourselves?

The reasons have come to me from thoughtful Chinese who have coped with challenges and threats more stark than any that we have yet faced. In their view, we developed a society that is open, self-renewing and respectful of human beings. We channelled aggression and competition into relatively peaceful activities such as democratic politics, civil society and sports. We germinated the institutions that make it possible for human beings to live without fear. The example must not be lost.

Section by Section

The first sections of this book restate our identity and the contribution to human progress of the four nations. The last part of the book connects the rejuvenation of our identity with practical politics. I give the four nations the sobriquet 'WISE' [Wales, Ireland, Scotland and England, along with all their ethnic and religious groups] because, to a part-Scots Irishman, none of the existing names ('Britain', 'United Kingdom' or 'British Isles') is adequate. Despite past antagonisms, I argue that the four nations belong together. I replace the conventional term 'working people' (i.e. those who are not rich or rootless, not part of the elite, aka 'working class', the 'poor', 'the people', 'deplorables', the 'Red Wall') with 'commoners'.

In **section 2,** *Why Was it WISE that Rediscovered the Environment?* Chinese environment correspondents make the link between environmental awareness and the social system evolved by WISE. They are quite clear why WISE were the first modern people to 'discover' the environment. This happened because of the kind of society we were, and perhaps still are. This is why the matter of WISE identity and the environmental issues facing all humanity are connected.

Section 3, *WISE: Revolutionary Nations,* starts with the tale of a young refugee who fled to Hong Kong because British rule was, in the 1960s and 70s, infinitely preferable to that in China. For, once five revolutions in thought had been made concrete in WISE institutions - legal equality, restraint on government, dispersal of power, participation and diversity – we had built the societies which much of humanity wants to emulate or join.

From China's history we can understand the preconditions of innovation. **Section 4, WISE:** *Innovation Nations,* covers one reason why these little islands, rather than vast China, had the scientific and industrial revolutions. It is counterintuitive that it was an Englishman, Joseph Needham, who revealed to the world how Chinese creativity had laid the foundations for Western modernisation. This then raised the question: Why was it not China but WISE that made the modern world?

The divergence between China and the Anglosphere from the 18th century was because our political systems developed differently. Why did they? Why did one mutate and adapt to new circumstances, whereas the other did not? Because political systems reflect culture, which is what groups and societies think life is, and should be, about.[16] To get a handle on that, in **section 5, *Why WISE?***, we compare the first President of the Republic of China, Sun Yatsen's, characterisation of China's culture with what anthropologists have told us about the Offshore Islanders. But is this insight still relevant?

Although imperialism is today generally lambasted as utterly evil and destructive, I cite some actual subjects of empire who have been rather more pragmatic in their assessment. **Section 6, *WISE in the World: Going Out*** redefines the British Empire as a positive influence, even as I excoriate oppressive episodes. The story of a local government representative in Hong Kong remind us how different was the British Empire from other empires.

Section 7, *WISE and the Invention of Liberty* tells of how a young Welsh fugitive, escaping from Hong Kong during the Japanese occupation of 1941, was succoured by people who knew and cared nothing of politics, only that a

---

[16] That definition comes from Mead, Lawrence M. (2019) *Burdens of Freedom: Cultural Difference and American Power,* New York: Encounter, p89.

fugitive was a fellow human being. Taffy then managed to join a faraway British contingent taking part in the Chinese war of liberation. In doing so, he was continuing a tradition of the Offshore Islanders, honed in a hundred struggles against invasion and continental despotism, standing up for the freedom of others.[17] What, in early centuries, was WISE self-defence, became a universal value.[18]

To introduce **section 8**, I quote an American writer on China who warned about her country's propensity to cloak its self-assertion in moralising. From ***WISE and the USA: Poor Relations,*** we see that our politicians, mesmerised by US power and poise, have accepted US claims of moral leadership at face value and egged on our US allies to grandstand. President Trump took the USA to task for that delusion and demanded that the West not exploit it. WISE must listen to Trump and unravel our dependence upon the USA. We should use our cultural affinity to be critical friends with the USA, not servile.

---

[17] "Whose freedom?" you might ask. The freedom of cultural communities not to be subsumed. Today, the Uyghurs and the Catalans, yesterday, the Tartars and the Sioux. In Shakespeare's Henry V, the common soldiers felt sorry for the French because of their perceived lack of freedom.

[18] What the circumstances are that give rise to the expression of altruistic values are the findings of Samuel Oliner's studies of altruism in Poland after the Soviet-Nazi conquest. See Oliner, Samuel (1988) *The Altruistic Personality: Rescuers of Jews in Nazi Europe* New York: Free Press, and also my (2024) novel, *To the River: why would you risk your life, and all that you love, for a stranger?*

It took a member of the CCP Central Committee to remind me that the British Empire was a WISE endeavour in which all four nations spread enlightened ideas throughout the world, see **section 9: *The Empire Was WISE***. Although Ireland broke away from the UK, and some Scots are considering doing so, this Chinese functionary, with his global and historical perspective, predicted that, in time, the four nations will come back together. Not to celebrate the past but to reaffirm their solidarity in a great endeavour of human civilisation, the sharing of their insights with the world.

In **section 10: *WISE Betrayed!***, the political class is accused of betraying the *commoners*. We start by listening to invidious comparisons of our political class with China's. A famous Chinese TV chat show host gets some things right but can't hit the nail on the head: In pursuing their own interests, both political classes have betrayed trust. The British sin by omission—they haven't cared enough to tackle our problems—whereas the Chinese chose to turn upon their people and subject them to expropriation and persecution. Both show how a political class pursues its own interests once the institutions and general indifference make that possible.

Section 11: *Is WISE Immune to New Fascism?* The Offshore Islanders were not seduced by the totalitarian ideologies of the 20th century because, from the time of Elizabeth I, a consensus gradually emerged that faith should be a personal, rather than a political, matter. A similar consensus had already held sway in China since the Enlightenment of about 500 BC. Confucius and his contemporaries dismissed supernaturalism[19] and advanced that happiness and harmony came from obeying laws of nature. In the 21st century, are the Offshore Islanders immune to the attractions of New Fascism?

In **section 12: *Key WISE: Respect,*** two Chinese asylum seekers fleeing religious persecution identify the key difference, as they see it, between their own society and that of the Offshore Islanders. It is how people without power, money or connections, or those who want to be different from the majority, are treated: With or without *Respect.*

At the start of **section 13: *So, What Is WISE?,*** a peasant grandmother in Maoist China rebels against the prevailing ideology. Despite all the dangers, she has managed to maintain her integrity and to adhere to the precepts of a society more wholesome than that which the communists forced upon it. The Offshore Islanders, too, must see through the propaganda of those who want to diminish their achievements and demonise them. This section reconfigures the identity of the Offshore Islanders, which is both pre-Empire and post-Empire.

In **section 14: *Reboot: Development, Democracy, Diplomacy,*** a Chinese naval cadet studying in Greenwich 150 years ago had a *road to Damascus* moment. If China's

---

[19] Gods were, from then, on more like Christian saints, models of good behaviour. Immortality was through the family: my children are my future, just as I am my ancestors' heir. It is an approach to life which ties in with modern genetics.

identity were to survive and its civilisation to persist in an age dominated by Anglo-American might, China first had to understand how the rise of the Anglosphere had come about, then revive China's economy, and, equally important, identify what must be saved. To survive in the Age of Asia, I argue that WISE today needs to concentrate on three reforms: democracy, development and diplomacy. This is our Sixth Revolution.

Section **2**

Why Was it WISE that Rediscovered the Environment?

One hundred years ago, we feared conquest by totalitarians, both communist and Nazi; 50 years ago, it was nuclear war that hung over us, and, as that danger receded, environmental degradation and species extinction alarmed us. Now, human beings are destabilising the global biosphere in multiple ways, and there are developments in science and technology, from AI to genetics, which menace as much as promise. The world faces bioterrorism, cyberwar and nuclear proliferation. Emigration from desperate communities threatens to overwhelm those more stable. In such a situation, what do the Offshore Islanders, their status, their opinion or their identity, matter?

....

A China Story

Shortly before President Xi came to power in 2012, Chinese environment correspondents told me about their work, raising consciousness about the relationship between humanity and nature. They were on a high about the potential of the environment issue to propel China towards

16

being a more open society. Environmental degradation had grown so large in the minds of all but the most dogmatic planners, that they were 'open[ing] them up to public discussion and debates… a spirit of participation is fostered.'[20]

It is no coincidence that, in Britain, consciousness of our interdependence with nature emerged just as the religious belief that humankind is above nature, and that it exists only for our exploitation, began to decline in the 17th century. When China became communist, it compelled faith in that old European dogma. That faith leeched away after the failures of communism were recognised in the 1980s.

Religion Versus Nature

Daoist and Buddhist thinkers, influential in East and South Asia for well over 2500 years until the arrival of the Europeans in the 19th century, saw human beings as part of nature and advocated harmony with the earth and all living things.[21] Hearing, from elderly Chinese peasants, about the years before collectivisation in the countryside, I understood that this was not just a philosophical abstraction but was

---

[20] A Chinese environment correspondent, quoted in de Burgh, H and Zeng, R (2011) *China's Environment and China's Environment Journalists* Chicago: Intellect, p83.

[21] Elvin, Mark (2006) *The Retreat of the Elephants: An Environmental History of China* Yale: Yale University Press

manifested in daily life. Animals could be as close as family members; nothing should be done to the soil or the waterways that damaged the ecology, even if it gave a quick fix; hunting was limited so that the hunted might recoup, and so on. They were ecologically aware because they had to be: The survival of their descendants was in play.

Perhaps this was rather eccentric. Most pre-modern peoples were ruthlessly exploitative of nature, as are the few remaining primitive tribes today.[22] In the West, the submission of nature to human whims has been baked into the prevailing religions. A humbler approach to the world of which we are a part, pioneered by those East Asians, only began to emerge in Britain 2000 years later.

Christianity and Islam had encouraged the idea that human beings are superior, made in the image of God, and that nature is provided for their sanctified domination and exploitation. These assumptions were also part and parcel of the secular religions of the 19th century, capitalism and communism, as they are of today's 'Westism,' in both its left and right versions.[23] 'Westism' is the belief that 'Western' modes of organising society and polity, including, in

---

[22] Ridley, Matt (1996) *The Origins of Virtue* London: Penguin, p220-224

[23] The adherents of identity politics agree with the so-called 'liberal imperialists' who have wanted to impose Westism on several Muslim countries, except that they appear to believe that Westism must be shorn of Westerners (whites) themselves and Western culture (the Renaissance, the Enlightenment).

particular, individualism and parliamentary democracy, are to be applied universally.

The First Environmentalists

When John Evelyn published a call to landowners to plant trees in 1664, he reflected a realisation, gradually emerging in the Anglosphere, that we are part of nature and that our environment has needs no less than we do. A century later, Benjamin Franklin in Philadelphia petitioned for clean air, and Malthus warned of the ecological destruction that he imagined would result from overpopulation.

In the 19th century, thinkers such as Emerson and Thoreau encouraged us to respect nature, and botanists and ornithologists advocated conservation. Evelyn's ideas about woodland conservation from two centuries earlier had practical results when, in 1855, in British India, the first permanent and large-scale forest conservation programme in the world was implemented.

Interest in and concern for nature was stimulated by the Enlightenment and applied through the voyages of exploration, of which the most famous is that of the Beagle, from which Darwin conducted his investigations. In 1859, Darwin published *The Origin of Species*, which further weakened the hold of the *sanctified domination* view of nature and encouraged those who wanted to limit our impact upon the environment.

Clubs and societies for the study and protection of nature proliferated. In 1865, the Commons Preservation Society was established, and its concern for public access was reinforced with the setting up of the Ramblers' Association in 1935. In 1889, the Royal Society for the Protection of Birds was founded.

Environmental concerns became more and more generalised, and the destruction caused by both world wars made people more aware of the fragility of the environment, at least in English-speaking countries. In 1958, Rachel Carson's *Silent Spring* exposed the damage caused by pesticides. In 1961, the World Wildlife Fund was set up, followed by a plethora of organisations, from Friends of the Earth (1969) to Greenpeace (1971) and initiatives such as what ultimately became David Attenborough's *Life Collection* (2005). James Lovelock formulated the influential Gaia Hypothesis in the 1970s.

Open and Closed societies

Until very recently, almost every significant lobby group, environmental campaign and book on this subject has been the product of people from Anglo-American societies. That is not surprising because, though originally not democratic in the way we now understand democracy, these countries were, at least by comparison with others, *open* societies.

In the 20th century, environmental awareness and the environment movement developed rapidly in English-speaking countries and, by the latter half of the century, elsewhere. Nevertheless, that century saw appalling degradation, probably much more severe than that caused by the industrial revolutions in Britain, the USA and northern Europe. Communism was the cause.

Communism, like the bible religions, holds man to be the master of the world, its owner to smash and grab at will, above nature and lord of it. Moreover, at the practical level of law-making and policymaking, communist societies do not allow the kind of questioning that could, in open societies, at least sometimes, hold back the worst excesses of exploitation.

The brave people who questioned the Three Gorges Dam Project in China, when completed in 2012, the biggest vanity project of politicians since the pyramids, redolent of toxic masculinity, went to prison. Thousands of communities were destroyed, millions of people were displaced, and the damage to the environment was incalculable; the price will be paid by generations ahead.

The Soviet Union inflicted more far-reaching and lasting damage on the material environment than any regime in history.[24] Since its collapse, the government of Kazakhstan has been struggling to reverse one of the world's worst environmental disasters: The fourth largest lake in the world, the Aral Sea, containing over a thousand islands, disappeared by 2010 thanks to ill-conceived irrigation projects ordered in Moscow decades before.

---

[24] John Gray excavates the philosophical origins of the Soviet disaster. See Gray, John (2002) *Straw Dogs* London: Granta Books, p138. He also reminds us that Lenin set in train the holocaust of 60 million people. 'The largest mass murder in modern times, perhaps in all human history.' (Ibid, p94)

Pollution in the former Soviet Union was the most extreme until China won that crown during the Russian-inspired development programme of the 1950s and 1960s. Mao Zedong's rule resulted not only in reducing living standards to pre-1930s levels by 1979,[25] but also to the murder of millions of China's educated people and peasant farmers who had the knowledge needed to work with nature.

Meanwhile, in Britain, planners created green belts around our cities and identified 150,000 miles of public footpaths to encourage people to enjoy nature. Awareness of the *cultural* ecology took more time to catch on, even in Britain. In the 1950s, Russian urban planners bullied the Chinese leaders into obliterating much of 14th century Peking, one of the wonders of the world and habitat of an intricate popular culture. At that time, 'modernisers' in Britain produced plans to complete the destruction of central London, which had been started by the German Air Force.[26] Fortunately, they failed, although Birmingham and other British cities were torn apart by greedy developers and indifferent politicians.

Moved by the writings of hundreds of proto-conservationists, such as Gilbert White (just look up a list of them in Wikipedia), commoners have worked to preserve the cultural achievements of their forebears and what they

---

[25] Deng, Kent (2012) *China's Political Economy in Modern Times* London: Routledge
[26] Bryson, Bill (2016) *The Road to Little Dribbling* London: Black Swan, p91

could of the natural environment. As early as 1810, the poet Wordsworth conceived of the Lake District as something akin to a national park. This was further emphasised in a parliamentary bill of 1908, originated by the Scots MP James Bryce, which sought to ensure access to mountains. Birkenhead Park has been called the template for all parks everywhere in the world.[27]

Anglo-American Leadership, China's Power

Not surprisingly, therefore, the pressure to get to grips, first with environmental degradation, then attenuated biodiversity, then ecology and now, most urgently, with climate change, initially came from the Anglophone countries. Fifty years ago, academics and activists imagined that they only had to control global corporations, mainly Anglo-American-run, to deal with the problems. Things are very different now. Under President Trump, the USA relinquished leadership on the issue and denied its importance.[28] Today, it is what happens in China that will determine whether the world tackles climate change. China accounts for 29% of global carbon dioxide emissions, the USA 15%. Emissions per capita are much higher in less populous countries.

Although China has repeatedly emphasised that it understands that climate change is a threat, has demonstrated

---

[27] Bryson (2016) *The Road to Little Dribbling*, p385
[28] President Biden thinks differently, but who knows how long that will last? And, anyway, the damage is done.

commitment to environmental action through air quality improvement and massive investment into renewable sources of energy, and pledges to reduce greenhouse gases, it is doubtful whether it can lead the world. So many powerful interests are in favour of continuing China's coal addiction.[29] The forces of environmental protection are weak, and journalists, such as the one I quoted above, have been emasculated.[30] A 2022 major feature film showed that the exploitative attitude of the ruling class towards the environment has not changed since the 1950s. *Cloudy Mountain* (China Film Corporation) celebrates the destruction of mountains in pursuit of road building. Ultra-nationalists and those who fear and hate 'the West' associate climate activism with Western imperialism; Anglo-American demonisation of China has been a boon for them.

Is there a constituency for the kind of self-discipline needed if the world is to reverse climate change? In the Anglosphere and Europe, thanks to openness and reasonably active media, many have understood the dangers and are adapting their habits. By contrast, the newly well-off in China and other populous parts of Asia appear to have no intention of limiting their demand for meat, cars, electricity

---

[29] Fossil fuel extraction is but a small part of our exploitation of the planet. See Conway, Ed (2023) *Material World: A Substantial Story of Our Past and Our Future*, London: WH Allen

[30] There have been exceptions: Chai Ling's documentaries and Cui Yongyuan's blog, for example. See de Burgh, H (2020) *China's Media in the Emerging World Order* London: UBP, pp21, 54, 88.

and foreign travel, all of which generate more greenhouse gases. Stewardship by families and communities ended when, in the 1950s, the Party seized ownership of land and property to be run by officials, whose highest priority is economic development but who have little interest in the long term.

And it will be the same in WISE, where the pandemic and the energy crisis are taking a toll on economies already suffering from generations of neglect by politicians. What politician will advocate putting climate change first when the pent-up anger of the left-behind demands growth at any price?

On the other hand, the free circulation of ideas means we are not limited by our politicians' imaginations. People are both agitating and acting. In accord with WISE tradition, rather than adopting an ideological approach, they are assuming personal responsibility and fostering local approaches. Thinkers have argued that it is not governments and NGOs that will provide the solutions, but the empowerment of small communities and local associations. It is property rights and duties, community stewardship, trusteeships and taxation nudging that we should consider as mechanisms to turn us from exploiters into protectors.[31] These, and doubtless many other ideas, emerge because our society is open and participatory.

---

[31] *Green Philosophy*, by Roger Scruton, argues that people respect the environment when they associate it with their home and that of their children. Matt Ridley (1997), in *The Origins of Virtue*,

A Role for the UK?

With this deep background, Britain should be leading the argument. Yet the well-known weaknesses of our economy, long, in Larry Elliot's grim expression, 'going south', mean that our politicians, perceived as shallow vote-pleasers, have little or no credibility. Not until we have turned around our own economy, addressed the regional and individual inequalities and elected a government which serves, not the interests of the cosmopolitan rich but the marginalised majority, can we hope to be taken seriously as a Thought Leader in the biggest enterprise of all: tackling global warming.

Aside from the USA, the other country with which we should be able to work closely and without whose partnership we cannot hope to influence global warming is China. The bridge between us exists; my former teacher found it in Taoism:

> Taoism coincides with the scientific worldview at just those points where the latter most disturbs westerners rooted in the Christian tradition - the littleness of man in a vast universe; the inhuman Tao, which all things follow, without purpose, and indifferent to human

---

gives Asian examples of how local communities conserved, but government schemes were destructive. Smith, Craig and Miers, Tom (2011) *Democracy and the Fall of the West* p86 mentions Iceland's introduction of tradable property rights in deep sea fishing as a means of preservation.

needs; the transience of life, the impossibility of knowing what comes after death; unending change in which the possibility of progress is not even conceived; the relativity of values; a fatalism very close to determinism...[32]

China is the country that our politicians, singing from a US song sheet, have done their best to alienate, on the grounds that it doesn't follow US prescriptions. But, if you wish to influence others, you need two qualities: a reputation for competence that gets you listened to, plus a willingness to understand their points of view and, therefore, the ability to deconstruct them with empathy and reason. Unfortunately, our politicians have demonstrated little of either.

The nations that produced John Evelyn, the first activism for conservation and environment and, most recently, Extinction Rebellion, have a responsibility to share their insights with the world. In the process, they may get authoritarian states to become more open, if only because openness is a precondition for recognising the environmental crisis and acting.

---

[32] Graham, A. C. (1989) *Disputers of the Tao: Philosophical Argument in Ancient China*, La Salle: Open Court, quoted in Gray, John (2002) *Straw Dogs*, p115. Dr Graham, whose lectures I had attended out of curiosity, came to see me when I was a patient in University College Hospital in 1971, and gave me a personal tutorial on the Tao, in words as in behaviour.

Section **3**

WISE: Revolutionary Nations

We Offshore Islanders are often lambasted for our conservatism. The persistence of a monarchy, outdated rituals and adherence to rules made in olden times, are all taken as indications of complacency. In fact, they camouflage the most radical social experiments ever made by human beings. The Offshore Islanders, with a succession of revolutions of the mind and ever-increasing participation in the processes, built the most successful human arrangements and then exported their principles worldwide.

....

A China Story

I was living with two fellow students in an abandoned temple on a hill in rural Shatin.[33] Each morning, we would walk down an earth track to the station and greet a guy about our age who lived in a hollow, or ditch, roofed with corrugated iron. He would be cooking breakfast over an

---

[33] After graduation, I worked in the PRC for six months, thereafter living briefly in (British) Shatin, then a rural part of the New Territories, the mainland section of the British colony of Hong Kong.

open fire for a schoolgirl in a neat white dress. He and his brother had swum from the mainland as teenagers, with their baby sister in a rubber ring. Xue and I came to know each other, and I learnt his take on China and Britain. He would say that it was not a revolution that had happened to his parents' generation, just a power grab. We British had had many revolutions, he thought. "You had revolutions in thinking; we only had rotation of power, one gang after another. Yours is the only nation which has been made by ordinary people standing up" was Xue's message.

Once he got to Europe to study (his sister and brother went to the USA), Xue repeated these views to me again and again. Yet it took me a long time to understand the import of what he said. I really had no idea of what life outside our islands was like, or that WISE seemed a fairyland for people like Xue, who had grasped the essence of it much more readily than I.[34]

Gradually, it came to me that the history of the Offshore Islanders is of their incubating specific ideas, many of which have transformed, and continue to transform today, the life

---

[34] In 2013, *The West You Really Don't Know* was transmitted on CCTV. It was a series of documentaries, written and presented by me, on the difficulties facing Westerners, which China should seek to avoid. While the PRC official line was that I exposed the dark side of the West, viewers from then to now (it is still shown in schools and is on Youku) have universally scoffed that they'd be happy if they could live as do those Westerners seen in the series.

chances of humankind, and how those ideas were gradually realised in our institutions and customs. Perhaps we can trace them back to the England of Alfred the Great (848-899). However, it is certain, whatever the provenance, that they were advanced by ordinary people in many struggles, particularly under the Norman and Stuart monarchies.[35] Centuries later, they were stimulated, extended and given theoretical underpinnings by luminaries of the Scottish Enlightenment. Another exponent was the Irishman, Edmund Burke.

These are the ideas: The country is created by the people, not by kings, so authority goes upwards from them rather than from the king downwards. Law is an asset of the people, not a means of control, and all are equal before it. Decision-makers and administrators are accountable to the people; power is dispersed throughout society and restrained by law; citizens are free to participate in public affairs and organise against government; the welfare of the people is the principal concern of government.

---

[35] Pre-Norman society was also a cruel place in which to be at the bottom: there was slavery, serfdom and (by our standards) horrific punishment for minor infractions. The point is not that the early Anglos were less barbaric, but that, despite this, they germinated the ideas that made us more humane and, eventually, but quicker than anybody else, practised them. I am indebted to Sam Fowles (2023, p16) for reminding me that in Scotland, at his 1306 coronation, Robert I declared himself ruler by 'due consent and assent' rather than by Divine Right.

What this means in practice astonishes many, even today. Italian, Turkish and Chinese associates of mine have all found it incredible that we think of ourselves as owning this country, as employers of politicians, able to make a citizen's arrest and the person whose task it is to put things right, instead of demanding that 'they' do it. They find it difficult to believe that I can, and have, set up a community association, charitable ventures, business enterprises, a critical think tank, a school and a college without ever asking permission to do so or being protected by some powerful person. In our country, I am commonplace. 'Almost the entire social order of the country arose from private initiatives.'[36]

Schools, colleges and universities; municipalities, hospitals, theatres; festivals and even army regiments derive from 'some public-spirited amateur, raising funds, setting out principles, acquiring premises and then bequeathing the achievement to trustees...'[37] In WISE, we believe that if something needs to be done, then the person to do it is you. 'Devices such as the limited liability company, purpose trusts, the banking system, the stock exchange, insurance, even national currencies did not come into existence by fiat from some central power.'[38] The concepts emerged gradually over centuries in different parts of Europe and were best realised in Britain. They were by-products of business dealings over generations, with the regulations

---

[36] Scruton, Roger (2017) *Where We Are* London: Bloomsbury, p28.
[37] Scruton, Roger (2017) *Where We Are*, p29.
[38] Scruton, Roger (2017) *Where We Are*, p194.

created from within, by the need for contracting parties to trust one another.

What are the institutions that came about to reflect and embody those key ideas and provide the framework for the initiatives and innovations of ordinary people? Not all were uniquely ours; some existed, for example, in Germany and Russia, before totalitarianism snuffed them out. What *is* unusual is that such a *combination* of institutions thrived here while disappearing elsewhere until, after the late 20th-century triumph of WISE values, they became the norm, or at least the expectation, over much of the world. Social media has enabled millions in closed societies to cascade them further.

Revolution 1: Equality before the law

Our greatest contribution to humanity has been the idea of law as property of the people, before which all are subject. Only a minority of humankind enjoys this, even today. Usually, the party in power, the police or military, make and are above the law. The revolutionary idea that all might have equal rights was subversive in most countries until recently. Usually, people fear the law as being merely the rules made by the powerful to preserve their power; they dread the forces of law and order.

It was in the 9th century that King Alfred systematised tribal laws and the idea of popular consent. After the Conquest in 1066, the Normans accepted the English administration and strengthened the existing system of impartial and universal law, even as they obliterated the indigenous nobility. Over the next 300 years, when rotten kings tried to circumvent the law, their subjects obliged them to obey.

The best-known such clash is the Magna Carta, 1215, signed on the site of the pre-Norman Parliament or *Witan*. It was only one of many restatements of the 'old rights' claimed for all subjects, of which the most basic was 'giving to every man and woman without distinction the right to justice'. At the root of them, we can already see people's belief that they had the right to remonstrate and a sense of moral equality, regardless of whether they were rich or poor.[39]

It permeated our culture. Shakespeare's plays treat kings and nobles as ordinary people, though with different challenges and grim outlooks. Nobles did not have a distinct legal status or intermarry only with other nobles, unlike in most continental countries, where they thought of themselves as a race apart.

Long after Shakespeare's death, visitors from the continent, usually elites themselves, were scandalised

---

[39] The reign of Henry III saw the return of Englishness to politics. This was personalised in the rivalry between Peter des Roches, of the 'European' party and the Englishman who succeeded him as Justiciar (prime minister) and was Regent of England from 1215-1232, Hubert de Burgh. See Churchill, Winston (2003) *A History of the English Speaking Peoples* London: Folio, pp224-7; Carpenter, D. A. (1990) *The Minority of Henry III* London: Methuen, pp134-145 and elsewhere. Hubert and his brother Geoffrey were both signatories of various editions of Magna Carta.

when they saw our nobs talking as equals in the pubs with their 'inferiors'. The French philosopher Montesquieu was amazed at the 'English spirit of liberty'. Such a spirit could not be expected to conform to church authoritarianism forever, particularly in the relatively non-authoritarian societies of northern Europe. From the Middle Ages onwards, there were periodic clashes between bishops who took their orders from Rome and kings who were sceptical of priests' claim to be the sole avenue to God. Popular revulsion against church corruption was expressed in heresies, nonconformist versions of Christianity, which were crushed ruthlessly by the Roman church.

Eventually, aware people seized on Protestantism as their alternative ideology. Just as our forebears had stood up for *legal equality*, Protestants believed in our *equality before God*. Christianity was being adapted to fundamental WISE values. Protestants emphasised our own responsibility for our own lives, reinforcing our native individualism and rejecting external authority. They also emphasised Jesus' championship of the humble and afflicted rather than the ritual and obedience beloved of the priesthood.[40]

---

[40] Much of the above comes from my pamphlet *Democracy in England*, Civitas 2016. There were authoritarian, even totalitarian, protestants, particularly in Scotland. For the folkways of Suffolk protestants transferred to Massachusetts, see Fischer, David Hackett (1989) *Albion's Seed: Four British Folkways in America* Oxford: OUP, Ch 1. In modern times, the Roman Catholic church would abandon its savage resistance (the Inquisition) and respond to the challenge by emphasising 'the social gospel'.

Equality is not serious unless people have equal access to information, enabling them to make reasoned decisions. Protestantism encouraged commoners to read and learn and was, therefore, a democratising force. By the Civil War of the 1640s, competing opinions were being published in pamphlet form. The publishing industry took off. John Milton theorised that society could not progress without media free of state control. For nearly two centuries thereafter, prototype journalists fought to resist the despotic impulses of monarchs and officials and to report for the public. In the 18th century, commoner education advanced rapidly.[41] Workers' welfare, trade and political organisations were set up in large numbers. WISE were regarded by foreign visitors as crazy for political news and, by the 19th century, had invented the idea of the professional, impartial journalist. Informed and confident, ordinary men and women became more and more involved in local affairs, on school boards and local councils. Equality before the law was to be complemented by equality of participation.[42]

---

[41] In the 'Georgian' period, bouts of repression were followed by reform. People always felt they had the right to riot, berate politicians and demand accountability. The aristocracy was smart enough to know that compromise was likely to be more efficacious than repression, which became ever less harsh. See Foreman, Amanda (2022) *The Georgians: Restraint, Revolution and Reform,* on BBC Radio 4.

[42] The supreme source is Thomson, E.P. (1963) *The Making of the English Working Class*, London: Victor Gollancz.

Common Law

About a third of the world's population today live in legal jurisdictions based on the Common Law of England.[43]

Insofar as it is possible for law to be 'made by the people', Common Law is that. Judicial decisions are based not on legislation ordained by politicians but on precedents from history, the demotic ideas of right and wrong, and the reasoning of judges. It is evolutionary. Part and parcel with Common Law has come trial by jury, an ancient Anglo-Saxon practice involving ordinary people in decision-making.[44]

Moreover, empirical studies have shown that common law systems provide the protections needed for enterprise to flourish. 'Neither the French civil law system, originating in the Roman legal tradition, nor the German and Scandinavian legal systems, were as good, to say nothing of non-Western systems of law.'[45]

The two fundamentals, equality before the law and law based on precedents, taken together with periodic

---

[43] Not Scotland, which, under a 'one country, two systems' approach, retained its own legal system after the unification of crown and parliament in 1707.

[44] Tombs, Robert (2015) *The English and Their History* London: Penguin, passim. Not being a historian, I have checked my assertions against others' works, in particular Tombs, to whose magnificent history I am greatly indebted. My own interpretations should not, though, be ascribed to him.

[45] Ferguson (2012) *The Great Degeneration*, p86 discusses this in detail. See also pp 90-93.

restatements of rights, such as the various editions of Magna Carta, encouraged people to trust and believe in the law, which is thereby rendered effective. Here is a list of advantages which we take for granted and which many others around the world lack:

1. People agree to use law rather than force to settle disputes.
2. People abide by legal decisions.
3. People feel protected by their laws.
4. A jury system where peers can witness accusations against them.
5. A lay magistracy ensures that justice is local, decentralised and comprehensible.
6. If people feel that laws are in their interests, not made in order to manipulate them, people will conform willingly, so the laws will be effective.
7. People feel they have rights AND responsibilities to uphold THEIR laws.[46]

The most radical dissidents in China today are the lawyers who have repeatedly made the point that the rule of law as it emerged in England is fundamental to a humane

---

[46] List adapted from Alan MacFarlane, personal communication, probably a synthesis of points made in Macfarlane, Alan (2014) *The Invention of the Modern World* Fortnightly Review: Odd. MacFarlane is the author of the influential *Origins of English Individualism* (Oxford: Blackwell 1978) and many other works.

civilisation. Chen Guangcheng and campaigner, He Weifeng, are both lawyers who have suffered from doing so. In alerting their compatriots, they follow in the footsteps of reformers of the early years of the encounter with the West and the constitutional lawyers of the pre-communist Republic.[47]

It should be underlined that, although unremarkable to Anglo-Americans, these ideas are seditious not only in China but in many countries. This makes their retention in the offshore islands all the more vital if those resisting tyranny around the world are not to give up hope that their own countries might evolve in the same ways.

Revolution 2: Restraint on government

As early as King Alfred, decisions were subject to discussion.[48] Subsequently, over the early Norman period, various agreements—versions of the Magna Carta—reasserted constraints on the monarch. In the mid-13th century, infuriated by the King's continued preference for fighting continental wars, his subjects yet again confronted a would-be authoritarian monarch and, this time, forced him

---

[47] See McGregor, Richard (2010) *The Party: The Secret World of China's Communist Rulers* London: Allen Lane, pp22-23 and passim. The CCP swept away the legal system carefully reconstructed under the Republic of China and, therefore, the protections it afforded.

[48] It is possible that the clan systems of the Celtic areas placed checks on the power of chiefs in analogous ways.

to call a parliament. The struggles of the 1260s have been understood as marking the rebirth of a common English political community.[49] During the next three centuries, the English revived pre-Norman culture, resisted a foreign church and asserted their rights vis-à-vis their monarchs.

Under Norman influence, the Scots, like the English, had their evolution towards a more consensual government stunted even as the administration of Scotland improved.[50] David I (1084-1153), of mixed Norman-Gaelic-Anglo-Saxon parentage, is reputed to have studied statecraft under Henry I of England in order to return home to stabilise Scotland. In part, this would be by importing Norman landlords, converting tribal chiefs into feudal lords[51] and imposing the Roman church over the native Celtic church.

There were popular movements against the Normans in both Scotland and England: William Wallace (1270-1305) had his English equivalent in Watt Tyler (1341-81). They both sought to revive traditional freedoms they considered usurped by foreign despots. Throughout WISE, Norman

---

[49] Tombs, (2015) *The English and Their History*, p76

[50] In the Gaelic areas of Ireland and Scotland, rival clans unendingly fought for supremacy, which was never permanent until the Norman-Saxon organisation was imposed, a process that went on well into the 18th century. Whether this was good is moot. It was certainly harsh. See Michael Frayn's play *Translations* for the mechanics of cultural oppression.

[51] The Dukes of Hamilton appear to have originated in a Norman family established in Leicestershire in the 12th century. The ancestor of the Anstruthers of Fife was a younger son of the Norman Count of Candela in Apulia. He arrived in Fife in 1100.

rulers gradually localised. The heirs of (initially Norman) King Robert I[st] Bruce and James Stewart, V[th] High Steward, who both married Gaelicised Norman noblewomen from Ireland, became the thoroughly Scots House of Stuart. A century later, Henry VII, who was mainly Welsh, became English.

Ireland was more complicated. The Norman incursions of the 12th century, like the Norse colonisation of the previous two centuries, were as much connected with local feuding as with Norman territorial expansion. Allied with Gaelic princes, Norman lords carved out territories for themselves from those of their defeated enemies. They also intermarried with the locals so that their descendants became culturally Gaelic and gathered to themselves followers and clan members.[52]

The 16th-century Reformation of northern European Christianity was not completed in Ireland. While many of the educated classes became Protestant, the poor remained in the old religion. When the government misguidedly tolerated foreign priests, who identified with continental powers and established themselves as local leaders, Roman Catholicism became associated with political dissidence. Hostility between the majority Roman Catholics and the elite minority who had conformed was exacerbated

---

[52] The descendants of William de Burgh, brother to the Justiciar (Prime Minister equivalent), Hubert Earl of Kent, rapidly Gaelicised. They married Irish princesses, and, for two centuries, probably spoke only Irish. Their followers took the names MacWilliam, Burke or Bourke.

by London's wrongheaded policies of suppression and colonisation, initiated by Queen Mary.

In the 1640s, parliamentarians in England and Scotland rose up in revolt against a king who wanted to reassert the 'divine right' autocracy at which many had bridled for centuries. Charles I (Stuart) was executed as a traitor, yet this was not a revolution as much as an affirmation of traditional rights in the face of 'Catholic', i.e. foreign-style, despotism. Compared with the violence of revolts on the continent in this period, the Civil War in England and Scotland was relatively mild. The battles were small, few were killed, and there were no mass persecutions, unlike in the later French Revolution.

The experiment with a republic, the Commonwealth, came to an end with the restoration of a limited monarchy in 1660. Antagonism between Catholics and Protestants did not. In 1688, Parliament invited a Protestant couple to take the throne in preference to James VII and II, who was scheming to re-impose the Roman church and faith-based government.

By the late 17th century, Parliament had established itself indisputably as the sovereign power. In 2022, the accession formalities of Charles III reaffirmed the monarch's subordinate status. By that time, the monarchy had transformed itself into what has been described as the *welfare monarchy*. The royal family remade itself as patron, promoter, and fund-raiser for the unfortunate. It justified its existence by service to the people. This is one of many limitations, moral and legal, on government, which have accumulated. The contrasting amassing of power by the central executive since the world wars is another story.[53]

Revolution 3: Dispersal of power

Until the early 20th century, what happened at the apex of the state was only part of politics, for another very important feature of our governance was—until recently—the dispersal of power. First, the institution of private property was a brake on the power of the state. The division of economic resources in society means that material power is effectively diffused.[54] Second, there developed a civil society of independent associations of every kind with which politicians did not interfere. Third, the dispersal of power between different *levels* of government and the dispersal of power *within* government both limited the possibility of politicians accumulating overweening power.

A paradox was that WISE combined an efficient central government, competent in tax-raising, with local decision-making and initiative. Security of property plus lack of interference in civil society and private activity gave

---

[53] This is very powerfully adumbrated in Craig Smith and Tom Miers's (2011) *Democracy and the Fall of the West* Exeter: Societas and in Sam Fowles's (2023) *Overruled: Confronting Our Vanishing Democracy in 8 Cases.*

[54] Smith, C and Miers, T (2011) *Democracy and the Fall of the West*, p34

people the confidence to be enterprising and innovative;[55] communities ran themselves. By the 13th century, WISE was a network of autonomous communities. By the end of the century, around 500 towns had charters of self-government and were represented in Parliament. Although the roles and personnel changed and responsibilities were extended, this continued to be the case right up until the 20th century.[56] Legal and constitutional changes strengthened civil society. Variations in the land laws in the 11th century led to changes in the legal treatment of corporate entities in the 19th century; the political revolution that transformed our politics transformed economics too.[57] The consequences were phenomenal. Britain's enterprise revolution happened almost everywhere, creating great cities of wealth and power from Glasgow to Birmingham,

---

[55] Ibid, p45. Chinese after the death of Mao (1976) were enterprising for an opposite reason: everything had been taken away from them, they were driven by desperation to try to rebuild what communism had stolen or destroyed. In 2024, many of the achievers appear to be doing everything they can to get their money and children out of China.

[56] What the USA has is the English system of the 17th century taken to its modern and logical realisation. See Freedland, Jonathan (1998) *Bring Home the Revolution: The Case For a British Republic* London: Fourth Estate. Power is dispersed between the central government and the 50 states, which make laws and run their own fiscal policy. Moreover, within the federal structure, there is a dispersal of power between the executive, legislature, and judiciary.

[57] Ferguson (2012) *The Great Degeneration,* p26

Newcastle to Liverpool. However, in the 20ᵗʰ century, this process went into reverse.

After 1945, many of our industries were overtaken by other countries, bought by foreign investors or eliminated in the years of Thatcherite reconstruction in the 1980s. Edgerton notes the political and social consequences: 'At local level, and through representation in the House of Commons, there was a profound diminution of business influence from the 1940s onwards. The bourgeois cities became cities without a bourgeoisie, only a service middle class; they had factories but few head offices; they were no longer centres of opinion or elites connected to national power. Local banks, stock exchanges, and commodity exchanges disappeared. Capitalist concentration, and nationalization, had denuded the industrial cities of their active, local, haute bourgeoisie.'[58]

The decline of the regional economies since 1945 has not been due only to the disappearance of industry but to the leeching away of local decision-making by London and the turning of local governments into agents of the national government rather than originators and drivers of their own economies. Reform of local government in 1963 and again in 1972 subjected localities to remote control, arguably eliminating the parochial pride and initiative which had

---

[58] Edgerton (2019) *The Rise and Fall of the British Nation: A Twentieth-Century History* London: Penguin, p313. Matt Ridley makes a similar case over Newcastle, as does Rod Liddle about Middlesbrough.

propelled development. Ironically, they were enacted in the decade that *Small Is Beautiful* was published.[59]

Today, the proportion of our public spending controlled from the centre is twice that in France, Japan and Italy and over three times that in Germany.[60]

Revolution 4: Participation

From the Norman Conquest onwards, critics of state power and rebels spoke of ancient freedoms being violated by the powerful. People were proud to obey constituted authority and revered 'the laws ourselves have made' but not to accept arbitrary power. The 1381 Peasants' Revolt was intended to restore traditional rights, as were later uprisings. Despite its apparent failure, its purposes were realised in the decades thereafter.[61]

---

[59] Schumacher, Ernst (1973/2010) *Small Is Beautiful: A Study of Economics As If People Mattered* London: Harper Collins. It is an economist's analysis of the advantages of small. A current application of some of his ideas can be found in Skelton, David (2019) *Little Platoons: How a Revived One Nation can Empower England's Forgotten Towns and Redraw the Political Map* London: Biteback

[60] Tombs (2015) *The English and Their History*, p888

[61] See Tombs, (2015) *The English and Their History*, pp119-22. Similarly attempting to restore traditional rights was the famous Jack Cade Rebellion of 1450. Tombs several times makes the point that WISE did not have class warfare—at least until the Chartists—but that all radical movements consisted of people of different social origins.

In the same 14th century, Wycliffe and his Lollards wanted the bible translated into English because this would free the people from dependence upon priests, the ideological commissars of the church. This can be seen as an expression of English individualism, or the belief that it is, by exerting our independence, that we are fully mature.[62] Nearly two centuries later, during the Civil War, the Diggers and Levellers went a stage further with democratising plans.

The elite was reminded of the popular will during the glorious revolution of 1688, when numerous meetings and demonstrations of (sometimes armed) citizens made demands.[63]

Not all Protestants were crypto democrats. Although opposed to royal or papal dominance, the Scots Covenanters and some English Puritans were anything but liberal. Nevertheless, ideas of dissent and diversity were well-seeded during the Civil War. It began to be acknowledged that a dissenter could still be loyal to the state, unless he were a Roman Catholic and thus in cahoots with a foreign political power, the Pope, with his kingdom in Italy.

---

[62] Few Anglos realise how specific this idea is to them and how weird it is to other cultures. MacFarlane and Hsu both identified how our culture extols independence and reinforces individualism, comparing us with East Asia. Macfarlane, Alan (2015) *A Modern Education* Cambridge: Cambridge Rivers Press; Hsu, Francis (1986) *Americans & Chinese*, Honolulu: University of Hawaii Press

[63] Tombs, Robert (2021) *This Sovereign Isle: Britain In and Out of Europe* London: Penguin, p100

Although people were constantly agitating for parliamentary representation, it was not until the 19th century that democratic mechanisms for elections to Parliament were introduced, and they too were forced on Parliament by popular tumult. The Great Reform Acts of 1832 and 1867 increased male participation while excluding women for the first time. Australia had the secret ballot and manhood suffrage in 1861, much earlier than the mother country,[64] and New Zealand enfranchised women in 1893.

When all women were allowed to vote in the UK in 1928, partly the result of popular agitation, it was the culminating moment in a long process. Participation in politics has been made possible for more and more people, usually following their protests.

Political participation at the national level is only part of the story. As Scruton reminds us, and as MacFarlane describes vividly,[65] our complicated society of multiple associations and initiatives was the product of individual or group enterprise, not state fiat. It is their sense of ownership of the country that makes WISE citizens so different from those of all societies except those countries which we ourselves have made. Today, this approach to life is being eroded by the accretion of bureaucratic power. The agents of the state perform more and more functions, or turn voluntary bodies into state proxies. Often barely

---

[64] Roberts, Andrew (2006) *A History of the English-Speaking Peoples Since 1900* London: Weidenfeld & Nicolson, p43

[65] Macfarlane, A. (2014) *The Invention of the Modern World*, Section 9

disguised lobbyists, 25,000 charities now get more than three-quarters of their income from the government; the taxpayer funds thousands of campaigning organisations.[66]

Revolution 5: Diversity

When Elizabeth I came to the throne in 1558, she decided that she would 'not make windows into men's souls'. She inaugurated the relegation of religious practices to the private sphere, with the exception that the rituals of the Anglican church were to be the establishment rituals. Given that Catholic-inspired revanchism was the biggest threat to the offshore islands and would continue to be until 1745, when the last Stuart-led invasion was defeated, this was not only far-sighted but also courageous. WISE society—with the sad exception of parts of Ireland—slowly but surely became outliers in inclusivity and in tolerating diversity.[67]

After World War II, the first wave of immigrants from the Caribbean met with some hostility from commoners who suspected that their jobs would be taken or wages lowered by immigration. The explanation, 'racism', was

---

[66] West, Ed (2020) *Small Men on the Wrong Side of History* London: Constable, p200

[67] For example, following the failure of the Reformation in Italy, state repression of the Protestants was severe and only lessened with the extension of the rule of the Kings of Piedmont-Sardinia, from 1848. In Italy, particularly in the papal territories, Jews were subjected to savage persecution until the collapse of Papal rule in the 19th century.

built on theories of 19th-century intellectuals, including Karl Marx, about racial differences, which were then widely believed in Europe but have since been shown to be unscientific as well as malign. They also contradicted the English tradition. Not only in the Empire were non-white people incorporated into the administration and armed forces, but at home. In the 18th century, we had a black mayor of London. In the Victorian age, several Indians were elected to Parliament,[68] an Indian sat in the House of Lords, and a Sephardi Jew became Prime Minister.

So, it is not surprising that three-quarters of Muslims in WISE believe that Britain is a good place to live for a Muslim.[69] Britain has gradually come to be seen as, in the words of one black politician, "The best place in the world for a black person to live."[70] Tony Sewell, founder of the educational charity Generating Genius, and commentator on the British Afro-Caribbean newspaper, *The Voice*, chaired a 2021 report of the Commission on Race and Ethnic Disparities which concluded that the claim of 'institutional racism' is not born out by the evidence.[71] Racism did emerge in politics in 2014 when the Labour Party, perhaps hoping to please its Muslim voters, was caught tolerating

---

[68] Edgerton, David (2019) *The Rise and Fall of the British Nation: A Twentieth-Century History*, p115

[69] Data cited in BBC Radio 4 *Analysis*, 170723

[70] https://unherd.com/thepost/kemi-badenoch-britain-is-the-best-place-in-the-world-to-be-black/, accessed 010523.

[71] https://www.gov.uk/government/publications/the-report-of-the-commission-on-race-and-ethnic-disparities, accessed 211122

antisemitic abuse and was widely condemned for it. Black Lives Matter,[72] one strand of identity politics, is irrelevant to Britain.

Outbreaks of anti-Muslim sentiment following terrorist attacks have also been generally condemned. Until recently, there has been little reaction to the quite colossal immigration. The UK population has been increased from 58m to 68m since 1997.[73] According to the EU, every country except Malta is more racist than Britain.[74] Could WISE be the least racist country on earth?

Summary

As early as the 9th century, the germs of equality before laws made by the people, rather than imposed by the elite; the possibility of unanimity in diversity; the dispersal of power and the idea of decision-making through discussion and

---

[72] It is odd that Black Lives Matter, an American movement whose contentions rest on very shaky foundations, has managed to set up in the UK such that even the captain of the England football team feels obliged to 'take the knee'. The title is offensive, as if the lives of those people killed by US policemen who are not black are less important. See how it has been adopted in the UK: https://www.aishnine.com/blog/dear-white-people-in-the-uk, accessed 190623.

[73] https://www.macrotrends.net/countries/GBR/united-kingdom/population-growth-rate, accessed 010523.

[74] European Agency for Fundamental Human Rights (2019) *Being Black in the EU* https://fra.europa.eu/en/publication/2018/being-black-eu, accessed 141222.

consensus; all these may well have been present. However, the putting into legal and political practice of those ideas took over a thousand years. It is not surprising that other countries have found it difficult to adopt them speedily.[75] WISE can aptly be characterised as revolutionary nations because of the successful transition from barbarism to what I will call (and explain in section 12) *Respect*. So far, we have not yet suffered a violent insurgency with the kind of repercussions that so disrupted France, Russia and China; in retrospect, they were reactionary revolutions, retreats into despotism and terror under Napoleon, Lenin and Mao.

Ours was the first Open Society, and this was an essential condition of the Enterprise Revolution, the Scientific Revolution and awareness of the environment. It brought about the greatest breakthrough in living standards in all history, the Industrial Revolution.

My pal Xue fled from a supposedly modernising China, in which he and his family had been expropriated and persecuted, to a colony where they could enjoy rights which had been taken away from them at home. They found relative freedom in Hong Kong because the colonial power had undergone a series of revolutions that Xue would call 'real revolutions', those of the mind, which changed behaviour and installed institutions and habits, making

---

[75] Except, possibly, in Germany after 1945. Germany's governance was redesigned with advice from British 'experts'.

life rather preferable to that in faith-based communism.[76] With unprecedented challenges before us now, it is to be seen whether WISE still has the revolutionary potential of our forebears. And whether the Open Society they created matters to us anymore.

---

[76] I don't want the reader to imagine that I am glossing over shameful episodes in British imperial history, such as the imposition of Black and Tans' terrorism in Ireland before and in Palestine after World War II, movingly documented by Caroline Elkins, op cit. My argument is that these do not change the historical assessment of the role of the Empire in world development (see Section 6) any more than the injustices of the Romans' conquests negate their contributions.

SECTION 4

Innovation Nations: WISE Contributions to Humanity and Their Economic Foundations

We have seen how WISE grew some habits and institutions which made them very different from most other societies except those derived from them—the USA, Canada, Australia and New Zealand—and those that have tried to copy them. Why the intellectual and industrial revolutions took place on the offshore islands, rather than in the richest and most puissant empire on earth, China, has been debated for decades. Whatever the answer is, it has a bearing on our future.

....

A China Story

Joseph Needham was a much-admired research biochemist at Cambridge University when, in 1937, three Chinese scientists arrived. With their help, he began to explore the history of science in China. He was astounded to realise that discoveries which had been fundamental to the emergence of European science had originated in China. Needham and Lu Gwei-djen continued these investigations for the rest of their lives, producing the multi-volume Science and Civilisation in China. *This book transformed views of Chinese civilisation, which modernisers of the 20th century had written off as worthless and ripe for demolition and replacement. In the manner in which Chinese leaders now talk of their country's past, we can see the influence of this book, so different is it from how previous generations spoke.*

Today, interest focuses on the question of why the Chinese innovations, which, when they reached WISE, changed the West irrevocably, did not cause Chinese society to develop similarly. Why did China not industrialise and modernise first? Why did science stop evolving in China after the 16th century? Why did European countries, adopting Chinese technologies, surpass China, then launch nautical explorations and finance scientific enquiry? Why was the spirit of Galileo suppressed in China but not, in the end, in Europe?

The answer that Needham found is that China's political institutions were inherently conservative. The Ming and Qing dynasties (1368-1911) repressed development in order to prevent the rise of a merchant class with which the imperial authorities might have had to share power. Although, in Europe, the Roman Catholic Church was more ideologically rigid than China's Emperors, it was forced to reform by competitors for material power (princes and emperors) and ideological power (protestants of many different cultures).

> *Lin Yifu, later of the World Bank, argued*[77] *that China's meritocratic system of selection to the civil service, so much admired by Voltaire and Leibnitz, channelled the energies of the ambitious into state service, meaning that commerce had little or no prestige or independence. Europe, on the other hand, incubated a cogitative merchant class, open to innovation and ideas.*[78]

Preconditions

There is a necessary though insufficient precondition for the kind of society that makes innovation possible: affluence. During the affluent Song Dynasty (960-1279), and for much of WISE history, leaders did not impose economic controls or religious theories that stymied development. While China remained wealthy after the Song, subsequent dynasties constrained both commerce and intellectual enquiry, though, by comparison with European Catholic countries, they were open and inclusive. That was not enough.

---

[77] Lin Yifu (1992) *The Needham Puzzle: Why the Industrial Revolution did not originate in China* Los Angeles: UCLA Department of Economics, working paper 650

[78] Moreover, these merchants were able to capitalise innovation such that they superseded the pre-modern modes of innovation by artisans and farmers and made possible systematic innovation by experts.

Back in WISE, the state of mind and the social conditions that gave rise to the entrepreneurship of the 17th and 18th centuries are enthusiastically described by Liam Byrne in *Dragons*.[79] Thereafter, not only did our Industrial Revolution bring about the greatest improvement of living standards in history, but the wealth it generated turbo-charged the scientific and cultural innovations of the Victorian period.[80] WISE today has culture industries which are particularly creative and exporting, from theatre to film to music and sports.[81] Soccer, rugby, cricket, golf, modern tennis, bobsleighing, bowls, croquet, racquets, table tennis (as Whiff Whaff), snooker, badminton and boxing were all invented here. We also created the rules for those sports we hadn't invented: hockey, polo, ice-skating, canoeing, lacrosse and downhill skiing.[82]

WISE are forever forming associations and clubs, joining together in joint ventures. From the 18th century, we not only set up mutual societies, businesses and cooperatives,

---

[79] Byrne, Liam (2017) *Dragons: Ten Entrepreneurs Who Built Britain* London: Head of Zeus. Section 1, The Nation's Foundations, is an excellent introduction to WISE entrepreneurialism, and the Conclusion looks to the future.

[80] West, Ed (2020) *Small Men on the Wrong Side of History* London: Constable, pp170, 173, 175

[81] Although the success may as much be due to the position of the English language. Chinese creative industries are extraordinarily fertile but have little purchase outside of China until they operate in English.

[82] Based on Roberts (2006) *A History of the English-Speaking Peoples Since 1900*, pp34-35.

but also made cultural innovations. Two of the most important cultural institutions invented here, which have been adopted everywhere, are the Joint Stock Company and Journalism.[83] WISE invented international maritime law,[84] and British (originally engineering) standards are the bases of international standards. From the 18th century, the Offshore Islanders were the source of most major scientific and technical advances, particularly in health.

It seems likely that this predisposition to invent derives from several factors.[85] First, the individualism, which, as will be mentioned in Section 5, was innate to our social organisation. This gave rise to non-familial forms of association and stimulated enterprise.

The second factor was the relative openness that came about following the Reformation. While our political system was hardly democratic until the 20th century, the legal and administrative framework nevertheless provided opportunities for commercial culture to thrive, for

---

[83] Chalaby, Jean (1996) Journalism as an Anglo-American Invention, *European Journal of Communication*, Vol 11, Issue 3

[84] The first modern bible of international Law was written by an Irish barrister: de Burgh, William (1868) *The Elements of Maritime International Law,* London: Longmans.

[85] David Willetts has reminded me that Landes (1999) theorised that the intellectual and industrial revolutions are dependent upon certain cultural traits. The Needham-Lin-de Burgh theory that I adumbrate above is complementary to Landes' in that 'we' accept the theory of cultural determination but identify different cultural traits. Landes, David, S. (1999) *The Wealth and Poverty of Nations: Why Some Are So Rich and Some So Poor* New York: W. W. Norton

intellectuals to opine and for inventors to create. Francis Bacon (1561-1626) could not have survived in much of continental Europe; Galileo, the astronomer, suffered under the Roman popes, and Lavoisier, the scientist, was guillotined by the French revolutionaries.

Thirdly, empiricism. The intellectual movement began with William of Ockham,[86] was developed by Francis Bacon and became, due to later English and Scots thinkers,[87] the basis of the Scientific Revolution. Instead of imagining the origins of phenomena and attributing them to gods, the empiricists observed, questioned and noted. This simple revolution in approach had immense consequences.

We can start in the 17th and 18th centuries when the Scientific Revolution—culminating in the work of Isaac Newton—turned into the (European) Age of Enlightenment. Although kicked off by Italian artists and inspired by pre-Christian Athens and Rome, it was in WISE that the most creative thinking took place.[88]

---

[86] Copernicus, the Prussian thinker, also contributed.

[87] John Locke, George Berkeley, Thomas Hobbes and David Hume, *inter alia*.

[88] We know that the steady accumulation of inventions and attitudes that preceded the Industrial Revolution in England was not only related to the European Renaissance and the Enlightenment. It was also fertilised by the technological sophistication and intellectual development of many non-Europeans, in particular, China and the Arab world. This acknowledgement by no means diminishes the fact that, since the 17th century, Anglo-American countries have put all others in the shade for the quantity and variety of innovations and discoveries.

The dynamo was the Scottish Enlightenment, which began in the mid-18th century. 'For near fifty years, a city that had for centuries been a byword for poverty, religious bigotry, violence and squalor laid the mental foundations for the modern world.'[89] Faith in ancient stories of genesis came to be supplanted by reason, theology by philosophy. Thinkers cast rational glances on politics, science, medicine and engineering. Scots questioned everything, from economy (Adam Smith) to human nature (David Hume), ethics (Francis Hutcheson) and civil society (Adam Ferguson).

When teaching at Edinburgh University in my twenties, I joined the Speculative Society, set up in 1764 for debating. Once, there were hundreds of such 'salons' in WISE, but only two remain, the other being in Dublin. London's Royal Society (the premier scientific academy) and the Royal Society of Arts, Commerce and Manufactures also date from this period of intense discussion and innovation. China has had several periods of particularly vigorous existential discussion, starting with the Chinese Enlightenment of the Spring and Autumn Period (770 to 481 BC) and, lately, the early 19th century through to 1949. After 1949, the Communist Party effectively abolished civil society, especially the

---

[89] Buchan, James (2007) *Capital of the Mind: How Edinburgh Changed The World*, Edinburgh: Birlinn, p1

salons in which people had met to think through the future of their civilisation.[90]

Inspired by explanations of existence more credible than those of before the Enlightenment, WISE men and women of every social background orientated themselves towards self-improvement, enquiry, analysis and discovery. Much resulted. Below is a chronological list of a few of WISE inventions that have improved the lives of everyone the world over.[91] In most cases, studies and experiments had taken place in other European countries and the USA over preceding decades, even centuries, forming the background to the ultimate achievement listed here. Yet this table—just a fraction of possible examples—illustrates WISE fecundity. It also shows the interrelationship of scientific research in multiple countries and why cross-fertilisation between Europe, the USA, Japan and China, in particular, is vital that we may continue to advance.

---

[90] Often by the simple expedient of murdering the discussants. I have touched on Chinese civil society in de Burgh, Hugo (2020) *China's Media in the Emerging World Order*, pp148 onwards.

[91] Based on the *Radio Times* list of *The 50 Greatest British Inventions*, with supplementary items. The thumbnails are drawn mainly from the *Britannica*. A richer and more diverting list is contained in Pope, Steve (2009) *So That's Why They Call It Great Britain* Cheltenham: Monday Books

invention	date	attribution	description
Acorn RISC Machine [later Advanced Risk Machine], ARM	1980s	Stephen Furber, Sophie Wilson, Hermann Hauser and the Acorn team	Revolutionised modern computing and mobile technology. Recently, Apple has chosen ARM architecture for its M2 and M3 processors, the best PC processors in the world. Amazon has produced the Graviton processor, based on ARM architecture, now in 50% of the new data centre rollouts. Other hyperscalers are doing so, too.
Anaesthetics	1847	James Young Simpson	Anaesthetics have a long history in several cultures, but the use of chloroform as a general anaesthetic was pioneered by Simpson in Edinburgh. It became common in Europe and the USA thereafter.
Antisepsis	1867	Joseph Lister	Lister published a paper which initiated the widespread use of antiseptic methods of killing germs in the treatment of wounds or in surgery.
Bicycle (modern)	1885	John Kemp Starley	Invention of the train drive rendered the old and unsafe penny-farthing bicycles redundant and provided transport for the masses.

invention	date	attribution	description
Blood transfusion	1665	Richard Lower	The first known successful transfusion of blood from one living being to another. In 1818, obstetrician James Blundell treated postpartum haemorrhage with a blood transfusion.
Cloning	1996	Ian Wilmut and Keith Campbell	Like most scientific advances, cloning has a long history, but the landmark experiment was the creation of the first mammal cloned from an adult cell, Dolly the Sheep, at the Roslin Institute.
Colossus computer	1943-5	Tommy Flowers, Max Newman and Alan Turing	The world's first electronic, programmable digital computer, Colossus, was developed to decode enemy cyphers in WWII.
Computer programming	1883	Ada Byron, Countess of Lovelace	As the person who realised the applications of Babbage's computer and writer of the first algorithm for it, she is considered the first computer programmer.

invention	date	attribution	description
DNA structure	1953	Francis Crick and James Watson	Modern molecular biology derives from the discovery of the double helix (DNA), a great leap forward in modern science, enabling us to understand how genes work. Genetics research has been further advanced by Paul Nurse, Leland Hartwell and Tim Hunt.
Electric motor	1822	Michael Faraday	'One of the greatest scientific discoverers of all time' (Rutherford) has so much to his credit that it is almost ridiculous to mention the electric motor. Yet this is the discovery of which more people are aware.
Electric telegraph	1837	WF Cooke and others	Starting from a 1753 article in the *Scots Magazine*, researchers in several European countries experimented with electrical telegraphy to transmit signals. In 1837, the same year that Samuel Morse patented Morse code, WF Cooke and Charles Wheatstone patented a system, the first to be implemented commercially.

invention	date	attribution	description
Electromag-netism	1831	JC Maxwell and Michael Faraday	Electric circuits and semiconductor devices are possible because scientists of the 19th century came to understand electromagnetism. This vital accomplishment was the consequence of many steps by different scientists, of whom the most important were Faraday and Maxwell.
Endoscopy	1894	John Macintyre	The first illuminated endoscope was made at Glasgow's Royal Infirmary, taking endoscopy, which had been attempted elsewhere, to a higher level.
Germ theory	1860s	John Snow	London doctor John Snow saved countless lives when he formulated a theory that germs were responsible for cholera.
Hip replacement	1962	John Charnley	Charnley designed the first replacement joint and performed the first successful hip replacement operation. He then instructed surgeons everywhere.

invention	date	attribution	description
Hydroelec-tricity	1878	William Armstrong	Hydropower had been used all over the world from early times, but Lord Armstrong, founder of Armstrong Whitworth Engineering, developed the world's first hydroelectric power scheme at Cragside in Northumberland.
Hydrogen	1766	Henry Cavendish	Although Robert Boyle had produced hydrogen gas in 1671, Cavendish is credited with identifying hydrogen as an element.
In vitro fertilisation	1978	Robert Edwards and Patrick Steptoe	The first successful IVF birth took place at Oldham General Hospital.
Jet engine	1930	Frank Whittle	RAF officer Whittle registered a parent for the jet engine in 1930 and successfully flight-tested his engine in 1941.
Keynesianism	1936	John Maynard Keynes	*The General Theory of Employment, Interest and Money* was not just theoretical, but it became a manual for politicians whose application of his ideas changed the fate of all of us.

invention	date	attribution	description
Marine chronometer	1761	John Harrison	Harrison took 30 years to design and build a clock that could keep accurate time while travelling. This enabled accurate navigation and safe long-distance travel.
Microwaves		See *Radar*	
Modern road construction	1820	John Loudon McAdam	In the 1780s, McAdam made a study of road construction, which led to the greatest advance in rod design and building since the Roman Empire. First applied in Bristol, his process was rapidly adopted in Continental Europe and the USA.
MRI scanners	1978	Peter Mansfield	MRI scanners use magnetic fields and radio waves to produce detailed images of the inside of the body. Building upon his predecessors elsewhere, Mansfield undertook the first successful scan of a human body part and shared a Nobel Prize for it with Paul Lauterbur.

invention	date	attribution	description
Nuclear power	1932	John Cockcroft, Ernest Walton, and Ernest Rutherford	Splitting the atom gave us new sources of energy, especially nuclear power.
Orthopaedics		Robert Jones	The 'father of modern orthopaedics' first developed surgical techniques for musculoskeletal disorders and then applied his discoveries to casualties of WWI.
Penicillin	1928	Alexander Fleming	Fleming said he identified penicillin, an anti-bacterial drug 'by accident'. This drug has saved millions of lives.
Photography	1839	Henry Fox Talbot	Early 'photographs' came in various forms, but Talbot was the first to invent a process for making permanent photographs which could be commercialised.
Plastics	1892	Alexander Parkes	Before Parkes, many attempts had been made to manufacture synthetic materials as substitutes for ivory or tortoiseshells. His was the first manufactured plastic, called Parkesine, used for combs, billiard balls, film and sunglasses.

invention	date	attribution	description
Radar	1935	Robert Alexander Watson Watt	During WWII, Watt, a meteorologist, was responsible for radio direction finding and radar technology, which now has innumerable uses. Among the originators of the studies in radio microwave optics was Jagadish Chandra Bose, who studied at Cambridge.
Reflecting telescope	1668	Isaac Newton	After centuries of attempts, it was Newton who built the first reflecting telescope, modern variations of which are still used in astronomy.
Seed drill	1701	Jethro Tull	The mechanisation of seed sewing made WISE farming more efficient, a fundamental factor in the British agricultural revolution of the 18th century.
Seismograph	1839	James David Forbes	After several earthquakes in Scotland, Forbes, already a pioneering geologist, constructed the first modern seismometer, the basis of all later improvements.

invention	date	attribution	description
Sewage systems	1865	Joseph Bazalgette	The most advanced sewage system ever yet seen was designed and implemented by Bazalgette, has been copied all over the world and is still in use, improving the health and wellbeing of hundreds of millions.
Spinning frame	1768	Richard Arkwright and colleagues	The mechanisation of spinning transformed first the English economy and then that of India and many other countries as cloth industries displaced cottage production.
Steam loco-motive and passenger railway	1802-5	Richard Trevithick	Trevithick was the first to harness high pressure steam successfully and construct the first steam locomotives.
Submarines	1878-9	George Garrett and John Philip Holland	Modern submarines essentially followed their designs, and by 1913, all the European powers had submarines for military purposes.
Telephone	1876	Alexander Graham Bell	The idea of a connection which can carry sound waves, such as the tin can telephone, has been around for centuries. Bell's personal experiments in communication with the deaf led to the invention that he patented in 1876.

invention	date	attribution	description
Tunnels	1908	Brunel	Brunel's designs revolutionised engineering and transport. The first tunnel under a navigable river, the Rotherhithe Tunnel under the Thames, is still in daily use.
Vaccines	1796	Edward Jenner	Although Lady Mary Montagu introduced smallpox vaccination to WISE from Turkey, Jenner developed this process and created the world's first generalisable vaccine.
Vaccines 2	2020	June Raine	Ours was the first country in the world to deploy an approved COVID-19 vaccine under June Raine, CEO of the Medicines and Healthcare Products Regulatory Agency.
World Wide Web	1989	Tim Berners-Lee	Half the world now uses the WWW to communicate with colleagues, friends and family, to access information, to go shopping and for countless other daily activities. Almost all of it is free because Berners-Lee decided not to patent his invention nor use any technology that required royalties.

The Economic Context – Global Britain, Past and Future

We have attributed our early history of innovation to fluid social relations, an open society, and competition between European communities. We should not forget that the relative wealth of much of WISE, well before our *'going out'*, and attested to in many histories, provided the essential foundation. Once families and individuals feel (what to them seems like) material security, minds can be turned to experiment and innovation. Matt Ridley's *How Innovation Works*[92] thinks through the relationships between technology and science, education and chance, serendipity and individualism. No matter how it came about, there was a lot of innovation in WISE from 1700. Thereafter, the role of the empire was to provide test beds and markets for the creativity of individuals and families and the investments of landowners.[93]

By the First World War, it was becoming clear that, in the modern world, the state would play the main part in innovation, or Research and Development (R&D). Previously, this game was played by individuals, often from

---

[92] Ridley, Matt (2020) *How Innovation Works: Serendipity, Energy and the Saving of Time* London: 4th Estate, Audible version

[93] British and Irish landowners invested their surpluses in infrastructure and industrial development in the colonies; this is the reverse of the lazy assumption that wealth went only the other way. Today's capitalists too prefer to invest abroad. Britain's commoners have not yet woken up to this; the reckoning is yet to come.

very modest backgrounds, or small companies. Between the two world wars, it was military-related R&D that was most fruitful. That chimed with the left's predilection for reducing the influence of private capitalism.

When the Labour government came to power in 1945, state leadership in every area of the economy reinforced what had worked during the war. Furthermore, there was a whole raft of new policies to encourage 'repatriation' and reduce UK dependence upon others. The 1951 Festival of Britain demonstrated not the Empire's (as in the 1851 Great Exhibition), but only Britain's, achievements in science and technology.

According to Edgerton, the government encouraged self-sufficiency in food, energy and manufacturing. There were import controls that allowed industries, particularly strategic industries, in manufacturing to develop and grow and invest in R&D. As a result, 'the British economy was the most manufacturing intensive in the world in the 1950s, barring Germany.'[94]

The subsequent Labour government, under Harold Wilson (1964-1970), where it did not nationalise to defend our national industrial capacity, made it clear that it expected firms to take account of the national interest.[95] Also, to be continued, was a state-led or inspired focus on science and engineering, heralding a 'technological revolution', in the

---

[94] Edgerton (2019) *The Rise and Fall of the British Nation: A Twentieth-Century History*, p264
[95] Ibid, p383

Prime Minister's words.[96] The British state was 'by far' the biggest investor in research and development other than the US and the USSR. Why else, when rational forces in the communist leadership were struggling to side-line their fanatics, was it the UK which was invited to provide an Industrial Technology Exhibition for China in 1973?[97]

The Conservatives, 1951-64, between the two Labour administrations, tended to concentrate on international affairs rather than domestic economic development. They did not disrupt the nationalist trajectory of the economy laid down by Labour, following the Second World War. There swelled a protected economy with significant state intervention and control.[98] According to Edgerton, it was not the welfare state which lifted the British people out of poverty but interventionist economic policies.[99]

Why Did This Momentum Stop?

It is tempting to answer that the Labour focus on home reflected the interests of the commoners and the majority

---

[96] Ibid, p347

[97] I was present in the Great Hall of the People in October 1972 when Zhou Enlai welcomed the UK's Foreign Secretary, the Earl of Home, to discuss technology transfer, so recognising the inferiority of communism in economic development. As the two leaders entered the Great Hall, the band of the Peoples' Liberation Army played *The Eton Boating Song*.

[98] Edgerton (2019) *The Rise and Fall of the British Nation: A Twentieth-Century History*, p450.

[99] Ibid, p375

of the population that had no skin in the imperial game. No doubt this is partly so. Influencers in the Conservative Party belonged to familial and school networks, which had supplied the managers and missionaries of the Empire, or which invested heavily abroad. They jibbed at swapping plumed bicorns and punkah wallahs for this sceptred but humdrum isle.

It was they who were particularly dissatisfied with Britain without an Empire. It became fashionable to subscribe to 'declinism'. We'd only been successful because of the Empire, it was surmised, so to retain status, we needed to belong to, or perhaps to become the leader of, some other international community. Those who might once have sought prestige and fruition in the Empire fantasised, after its demise, about running the vanquished continentals.

Some facts support the idea of WISE 'decline', although today's historians emphasise that it was a relative, rather than an absolute, decline. The USA had overtaken us as an industrial power, and from the moment it entered the Second World War, our inferiority was obvious. Come the peace, we had to contend with revival on the continent and new national economies in former imperial territories.

Manufacturing industries re-emerged against which ours could not compete. Not only did WISE lose its share of world markets, but also much of the home market. The UK became a net importer of manufactures,[100] and manufacturing output fell much faster than that of the

---

[100] Edgerton (2019), pp452-3

economy as a whole. High interest rates exacerbated the problems.

In pursuit of integration with Europe—not illogical, since the continental countries had always been our most important trading partners—Wilson's nationalist approach to economics and international affairs was deliberately downgraded. Perversely, the patriotic Margaret Thatcher helped by adopting internationalist solutions to what were perceived as the problems of our economy. Her government sold off our infrastructure and key industries to private investors and foreign predators in the name of efficiency. This was also justified by the 'free market' ideology that became all the rage.

It was argued that producers had 'captured' much of industry to serve their interests rather than those of the rest of us, that decisions were made by unproductive state employees, that private enterprise was frustrated by government bureaucracy and regulation, and that our economy was becoming East European. As it was by now well known that communism impoverished everybody except a party elite and put an end to initiative and enterprise, the charge that the UK was going down that path got home.

Ideas have consequences. 'The idea that radical invention came from freedom, not from social demands, and from genius rather than from organized research', returned.[101]

---

[101] Edgerton (2019) *The Rise and Fall of the British Nation: A Twentieth-Century History*, p192

Perhaps this happened because it so well accorded with our interpretation of the 17ᵗʰ and 18ᵗʰ centuries, and perhaps because it contrasted with the failed statism of the communist countries. If in no other way, this very persistent trope may now have been proved wrong by the scientific ingenuity of massive, state-funded R&D enterprises in China.

The results of the Thatcher Revolution were mixed and are disputed. Many of our manufacturing industries, previously sheltered by nationalisation, were allowed either to collapse or to be bought over by foreigners. According to Edgerton, we ended up unlike any other major capitalist economy, in that we have no national major car, chemical, electrical, engineering, or electronic firm operating on our territory.[102] We had introduced railways all over the world but no longer built trains. Private purchases and government procurement no longer 'bought British', companies no longer did research for national reasons, and national champions of R&D programmes were abolished.[103]

The expectation was that new, modern enterprises would arise from the ashes of the old, yet very few large new enterprises were built. Where there was entrepreneurship, according to Edgerton, it was foreign.[104] Attempts to create a shareholding democracy failed, and the proportion of shares held by individuals was lower in 1989 than in 1975.

---

[102] Ibid, p474
[103] Ibid, p486
[104] Ibid, p469

And What of Today?

Despite all these troubles, plus the vast success of the USA and China, WISE is still among the world's main trading, financial and manufacturing nations. 81% of GDP is provided by the service sector. The most important industries after services are aerospace, pharmaceuticals and North Sea gas. Our tech sector is valued at number three, behind the United States and China.[105] Given that Anglo-America's began 300 years ago, and China's 30 years ago, this shows us quite how amazing China's advance has been.

Our share of world manufacturing output was about 23% in the 1870s but 5% by 1973, reflecting more the rise of the rest than our diminution. Today, manufacturing amounts to 10% of our economy. There have been many explanations for this, including lack of innovation and cultural attitudes, but the inflow of low-cost manufactured goods, from Asia from the 1970s onwards, mattered.

Because our agriculture is efficient (by European standards), we produce around 65% of our food. Nevertheless, we are the world's fifth largest importer (and fifth largest exporter) with a trade deficit that has significantly widened in recent years. Regardless of Brexit, 52% of UK imports come from the EU (49% of exports go to the EU). The UK's second biggest export market is

---

[105] https://www.gov.uk/government/news/uk-tech-sector-retains-1-spot-in-europe-and-3-in-world-as-sector-resilience-brings-continued-growth, accessed 161023. The data cited here should only be taken as notional. Revisions are continuous.

the USA (20.5%), and the fastest growing export market is China (4%), although Ireland, at present, matters more (6.9%).

London is very important to the economy. The cultural centre of the world, in which over half the population is not UK-born, is the largest city in Europe. There are over 500 banks in London, making it the leading centre not only for banking but also for insurance, foreign exchange trading and energy futures. It is a global hub for business and is often referred to as one of the world's three command centres; the others being New York and Tokyo. The UK has been the leading destination for foreign direct investment in Europe. This is not necessarily positive since direct investment also often means the buying up of UK companies, with the long-term implications usually being bad for Britain.

We produce many more Nobel Prize winners for science per head of the population than the other advanced nations.

Despite all these advantages, the trends are negative. Governments have set out the *Export Strategy 2021, the UK Innovation Strategy: leading the future by creating it* in 2021, and established the *Advanced Research and Invention Agency* in 2022. Will these be enough to reverse the direction?

Situation Report - What's Bad?

Although economists, business leaders and financial journalists have been warning of the dire state of the economy for decades, members of the political class have rarely come clean about our future but seem to want us simply to accept the decline they have willed on us. British economic growth is set to be the worst in the G20, apart from Russia. It need not have been like this. In the 1990s, our economy was racing ahead, but we had structural problems that the politicians avoided tackling. Here I list the economic problems squeezed down from many policy papers and research briefings:[106]

- de-industrialisation
- lack of investment
- low productivity
- resource dependency
- debt [see Section 10]
- reliance on two exporting service industries
- the sale abroad of our companies
- no foreign policy to serve our long-term interests
- decadence of our provincial economies
- polarisation [of rich and poor, regions and families]
- unemployment [now often given as over 9million]

---

[106] The data comes from diverse sources, especially Resolution Foundation, Civitas and IPPR. I have also followed the many publications of (the Labour Party's) John Mills, for example, Mills, John (2020) *The Elephant in the Room: Why UK living standards may be lower in 2030 than they were in 2019 or even 2007 and what we can do to stop this happening* London: Civitas. Then there are McDonnell, John (ed) (2018) *Economics for the Many* London: Verso, and Mitchell, Austin (2017) *Revenge of the Rich* London: Biteback

Situation Report – What's Good?

Even since the material advances of the USA, Germany and East Asia, WISE inventiveness is the extraordinary success story of the modern world and, indeed, its foundation. China is catching up very rapidly, possibly because the dynamics of innovation have changed. Creativity is now incubated less in university departments, rarely in the garages of eccentric inventors, and more in huge R&D departments of well-funded conglomerates, of which China has many. 'China is outpacing the west in areas such as robotics, quantum computing, virtual reality and weapons systems'.[107] Does this mean that the UK is out of the race?

Despite inadequate funding, poor salaries for researchers, and a limited market in which to exploit its discoveries, the UK still has three of the world's leading universities and 11 of the 100 best. The UK has 1% of the world's population but accounts for nearly 12% of total academic citations and 16% of the most highly cited studies. However, the total R&D investment by industry, universities and government is half that of Germany and miniscule by comparison with the USA or China.[108]

---

[107] Gray, John (2023) *The New Leviathans: Thoughts After Liberalism.* London: Allen Lane, p23

[108] https://www.ons.gov.uk/economy/governmentpublicsectorandtaxes/ researchanddevelopmentexpenditure/bulletins/ukgrossdomestice xpenditureonresearchanddevelopment/2020#:~:text=1.-,Main% 20points,period%20available%20using%20improved%20 methodology, accessed 220523

The *UK Innovation Strategy* published in 2021[109] identifies seven technology families in which the UK has strengths and opportunities to lead. They are Advanced Materials and Manufacturing; AI, Digital and Advanced Computing; Bioinformatics and Genomics; Engineering Biology; Electronics, Photonics and Quantum; Energy and Environment Technologies; Robotics and Smart Machines.

China's Past, Our Future

Centuries before the arrival of Western missionaries in the 19th century, China was potentially an open society, as we, too, were becoming. It did not matter to what religion you belonged, as long as you behaved. In behaving, you accepted the political system, relatively open to innovation and ideas during China's Song Dynasty (960–1279) and increasingly inclusive in England from the 18th century. Had the Song not been overwhelmed by the militarist Mongols, it might have been China that taught the world openness, rather than WISE. [110] The fall of the Qing, another military

---

[109] Department for Business, Energy & Industrial Strategy (2021) *UK Innovation Strategy* https://assets.publishing.service.gov.uk/government/uploads/system/uploads/attachment_data/file/1009577/uk-innovation-strategy.pdf, accessed 210523

[110] Emmanuel Todd's theories (op cit) of the relationship between family form and political system render a less authoritarian political arrangement in China unlikely. However, as we have seen in Hong Kong, authoritarianism and openness can be compatible, such that China could have developed as did Hong Kong.

dynasty, in 1911, inaugurated a period of openness and experimentation, showing us the rich promise of Chinese civilisation, once liberated. This ended in 1949[111] when replaced by ideological repression.

Since the death of Mao Zedong in 1976, Marxist ideas have been laughed out of court by most Chinese.[112] At the same time, many have been taught to believe that Anglo-America is doomed to inevitable capitalist decline, 'consumed by its own internal political contradictions'.[113] The evidence for this is found both in the performance of the economy and in the fracas of US political and cultural wrangling. Yet what is ignored is the constant ability of open and competing societies to innovate and reinvigorate themselves. Also overlooked is that, being willing to disagree without destroying each other, is a firmer basis for cooperation than forced unanimity. Our political system—certainly not perfect and in urgent need of servicing[114]—is the Anglophone nations' trump card, even in the 21st century.

Creation and innovation are much more competitive globally than when the UK gave the above-listed innovations

[111] The best account for the general reader is Dikötter, Frank (2013) *The Tragedy of Liberation* London: Bloomsbury

[112] Shi, Yinhong (2004) The Issue of Civil Society and its Complexity, Section 18. In: Sato Yoichiro (ed) *Growth & Governance in Asia*, Honolulu: Asia-Pacific Centre, p230. I quote from this in my *China's Media* (Legend, 2020), p199.

[113] Rudd, Kevin (2022) The World According to Xi Jinping in *Foreign Affairs*, November/December 2022, p111

[114] The urgency is well described in Smith, C and Miers, T (2011) *Democracy and the Fall of the West,* Section 6.

to the world. Every government—almost—wants its people to star in innovation. The richest countries, as well as those with the biggest internal markets, can easily outpace the smaller countries. The scientific approach to life has become universal, as superstitions and religions are regarded as aesthetic rituals rather than authorities. Tradition matters little in the sciences' hinterland; the quality of school education matters most. Schooling in East Asia is consistently better in the sense that it pulls up more people to high standards with greater ease than in the Anglophone countries. Do our clever young still opt for science, industry and invention, or are they cajoled into safe caretaker jobs in the professions, public service or intellectually undemanding service industries? We need the answer to these questions, and we need competition, at home and abroad, if we are to avoid imperial China's fate.[115]

Faced with doubts about our preparedness at home and the competition from global R&D abroad, Sir Paul Nurse asked the question: 'Can we go on innovating?' The Nurse Review[116] answered: Yes, if we select our areas of specialism

---

[115] And, perhaps, the fate that awaits the China of today. Although John Gray, in *The New Leviathan*, argues that the Chinese model will win out and the West will copy it in order to keep up, he also admits that recent policies have severely damaged China and limited its prospects. This view is widespread, in China as elsewhere.

[116] Nurse, Sir Paul (2023) *Independent Review of the Research, Development and Innovation Organisational Landscape*, OGL https://assets. publishing.service.gov.uk/government/uploads/system/uploads/ attachment_data/file/1141484/rdi-landscape-review.pdf, accessed 210523

carefully, support R&D effectively and avoid a brain drain of best talent abroad. To achieve these things, we need political leadership which is focused on development, aware of advances elsewhere, conscious of our national identity and its ability to motivate and mobilise, and is determined that the Offshore Islanders' achievement be not an excuse for snobbery but an inspiration to roll up our sleeves and reboot.[117]

---

[117] In Tomasi's novel, *The Leopard*, the Prince of Salina regretfully notes that his titles will be inherited by people who do not see the responsibilities that they imply, but only the social distinction they supposedly confer.

Section 5

Why WISE?

How was it that the polity brought to life by King Alfred in a backwater of Europe came to remake empires throughout Asia and Africa, build new countries in the Americas and Australasia, persuade humanity to speak English, and to see Britain as lodestar?

....

A China Story

For the man who was to become the first President of the Republic of China and 'Father of the Nation', Sun Yatsen, the Open Sesame into modernity for China was to learn from Britain. Sun was profoundly influenced by his experience of British schooling, the Anglican church and the medical education he received in Hong Kong. He admired what he thought of as our collectivism.

'The Chinese people have only family and clan solidarity; they do not have national spirit...they are just a heap of loose sand...' *was an observation of his that many took to heart. They thought of Chinese individualism as a defect, they wanted the Chinese to identify with a nation-state rather than 'merely' as culturally Chinese.*[118] *Thus,*

---

[118] A minority of my students, over the 20 years when I have had many Chinese in my classes, disliked being referred to as

Christianity or Communism were adopted by reformers consciously seeking one or other ideology with which to break family ties and bind Chinese together under new management, relating themselves only to the Party/State. Communism's clobbering of Chinese traditional society was simply a more violent and destructive version of what Westernisers had been seeking to do since the early 1900s.[119]

Whether they have succeeded is debatable. China's spontaneous and massive development from the late 1980s (as we shall see in the next section) came about because communist collectivism was rejected as disastrous. This did not denote a turn to Anglo-American individualism but the revival of traditional, family and network-based enterprise.[120] *As George Orwell put it, 'Nations do not escape from their past merely by making a revolution.'*

Zhongguoren (citizens of the Chinese state) and preferred to be called *Zhonghuaren* (those of Chinese civilisation), so great was their antipathy to the conflation of the Party with the nation.

[119] Radicals lamented the nature of Chinese society, variously termed by anthropologists 'the differential mode of association' or 'network society'. See de Burgh, H (2020) *China's Media in the Emerging World Order*, section 5, for a summary. In effect, both KMT and CCP tried to coerce the Chinese into becoming Anglo-Americans in their relationships and/or to atomise them.

[120] This contradicts the, otherwise very illuminating, argument of Lawrence Mead that Anglo-American individualism is the driver of human development. His insistence upon the primacy of culture is a courageous corrective to current shibboleths. See Mead, Lawrence M. (2019) *Burdens of Freedom: Cultural Difference and American Power*, New York: Encounter Books.

David Goodhart, writing about the UK today, has identified the reverse problem of identity in his book *The Road to Somewhere*.[121] He thinks that the majority of us have a very solid sense of identity with the nation and the community, but that the chattering classes—the opinion-formers and decision-makers—have lost it.

Wise Identity

Until recently, we Offshore Islanders were not troubled about our identity. Many thought of ourselves as the most fortunate beings on the planet, the freest and among the richest, victors in every war and models in every sphere. We gave the world the global language, the mother of parliaments, Association Football and Protestant Jesus. We were not entirely wrong in thinking ourselves distinct from even our closest neighbours, although we probably could not explain why.

Indeed, as noted in Section 4, since the 18th century, the Offshore Islanders have evolved institutions, invented artefacts and transmitted ideas that are transforming the world into a better place for most people. Other societies have gone through periods of great energy and innovation, from Tang Dynasty China to the Abbasid Caliphate, from Renaissance Florence to Hanseatic Germany. However, it was our creativity that led to world transformations; in particular, the scientific and industrial revolutions. Why? And does our early start really matter anymore, now that

---

[121] Goodhart, David (2017) *The Road to Somewhere* London: Hurst

we are being overtaken? Others are richer, more powerful, have better health services or are registering more patents.

We should know why we did so well, so that we don't inadvertently ruin the curious combination of elements that went to make up our success. We must cast aside the sweeping assumptions of the Marxists, who attributed the rise of the Anglos to plentiful coal or surplus labour.[122] Naturally, there were many factors contributing to our evolution, from temperate climate to island status, from a melting pot of races to the discovery of iron.[123] One factor above all gave us the impetus to rise above our neighbours and make us their teachers: family form.

Origins of Detachment

Until recently, families in most human societies came in various communal or extended units in which people were not private individuals but cogs in a big machine. Yet, at least for the last thousand years, Anglo offspring[124] have

---

[122] Marx believed that economics determined everything, whereas we now know that culture is an equally significant determining factor in the life of an individual or a society and that culture may determine economics.

[123] David Landes overviews the environmental factors in Landes, David, S. (1999) *The Wealth and Poverty of Nations: Why Some Are So Rich and Some So Poor*, ch 1.

[124] I am writing about pre-British times but prefer 'Anglos' to 'English' because the people I'm writing about include not only the English but most of the Scots, many of the Welsh and probably those Irish descended from Norsemen and Scots.

split off from their parents relatively young and decisively. Children were on their own early. They were admired by their relatives, not for their conformity and dependence, as in, say, the Mediterranean, but for their independence.[125] Modern Anglo-Americans reinforce this during socialisation with their stress on individuality and personal assertion.[126]

Family form greatly influences a culture's politics, religion and economic development; this helps to explain why our society evolved as it did.[127] 'Authoritarian relationships between parents and the children lead to authoritarian ideologies, liberal relationships to liberal political concepts.'[128]

Among the consequences of relatively detached relationships were: Except in aristocratic families, Anglo fathers were not obliged to leave their property to a member of the family, but were free to do with it as they wanted;[129] Anglo children had to make their own way

---

[125] Todd, Emmanuel (1985) *The Explanation of Ideology: Family Structures and Social Systems* Oxford: Blackwell, p100.

[126] Hsu, Francis L. K. (1981) *Americans & Chinese* (3rd edition), ch 3

[127] The most succinct summary of Anglo social formation is in the first section of Willetts, David (2019) *The Pinch*, London: Atlantic Books. Willetts bases his analysis on Macfarlane, Alan (1978) *The Origins of English Individualism*, Oxford: Basil Blackwell, who first revealed the uniqueness of the predominant family form in these islands.

[128] Todd, Emmanuel (1987) *The Causes of Progress* Oxford: Blackwell, p145

[129] Until inheritance tax made finding better ways of preserving fortunes necessary, British landed families prevented heirs from disposing of their estates by the device of entail, ensuring that estates devolved only by primogeniture.

and find their own means of support. More likely to be educated and able to own property, daughters at least had the inklings of liberty and were not mere chattels, as in other parts of Europe. Educating women is a sure-fire way of changing a society, which is why religious zealots denigrate it – always.

To continental observers, pushing youths out from the family home was thought quite barbaric, as was the personal, as opposed to familial, ownership of property and the protection of the law for property holders, necessary for a society in which family inheritance could not be taken for granted. Yet these oddities (by European standards) were preconditions of our social evolution and the enterprise revolution, which preceded both the Industrial Revolution and overseas expansion.

Just think about it: the spirit of individualism led to self-sufficiency and then the self-esteem of the smallholder or artisan. Enterprises compete, and competition inspires ingenuity and innovation. Every farmer and tradesman was proud to 'stand on his own two feet' and thought himself the equal of anybody.[130]

---

[130] It was exactly this spirit of independence and enterprise that the communists suppressed so bloodily in both the Soviet empire (starting with Lenin's liquidation of the Kulaks) and China in the 1950s. To make a slave society, you first have to eliminate people who know how to do things better than you do.

Detachment and Collaboration

Anglos are individualised, yet paradoxically, their detachment from family led to collaboration. Denied the secure support of parents, they required non-family arrangements for protection, insurance and mutual encouragement. Individuals bonded together in associations of need, or professional lobbies and in religious and hobby communities; 'They were very effective in creating local and civic institutions... The vigour of historic civil society in England or the USA is not some universal trend. It depends upon some very unusual and shared features of our two countries. England and America share a similar civil society because they share the same (rather unusual) family structure.'[131]

So, thanks to the instincts—independent, egalitarian and communitarian—of our forebears, we evolved the institutions that enabled us to step from pre-modern society to 18th-century commercialisation. From the 13th century on, we were exceptional in other ways too, for our relationships were increasingly governed by law. In the rest of Europe, kin relations determined everything, as they still do in much of the world.[132] As Tombs so well describes,

---

[131] Willetts, David (2010) *The Pinch: How the Baby Boomers Took Their Children's Future - And Why They Should Give It Back*, p19, quoted in de Burgh (2021) *China's Media in the Emerging World Order*, p139.

[132] The subsequent paragraph is a paraphrase of sections of Tombs, Robert (2015) *The English and their History*, London: Penguin, pp881-883.

by the 1700s, there was long established administrative unity, as well as an ancient tradition of participation and representation in government. Our Common Law was trusted and effective, and power could be seen to be restrained by law. We traditionally obeyed constituted authority and revered 'the laws we ourselves have made'.

Whether this WISE version of communitarianism – the idea that the individual flourishes only through his or her social relationships - will persist following massive immigration from cultures which are very different, we cannot know. For the moment, we are a less homogenous country, with Scots, Sikhs, Hindus and various sects of Muslims often in conflict with each other. If we are to avoid becoming another Lebanon, some serious thinking is needed about how diverse people can be assimilated.

Predilection for Enterprise

The lonesome Anglo could not stop at associating; he had to be enterprising to survive. Driven by the creativity of individuals, for much of modern history, England was ahead of continental Europe in economic, as of political, development. From as early as the 14th century, it was the wealthiest country in Europe as well as the best governed. From 1713, Britain was rightly seen as rich. By World War II, Britain was second in wealth to the USA.[133]

---

[133] Tombs, Robert (2015) *The English and their History*, London: Penguin, pp372-380

How was this? Throughout the world, for centuries, despots and their intellectual supporters have claimed that commerce is despicable and exploitative and that a harmonious society can only be created where the desire to do business is curtailed and controlled by the state. Monarchs and party general secretaries have wanted to seize the fruits of commerce, and bookworms have fantasised about a society in which capitalists and landowners are brought low, in which everyone is equal and receives the same allocation from a disinterested bureaucracy.

From the 14th to the 17th century, the Offshore Islanders also struggled over whether and how enterprise should be regulated and, possibly, smothered by the state. During the Civil War, state power was challenged, and our political and legal institutions reached a stage that ensured enterprise could flourish, that we could trade freely and build durable and capitalised businesses.[134] Although some of the advantages were enjoyed in other European countries, for example, free movement, competition for the clever and skilful and curbs on despotism,[135] our businesspeople were freer and more secure than their counterparts in most of the world.

Northern Europeans, generally, were curious. They hoovered up all sorts of know-how from elsewhere,

---

[134] Lipson, E. (1944) *A Planned Economy or Free Enterprise: The Lessons of History* London: Adam and Charles Black, p26

[135] The consequences of this over the subsequent century are described by Ridley, Matt (2011) *The Rational Optimist* London: Fourth Estate, pp 220-223.

communicating with and abetting each other to bring about the Scientific Revolution of the 17th and 18th centuries. Scotland was the epicentre of new thinking. Throughout WISE, knowledge was exploited and put to practical use in the Industrial Revolution. This is because WISE societies were already enterprising; technological innovation was being initiated by people who, though largely ignorant of science, were skilled entrepreneurs.[136]

The differences between our 'going out' into the world and that of the Spanish and Portuguese are marked. Those two countries imposed a despotic ideology on their colonies at great human cost. The failure of Latin America to achieve anything like the advances of the USA has long been attributed to cultural differences; the two versions of Christianity were the ideological representations of those cultures.

Ideology

Our Stuart monarchs had claimed the Divine Right of Kings as justification for authoritarian control of ideas and behaviour, but this was anathema to individualistic citizens.

Both sides in the Civil War (1642-51) thought of themselves as Christians; there was no possibility of anything else.

---

[136] On the relationship between enterprise, technological development and science, see the wonderfully illuminating book by Matt Ridley (2020) *How Innovation Works: And Why It Flourishes in Freedom* London: Fourth Estate.

However, the Reformation (1534 and 1560)[137] had put the 'old believers', in an authoritarian church and authoritarian government, on the back foot. The mental changes that the Reformation institutionalised had been marinating over some three centuries. Christendom's early protest movement, the Waldenses, criticised the totalitarianism of the Roman church in the 1100s. They rejected the right of priests to hide the bible (with its anti-establishment messages and subversive incongruities) from the people. They initiated the long trek to civility and literacy, which started with translation of that bible into languages spoken by ordinary people and then to its printing and wider diffusion. The New Testament[138] was used to give divine sanction to egalitarianism, the striving to create and build (as opposed to fatalism), mastery over nature, esteem for manual labour, personal property rights, duties of rulers towards their dependents and respect for the humble and poor 'who are always with us'.

The Waldenses survived many attempts to exterminate them by the popes.[139] According to Landes, it was through

---

[137] 1534 in England and Wales, 1560 in Scotland. In Ireland, the process, which never covered more than a fraction of the population, took about three decades, culminating in the Irish Act of Uniformity of 1560.

[138] The New Testament comprises manuscripts collated in the 4th century AD, as opposed to the Old Testament, dating from several hundred years BC.

[139] Up to the 19th century. During WWII, the Waldenses of northern Italy rescued many Jews from Nazi persecution and hid them in the mountain fastnesses to which their own ancestors had fled Catholic death squads.

those Waldenses, the Lollards in England and the Lutherans and Calvinists on the continent, that 'this Judaic-Christian tradition entered into the European political consciousness.'[140]

Nowhere more so than in WISE. For centuries after the Reformation, Protestantism was the ideology which explained and justified our rise and expansion. Merchants felt sanctified; colonists kidded themselves that they were obeying God's commands as they built America or reorganised Africa; earnest bible readers championed the human rights of chimney sweeps at home and slaves abroad. Soldiers were blessed by their chaplains as they set out to 'to right wrong, to overcome evil, to suffer wounds and endure pain, if need be; but in all things to serve thee, bravely, faithfully, joyfully, that at the end of the day's labour, kneeling for thy blessing, thou mayst find no blot upon my shield.'[141]

Social Implications of Enterprise

Countries where the economy is run by a central directive in which equality is imposed, and where decisions are made by political officials, are harsh, unkind societies. Initiative is frowned upon and corruption is extreme; ask the East Europeans, if not the Chinese.

---

[140] Landes, David, S. (1999) *The Wealth and Poverty of Nations: Why Some Are So Rich and Some So Poor*, p34

[141] *A Knight's Prayer*, placed over the bedhead of many protestant boys, including the author's, in the last two centuries, is believed to be from an inscription at Chester Cathedral.

Commercial society is civilising. Business brings people together; they form associations, alliances and friendships. To survive in business, they must be pragmatic. They exchange ideas and change their opinions as they learn new things. People doing business need a good reputation in their communities; they need to get on with others and be known for fair dealing because they are accountable to their customers.

More and more people want to participate in opinion-forming and decision-making; intolerance and cruelty diminish. The arts flourish, and concern for others, given concrete form by charities and foundations, seems to be a by-product of commercial success because so many rich businesspeople look for ways of sharing their wealth and time with others.

Intercourse stimulates innovation. We stole many ideas from abroad because our traders and explorers were always open to them. Pre-modern, we learnt from the Romans, the early Christians and the Normans. The Italian Renaissance and the German Reformation fertilised us. Wherever we went, we picked up new notions and absorbed them. For example: Enlightenment Europe admired what it thought were great Chinese achievements: the absence of transcendental religion and no hereditary aristocracy. At a time when our military and civil services were nepotistic and corrupt, British pragmatists observed that Chinese officials were selected through competitive, written examination. A century or so after this discovery, we enacted the Northcote-Trevelyan Reforms, which inaugurated the same, laying the foundations for an administrative culture that has generally been truthful and public-spirited.[142]

Social Implications of Pragmatism

It is a mark of their self-absorption that many Britons claim WISE is particularly class-ridden, and that we are unusual, in being divided by accent, dress, tastes and sports.[143] They are wrong. Any Briton who has lived in—and spoken the language of—almost any other society knows that class distinctions are universal phenomena and, probably, that WISE is far less class-ridden than most other societies.

It was noticeable to foreign observers as early as the 18th century that rich and poor could talk to each other as equals when they shared the same intellectual or sporting interests. There were no distinctions of dress as were enforced on the continent, and nobles did not have legal status separating them from commoners.

People did recognise class distinctions, but without necessarily accepting inferiority or superiority. In the 19th and 20th centuries, cultivated members of the *haute bourgeoisie* drew a distinction between themselves and the aristocracy that was not very flattering to the aristocrats. It was a matter of pride to many others to claim to be

---

[142] See Chang, Y.Z. China and English Civil Service Reform in *The American Historical Review* Vol. 47, No. 3 (April 1942), pp539-544.

[143] Wittily observed by Kate Fox (2005) in *Watching the English: The Hidden Rules of English Behaviour* London: Hodder

working class, and even as their involvement in local politics and school boards grew, they did not give up that membership. We did not have class warfare until the Chartists; radical movements were made up of people from diverse backgrounds.

We were distinguished from those across the channel by our social mobility. Provided those 'trans' class adopted the traits of those among whom they wished to move, swapping, for example, a cloth cap for a hacking jacket, they were accepted. The aristocracy did not require their wives to be armigerous, as did the Spanish nobility. In the novels of George Eliot, lords speak in local dialect. Not until the public school system was entrenched in the late 19th century did accent become a measure of one's class. We are, relatively speaking, free of class prejudice or the impediments to social mobility that exist in countries as diverse as Italy and India, Argentina or Armenia. When our politicians dishonestly claim that class distinctions hold people back, it is in order to curry favour with categories whose grievances they nurse.[144]

Summary – Unity in Diversity

Our commonality, 'somewhereness', to adapt Goodhart's expression, emerged from a hotchpotch of ethnic backgrounds and religious affiliations. That which brought us together had more pulling power than that which made us different.

---

[144] The most sensible, as well as the most succinct, report on social mobility in the UK is to be found in Saunders, Peter (2010) *Social Mobility Myths* London: Civitas.

The Offshore Islanders evolved to be the least worst society, in large part because their predominant family form engendered respect for difference and inspired enterprise, cultural and economic. The exceptional humanism, what I term *Respect* and write about in section 12, was a by-product, because communities in which people are secure and able to support themselves can be kind and allow the play of altruism. Curious though this may seem, detachment bundled cooperation.

This is not to say that our society is/was superior, but that it was appropriate for the times. Today, China, although with very different social organisation, has undertaken the industrial and information revolutions at ten times the speed of ours, so we cannot be complacent that we still have the Open Sesame. Moreover, our family form may have altered because of political manipulation, changing conceptions of womanhood and immigration too high to absorb and acculturate.

A successful society can unite because it knows what it is defending, feels independent of competitors or aggressors. Members best collaborate and are brought together by sharing a common identity. In the past, these things grew out of our distinct family form. Our society enjoyed material progress and security, if not contentment.[145]

---

[145] It could be argued that the relatively detached nature of Anglo-American relationships (by comparison with the intensity of Mediterranean families, for example) can result in anomie and depression, as well as spurring achievement. Human beings are more likely to be happy if they have close social relations; other cultures may do better at this than ours.

Being aware of the relationship between family form and development does not mean that we should attempt to recreate the past, but that when seeking to rejuvenate our society and economy, we should pay attention to the affective roots and the circumstances in which our heirs are to be raised.

Today there is a question mark over our future, such are the challenges facing us. This section seeks to explain why we achieved what we did, not how we can progress in the future, for which different conditions will need to be fulfilled. What is certain is that our community needs to reassert and share its exceptional identity, the foundation for mutual trust and collaboration.

Section **6**

WISE in the World: *Going Out*[146]

'The past is a foreign country', so why do we have to mention the Empire? Because, since leaving the EU, we appear to be struggling to work out a post-EU identity and have been accused of wanting to resuscitate The Empire. Simultaneously, an attack on Western civilisation, first made in the USA, has extended to the offshore islands. It is said that all our interactions with the world have been only exploitative and destructive. Such claims should be recognised for what they are: a kernel of fact expanded into a morass of malevolent polemic. In this section, I explain the British Empire through the perspective of future generations to identify its meaning for humanity while relegating it to the position of a deviation in the evolution of WISE itself.

---

[146] 'Going out' is a Chinese expression, which I use for WISE. Since the 1990s, Chinese entrepreneurs, engineers, health workers and others have been emigrating in a process known in China as 'going out' or 走出去。For individuals, travelling abroad provides opportunities; for the country, creating relationships on every continent provides resource security and alliances. Just as the British once sought to circumvent the hostile Catholic powers of Europe, China seeks to elude the US ring of military bases and political alliances intended to hem in China.

A China Story

Stepping down a corridor over sleeping infants, plastic buckets of laundry, tatty bundles and snoring labourers in torn shorts and string vests, I glanced through steel grills into rooms containing a dozen or more bunks walled with chicken wire. Each bunk was the home of somebody, or a mother and child together. This was the 1970s.

They were some of the two million refugees who had made it through the currents and past the machine guns to swim the 4 km from Shenzhen to British-run Hong Kong.[147] I was a teenager in the company of a haughty Englishwoman, Urban Councillor Elsie Elliott, investigating cases of abuse or corruption. Several evenings a week, she would hold a surgery in a room in one of these blocks and hear the troubles of the homeless, hawkers, prostitutes, squatters, newly arrived refugees and the sick. Several interpreters helped her understand the cases (her customers were from all over China), and then she would summarise them in English, for me to type up the record. To her, every man or woman, no matter how destitute or desperate, was a human being owed the same Respect *that she would show to the Governor or a community worker. Her* Respect *for all was the wonder, not only of the refugees who were used to being despised but also the journalists, police inspectors and civil servants whom she tried to co-opt and often lambasted.*

---

[147] Chen Bing'an: *The Great Exodus* 大逃港 Salt Lake City: American Academic

Shame at the Empire

When I first came across China's modern history at school and how the British had inaugurated the collapse of the Chinese monarchy and nearly 200 years of chaos and suffering in China, I was ashamed of the British Empire. In 1839, Chinese officials asked British traders to stop importing drugs into their world. Britain retorted with violence and then annexed Hong Kong.

To an idealistic Irish boy with a leftist mother, that clinched it. Imperialism was all bad. Once I got to Hong Kong, Councillor Elliott fired up my anger at the colonial authorities such that, in a mass demonstration against British rule, I got knocked about by a policeman and could tell myself I was a freedom fighter.[148]

The Victims' Version

And yet it was in Hong Kong that, a little later, I came across a more nuanced view of the British Empire than either the heroic one I had read about in the novels of Henty or the guilty one later taught at university. As I got to know more Chinese people, they told me that, apart from the safety from

---

[148] The demonstrations were against the rule (1971-82) of Sir Murray MacLehose. He carried out many reforms in the governance of Hong Kong, including setting up the Commission Against Corruption, the proposal for which is credited to Elsie Elliott. Many years later, I made a documentary about MacLehose for STV, an extended interview.

persecution it gave to innumerable peasants and workers, British Hong Kong provided a refuge for dissenters, liberals, intellectuals, artists and writers. First, under the monarchy, and later, after the communist conquest, Hong Kong was a refuge, without which, modern Chinese civilisation would have been much poorer.[149] I began to understand that the British Empire had long had this dual aspect – power hungry but also nurturing freedom and responsibility.

The suffering of the Chinese people in the first 30 years of communism was appalling, with mass starvation and many more killings than those inflicted by the savage Japanese occupation, of 1937 to 1945. The refugees in Hong Kong were spared that, thanks to the British administration. HK also allowed a relatively free press, freedom to associate and discuss, plus the rule of law, all of which had been abolished on the mainland. In the '80s and '90s, after Maoist barbarity had been curbed, Hong Kong was thought of by reformers in China as a model for the economy and media as well as a safe house for Chinese culture.

Once I had realised that the view of the Empire as malign is much too simple and often wrong, then the door was open to a complete rethinking. When looked at from a wide, historical, perspective, rather than the point of

---

[149] For a few weeks in my teens, I lived in an HK hostel full of Russian refugees whose parents had sought safety in Harbin but who were now hoping to flee to Australia under an UNRRA programme. They were keen to explain to me the horrors of life under communism in both USSR and People's Republic of China (PRC).

view of offended elites, it is indisputable that the British Empire set standards and raised expectations, disseminated humane values, opened closed societies and gave hope to the oppressed everywhere, not just in Hong Kong. We introduced modern medicine, advanced communications, public education and leadership training to the huddled masses of Asia and Africa. Doing so upset local despots and sometimes marginalised traditional customs such as widow burning or human sacrifice. Resentment of the British today, whether the hostility of Muslim elites or Hindu nationalists, is the delayed response to the subversion described so well in *Things Fall Apart*.[150]

There Are Empires and Empires

It is easy to emphasise the mistakes and wrongdoings of the Empire. In the takeover of India or the colonisation of Native American lands, things were done that we condemn today but which were typical of the times.[151] Yet, when we

---

[150] The great novel of Chinua Achebe, first published in 1957.

[151] The dehumanising of Africans and the devastation of communities are recounted graphically in French, Howard W. (2021) *Born in Blackness: Africa, Africans and the Making of the Modern World, 1471 to the Second World War*, New York: WW Norton. Biggar (2021) lists every imaginable horror and dereliction of duty, see Biggar, Nigel (2021) *Colonialism: A Moral Reckoning* HarperCollins Publishers. Kindle Edition. p338. Elkins details many shameful episodes and clarifies who was responsible, as well as the efforts to expose and halt them. Elkins, Caroline (2022) *Legacy of Violence: A History of the British Empire*, London: Bodley Head.

contrast the British with other empires, both pre-modern and modern, we can see that the effects of the British Empire were quite different from those of others.

The Roman and Mughal Empires were all about acquisition: Taking the resources of the conquered lands to benefit Rome or Delhi. The Ashanti and Zulu Empires were exploitative and violent. The savagery of Spain's occupation of the Americas is revolting.[152] The Soviet Russians were genocidal authors of innumerable atrocities.[153] The German Empires—whether in Africa in the 19th century or Eastern Europe in the 20th—were more systematically genocidal; they sought to kill all the educated and enslave the rest as a prelude to their total liquidation. The Japanese in China and Korea behaved similarly. They stole resources and whole industries; the people they did not starve to death were their playthings. No wonder that, in the 1940s, Indians generally preferred British rule to Japanese 'liberation'. In the Soviet Empire, Lenin initiated the slaughter of vast numbers of peasants who might doubt his right to steal their livelihoods, to say nothing of other potential opponents, especially the educated, the enterprising and whole ethnic or religious minorities. Only Mao Zedong competes with Lenin in barbarity.

---

[152] Landes, David, S. (1999) *The Wealth and Poverty of Nations: Why Some Are So Rich and Some So Poor* New York: W. W. Norton, pp76-77

[153] Ferguson Niall (2006) *The War of the World: History's Age of Hatred* New York: Penguin, Section 4

Caroline Elkins' *Legacy of Violence* sets out to show the worst aspects of the British Empire and wants us to believe what Nigel Biggar[154] finds conclusively to be false: that barbarism was the organising principle of the British Empire. She does, nevertheless, admit that its rule was quite different from that of totalitarian regimes. Her exposures are a corrective to some more idealistic histories, such as that of Jan Morris.[155] They serve to remind us how repulsive the behaviour of human beings can be, anywhere, when they have untrammelled power over other human beings. Imperialism features in all centuries and all parts of the world. Racism and violence are human conditions which some civilisations have sought to mitigate, but most have not.

What saves our forebears from being on a par with the empires of the Belgians of the 19th century or the Spaniards or Turks of earlier is what Elkins terms their 'Jekyll and Hyde' character. [156] In WISE, some had a conscience. Those who committed gross acts of violence, such as Eyre in Jamaica, or of corruption, such as Clive, were brought to trial. Yes, we had brutes, racists and malevolent fools like those whose reaction to the Easter Rising turned a putsch into a revolution, or those who commanded the incineration of entire villages in Palestine or Malaya in the

---

[154] Biggar, Nigel (2021) *Colonialism: A Moral Reckoning*
[155] Morris, James (1979) *Pax Britannica* (3 volumes) London: Faber
[156] Elkins, Caroline (2022) *Legacy of Violence: A History of the British Empire*

1950s. Yet we also had people like Emily Hobhouse who stood up for the Boer families persecuted by Kitchener and officials such as Edwin Montague, who called out crimes in India. Caroline Elkins reminds us that we failed to live up to our own humanitarian standards or to the Geneva Conventions on many occasions. Yet, because we acknowledged those conventions and cited those standards, they could be used against us to challenge not only lapses but also governance itself.

How many Japanese monsters were called out by their fellow countrymen? Were Arab or Ashanti enslavers made to feel shame by their compatriots? Who in Germany condemned the genocide of the Herero and Nama?[157]

Going Out – The Beginnings of Global Britain

It all started in the 16th century, when Spain declared herself our enemy, with our adventurers sailing abroad to plunder Spanish ships returning from Latin American colonies with loot. Before long, our traders and buccaneers started to head for Asia. The most famous of all the trading bodies, the East India Company, was founded in 1600.[158] It came to dominate India, and its responsibilities were taken over

---

[157] In 1980, CCP General Secretary Hu Yaobang apologised to the Tibetans for Chinese misrule and started to reverse the CCP's colonialist policies. Hu stands out, as an unexpectedly civilised man, at the top of the CCP.

[158] Dalrymple, William (2019) *The Anarchy: The Relentless Rise of the East India Company* London: Bloomsbury, Audible edition

by the British government only after the Indian Mutiny of 1857. Public opinion in WISE was demanding that a commercial company should not rule a whole continent and its 584 princely states. The 'mutiny' against it had different reasons in different parts of India, and most of those who suffered, contrary to missionary propaganda, were Indians, not whites. It was put down mainly by Indian troops and was not a 'war of independence' but about particular complaints. Missionary interference with local religions, competition between British and Indian businesses and the deposition of the ruler of Oudh on 'moral' grounds were the main causes.[159]

Once our government had taken over management, we come across the great paradox of the British Empire: the more it was run from London, the less Britain benefitted. Once London had sent out trained administrators, Scots engineers and doctors, Irish soldiers and Welsh chaplains, the imperial domains became increasingly a burden paid for by the British taxpayer. Even Disraeli, romantic about Empire, saw them as millstones around our necks and predicted that all the colonies would be independent before long.[160]

---

[159] Ferguson, Niall (2011) *Civilization: The West and the Rest* London: Penguin, pp 148-9

[160] Roberts, Andrew (2006) *A History of the English-Speaking Peoples Since 1900* London: Weidenfeld & Nicolson, p80. On the empire as a financial liability, see also Tombs (2021) *This Sovereign Isle: Britain In and Out of Europe*, p30.

WISE enterprise, catapulted into the wider world thanks to the Empire, changed global infrastructure. It was WISE capital, know-how (IP) and skills that established railway networks on every continent. Global shipping was mainly British. The international telegraph arrangements were made by us. Our industrial and regulatory standards have been adopted worldwide. The City of London became the global financial centre, and our law courts became the resort of the aggrieved of the world.

Empire as Responsibility

Our politicians and administrators came to advocate that our duty, as imperial rulers, was not only to liberate the poor from the burdens of rapacious landlords and chiefs but also to help develop the institutions of modern society, such as reliable public administration, healthcare and schooling. The ultimate aim was self-government. Some in WISE, particularly the religious, were arrogant, asserting superiority, but many others respected the cultures of the lands in which they served. My father was not unusual in being competent in two Indian languages, learnt while a soldier on the Northwest Frontier. His cousin, another soldier, wrote a guide to a historic Indian religious site. Much more significant than they, Warren Hastings, a founder of the 18th century Indian Empire, had been a model in his respect for Indian institutions and learning. Many other WISE scholars followed in his footsteps, preserving and honouring the cultures of the peoples in their care,[161] which no amount of malicious deconstruction, such as that of the inventor of 'orientalism', Edward Said,[162] can expunge.

More valuable to the huddled masses of Asia and Africa were modern medicine, advanced communications, public education and the nurturing of leadership. Although the regimes that have followed British rule in many countries have sought to blacken the record, their more honest compatriots have acknowledged that British rule was infinitely preferable for most of the populations than what came before or after. Plus, it brought the benefits of modernity and raised expectations.[163] Ideas of equality,

---

[161] The fact there are so many cultural artefacts of other peoples in our museums has been a matter of criticism recently, but it can equally be seen as an act of preservation and respect. Ideologists have wreaked havoc on their traditional cultures in many parts of the world, so that those wanting to restore memory of them need to visit the UK. It is rather topical that a senior curator at the Ashmolean is a Uyghur from China.

[162] Said, Edward W. (2003) *Orientalism* London: Penguin Random House. Said has long been exposed as a propagandist rather than a scholar. Biggar (2021) Ch 3 found that ancient Hindu culture was rescued from oblivion by British orientalists.

[163] Such as the anti-colonialist writer Chinua Achebe, about which see an article by Bruce Gilley, 'Chinua Achebe on the Positive Legacies of Colonialism', to be found at: https://web.pdx.edu/~gilleyb/Achebe_Final_AsPublished.pdf, accessed 161122. Nirad Chaudhuri went further, writing that 'all that was good and living within us was made, shaped, and quickened by [the same] British rule'. Chaudhuri, Nirad (1951) *The Autobiography of an Unknown Indian* London: Macmillan, Dedication. I am indebted to Gareth Stanton for introducing me to Chaudhuri and so many

accountability and individual rights seeped into Asia even if Asians rejected other aspects of the societies whence they came.[164]

Empire as Enlightenment

Kishore Mahbubani, predicting the end of Western domination of the world, nevertheless ascribes 'the enormous improvement in the human condition' to 'a slow process of Western ideas and best practices seeping into other societies,'[165] for which the principal vehicle was the British Empire.

In a lecture in 2005, the Prime Minister of India stated that '[India's] notions of the rule of law, of a constitutional government, of a free press, of a professional civil service, of modern universities…[]…our judiciary, our legal system, our bureaucracy and our police are all great institutions, derived from British Indian administration, and they have served our country exceedingly well.'[166]

A recent study of the Nigerian media describes how, emerging under British auspices in 1849, they espoused liberal ideas of a free press and watchdog journalism and often challenged the British authorities. Today, they are

other post-colonial writers when I took his MA course in post-colonialism at Goldsmiths' College many years ago.

[164] Mahbubani, *Has the West Lost It?* (2019), pp11, 25 and elsewhere.

[165] Mahbubani, *Has the West Lost It?* (2019), p11

[166] Quoted in Biggar (2021) *Colonialism: A Moral Reckoning*, p347.

the most politically vibrant media in Africa and 'at the forefront of democratic development in the country.'[167]

Withdrawal

So, it is not surprising that, in the 1940s, peoples of the Empire came to the aid of WISE against fascism. WISE could not have survived without the Empire, but after the Second World War, WISE could no longer sustain it. Our leaders hastened to offload the responsibilities onto the men and women they had prepared for independence.[168] You can say that the Empire burnt itself out, saving the world from fascism. Perhaps, also, the Scots engineers, Irish soldiers, English district officers and Welsh teachers had lost the missionary urge, and, along with Attlee, Prime Minister from 1945 to 1951, they wanted to expend their idealism in righting wrongs at home.

To imagine for a moment the world without the British Empire is to see the persistence of tyranny in advanced lands and barbarism in the backward, without the hope kindled

---

[167] Umejei. E. and Suleiman, S. (2021) 'Ten Years in Nigeria' in de Burgh, H. and Lashmar, P. (2021) *Investigative Journalism* (3rd ed) London: Routledge, p206. By contrast, it is argued elsewhere that Indian journalism has deteriorated 'since India inherited its liberal press laws from the British Raj'. See Sonwalker, Prasun (2021) India's Paradox in ibid, pp175-186.

[168] This is a simplification. Attlee's government 1945-50 turned a blind eye to exploitation and oppression in places which it wished to keep under control.

by knowledge of WISE and its values. There were crimes committed during the two hundred years of WISE *going out*. However, when the mistakes and the cruelties have receded into distant memory, its legacy is what its subjects have wanted to name 'liberalism' or 'democracy'. As I explain elsewhere in this book, I prefer to call it *'Respect'*. *Respect* for all human beings, no matter that they differ from ourselves.

Mahbubani goes much further in claiming a positive contribution from the spread of what he calls 'Western reasoning.'[169] 'The national liberation of colonized societies,' he writes, 'was much less significant than the intellectual liberation.'[170] He identifies three learnings: rulers are now accountable to the people, not the other way round; people are no longer fatalistic but believe they can improve their lot; rulers now aim to practise governance, not politics. These revolutions, like those in WISE centuries before, are changing the world for the better.

The *meaning* of the British Empire—quite unlike other empires—is that it exemplified reason and disseminated the idea of *Respect*, the champions of which imposed duties upon themselves to serve humankind.

Shaping the Modern World

I deal with the significance of the Second World War to our story in section 7. After that war, Britain was on a high as

---

[169] Mahbubani, *Has the West Lost It?* (2019), pp11-15
[170] Mahbubani, *Has the West Lost It?* (2019), p21

the saviour of the world, but was broke. The dependencies had become a costly liability. For politicians of the left, at that time, Empire did not signify the leadership of a family of nations. Rather, they saw Empire as the *exploitation of Britain* by rich internationalists, whether businessmen or the sons of the elite, enjoying 'outdoor relief' as the administrators of the Empire. Our economic policies were driven by the financial interests of overseas investors.[171] George Orwell was the best-known exponent of the view that British overseas investors betrayed the nation.[172]

The Labour government, in Edgerton's analysis, adopted a patriotic programme of economic nationalism (see Section 13), which was successful. Yet it is curious that, despite this, and despite the prestige of being the moral winner of the Second World War, many of the political class swore by 'declinism': the idea that Britain amounted to little. They could not see that the Empire had been tangential to Britain's achievements and that our country did not need to be ensconced in some greater grouping in which the British political class would set the tone. Although the Attlee government, and the later Labour government of Wilson, walked the walk—achieved economic nationalism—they did not talk the talk: persuade themselves that Britain was

---

[171] Edgerton (2019) *The Rise and Fall of the British Nation: A Twentieth-Century History*, p128.

[172] Orwell, George *The Lion and the Unicorn: Socialism and the English Genius,* and Montague, Ivor, *Traitor Class*, both published in the 1940s.

enhanced, rather than diminished, by the evaporation of the Empire.

So, with US pressure, the Labour right and the Conservative left pushed and pushed at the door of the EU (as would become) in the hope of becoming arbiters of this new empire in the making. They offered sacrifice after sacrifice—our fishing industry, our obligations to the Commonwealth, acceptance of the appalling Common Agricultural Policy (CAP, notorious for protectionism and dumping)—until, under Prime Minister Edward Heath, we joined. Prime Minister Blair even wanted us to join the Euro, which rational economists correctly predicted would destroy industry and employment.[173] The welfare of the commoners was nothing to those promoting the fantasy of a united Europe, counterweight to the USA.[174]

Well before our entry into the EU, the USA had obliged Britain to hand over international assets in order to enhance its own empire. One significant difference between the two was that Britain had, in time, accepted responsibility for the welfare of its dependents, administering to the highest standards of the times. By contrast, the USA preferred to rule through commercial and military pressure rather than

---

[173] Tombs (2021) *This Sovereign Isle: Britain In and Out of Europe*, p47

[174] The enthusiasm of the Germans and Italians was understandable, given the mortification of their decent folk for what their armies had done. The French wanted to tie Germany up, deluding themselves that Europe would be run by France. Later, the Eastern Europeans were enthusiasts for the new Habsburg Empire to protect them from any revival of Soviet imperialism.

direct government, the model seemingly being adopted by China today. To compensate for its loss of sheer power, the UK collaborated hard to create an international order in which nations would be protected from and by each other. Decisions affecting many countries would be debated, as far as is possible, in the open.

The UK maintained the Commonwealth in order to reassure the countries to which it was giving independence that they were not to be abandoned. Countries that were never colonies of the UK, including Mozambique, Togo and Rwanda, have joined since. The UK has been a founder member of the G7, the G20, the International Monetary Fund, the Organization for Security and Co-operation in Europe, NATO, the United Nations Security Council, the World Bank, the World Trade Organization and the Asian Infrastructure Investment Bank. Those are some of the positive contributions of the UK to the world, following the dissolution of the Empire. Unfortunately, because of our politicians' failure to understand that they should reinstate our pre-imperial identity rather than attempt to prolong a role as the world's prefect, they have involved us in some shameful episodes.

From Championing Self-determination to the *Two Whatevers*

The decline in status and confidence associated with the 1960s and 1970s was arrested by Margaret Thatcher's government. There are many questions to be raised over the effects of her economic reforms.[175] At least, her successful liberation of the Falklands showed that the British were still competent in war and by the 1990s, there was exhilarating evidence of economic boom.[176]

Unfortunately, the Falklands' success inspired a generation of political leaders to imagine themselves as crusaders, and the booming economy convinced them that we were above financial prudence. Stupid and immoral decisions were taken by politicians from Blair to Truss that have led to the ruin of millions of lives and the destruction of three countries. We should not forget the expenditure of trillions of taxpayers' money that should have been invested at home rather than burnt on foreign battlefields. Furthermore, we succeeded in alienating much of the world.

We have not just been lackeys of the USA but fomenters of trouble. It was PM Blair's forceful advocacy that pushed the United States into a 'liberal intervention' in Kosovo. That took place in 1998-9, but its repercussions, and those of the invitations to Georgia and Ukraine to join NATO, have lasted. Russia was turned against the West, and this led to the Crimean annexation, the invasion of Georgia and the attempted conquest of Ukraine.[177]

---

[175] Edgerton interrogates them in (2019) *The Rise and Fall of the British Nation: A Twentieth-Century History*

[176] The Suffolk where my mother lived went from grimly depressed to affluent; Edinburgh and Glasgow, where I was, transformed back into dynamic commercial centres. Yet wealth was unevenly realised over the four nations.

[177] See Milne, Seumas (2013) *The Revenge of History* London: Verso.

Blair was emboldened by his Balkans adventures, so we had 'a mournful legacy of death and destruction that destabilized the [Middle East]'.[178] As is now only too famous, Iraq was wrecked, and the lives of at least 10 million people were smashed because Blair and his acolytes fed false information about Iraq's capabilities to the USA. He justified his assault on Iraq by equating that country with Nazism, a smear, ignorant, ahistorical and dishonest, being used today on China.

Prime Minister Blair was an evangelist, whipping up US politicians to realise their 'manifest destiny'. New Labour built two aircraft carriers which could only be used in tandem with the USA.[179] Our foreign policy became, in effect, one of 'two whatevers': Whatever the USA wants, we give, and whatever the USA attacks, we attack. Once he had left British politics, Blair took a job created for him by President Bush, then, diversifying, 'work[ed] for some of the vilest torturers and dictators on earth.'[180]

Prime Minister Cameron's 2011 intervention in Libya caused a migration crisis and destabilised the Sahel region, ruining tens of millions.[181] In June 2011, the UK Foreign

[178] Bacevich, Andrew J. The Reckoning that wasn't in *Foreign Affairs*, March/April 20213, pp6-21, p12
[179] Edgerton (2019) *The Rise and Fall of the British Nation: A Twentieth-Century History*, p514 et seq
[180] Edgerton (2019) *The Rise and Fall of the British Nation: A Twentieth-Century History*, p519
[181] https://committees.parliament.uk/work/2785/libya-examination-of-intervention-and-collapse-and-the-uks-future-policy-options-

Secretary Hague opined, off-the-cuff, that the Syrian president 'must go'.[182] He had no suggestions as to how Assad, the leader of a threatened minority fighting for life, might reform, might be made to go, or might be replaced. No matter, 'Assad must go' became British policy.

Aggression in Iraq and intervention in Syria were both stupid and barbaric. Why stupid? Because the governments of both Iraq and Syria, though as cruel as any Middle Eastern government, were both enemies of the West's greatest enemy, militant Islam.[183] They were also relatively tolerant of Christian, Jewish and Muslim dissident minorities, whereas those who sought revolution were not.

So it came to pass that, because Secretary Hague wanted to sound important and Cameron to distract attention from failings at home, Britain supported rebel groups in Syria that were more vicious than the ghastly government. We thereby helped ISIS to establish its terrorist state,

---

inquiry/news/103285/libyan-intervention-based-on-erroneous-assumptions-david-cameron-ultimately-responsible/ accessed 220224

[182] https://www.bbc.co.uk/news/uk-politics-13837850, accessed 161122.

[183] It is quite wrong to blame Muslims in general for the rise of militant and violent terrorist groups. The USA conjured up the Taliban in order to counter Russian influence in Afghanistan in the 1970s. Israel is widely believed to have made the rise of Hamas, now its deadliest enemy, possible, in order to undermine the PLO. In trying to remove Assad in Syria, the Obama administration supported ISIS directly and indirectly. Mahbubani, *Has the West Lost It?* (2019), p55-56.

which was 'carrying out beheadings, mass rape, attempted genocide, destruction of historic sites, and [] launching attacks in Europe.'[184] Ten million Syrians fled their homes. Uncountable numbers were butchered. 'Syria is less free, more brutal, poorer, more corrupt and devastated by years of intense fighting.'[185] Iran has grown much more powerful.

Since 1997, Britain's foreign policy has been obedient to the US dogma that 'the fate of humankind hinges on the outcome of a cosmic struggle between democracy and autocracy' and that we know much better what is good for foreigners than they do themselves.[186] The results, of what I call 'Westism', have not been bad only for the inhabitants of those countries we helped to wreck. British interventions were defeated in Iraq, trounced in Afghanistan,[187] mocked in Libya and exploited in Syria. In all cases, they left them much worse off, their peoples angry as never before. From among the Islamic countries whose total numbers will soon outnumber Christians, we swelled the ranks of those who hate us. This was not because our military were not

---

[184] Snell, Arthur (2022) *How Britain Broke the World*, p196.

[185] Snell, Arthur (2022) *How Britain Broke the World*, p203.

[186] Bacevich, Andrew J. 'The Reckoning that wasn't' in *Foreign Affairs*, March/April 20213 pp6-21, p12. The attribution is to Biden, but the sentiments predate him.

[187] The senior Mandarin at the Foreign Office, Simon McDonald, recommended withdrawal from Afghanistan to ministers in 2010, but they did not take that decision for eleven years and only when it had, in effect, been made by others. Lambert, Harry (2023) 'Britain should not make an enemy of China' in *The New Statesman*, 19-25 May 2023.

brave, skilled, or competent. It was because, from Blair to Cameron, our politicians were indifferent, and sent them into battles they could not win.[188]

The rout from Afghanistan is seared into everybody's memory, so I don't need to use that example, too.[189]

In the 2020s, the UK has not only continued to be sycophantic to Saudi Arabia, arguably the most destabilising regime in the world, as well as one that is brutal, corrupt and genocidal, it has also, on US orders, demonised China. There are many things wrong with China's rulers, but demonising China has no effect other than to fortify xenophobic and aggressive forces there, and make collaboration on the world's big issues, more difficult.

Not content with trying to rupture relations with China, some politicians got going on alienating India, too. Prime Minister May tried to stop Indian students from studying in Britain, or any students from staying on for a couple of years for work experience, while beseeching India's decidedly unattractive leaders for a trade deal.

With such ineptitude, it is hardly surprising that when Western leaders sought help from the Saudis and Emiratis

---

[188] For a detailed analysis, see Elliott, Christopher L. (2015) *High Command: British Military Leadership in the Iraq and Afghanistan Wars* London: Hurst and Company.

[189] Although published well before the scuttle of the Western forces from Kabul, Sherard Cowper-Coles' 2012 book is revealing of the chronic incompetence and incidental savagery of the US-led war on Afghanistan. *Cables from Kabul: The Inside Story of the West's Afghanistan Campaign.*

to get around the energy crisis caused by Putin's wars, they were refused. This was despite the fact that the US had been their guardian, and the British their best suppliers of arms and diplomatic help, for generations.

Has our political class so screwed things up that Britain's influence in the world is finished? A glance at Germany is enough to tell us that renaissance is possible. If Germany can recover its international standing after giving us (in living memory, just) the worst government and military the world has ever seen,[190] then surely, we can recover from the sordid buffoonery of our last few Prime Ministers?

Conclusion

During the three hundred years in which WISE made the modern world, there were many injustices and much suffering which cannot be excused or forgotten. The descendants of victims of the British Empire, like the victims of the Ottomans or the Japanese, can hardly be comforted. Yet, for humanity as a whole, the eruption of WISE in the world has been a liberation. Hundreds of millions live healthier, more educated and safer lives than their forbears because WISE standards and expectations

---

[190] There is not much to choose between the Hitler regime and that of Lenin and Stalin, except that Hitler industrialised genocide, whereas his Russian confreres, in wiping out inconvenient nations, races and cultures, imitated Genghis Khan.

replaced fatalism and subjection.[191] The fiercest denigrators of the British Empire have been those who want to deny their people those advances: Mao Zedong, smashing a civilisation in his lust for power; President Putin of Russia, reviving medieval belligerence; Islamist fanatics destroying the lives of others to earn access to an imaginary paradise.

WISE does not need to be trapped in a vision of the world determined either by nostalgia for the Empire or by shame at it. WISE is much greater than the British Empire, which is why the British Empire was like no other in its positive effects. Recognition of WISE achievement and benefits to humanity should be the *first* principle of our international strategy. Our political leaders must face down the subversion of European civilisation and WISE institutions, that we may survive and continue to make our contributions.[192]

The *second* should be a rejection of the division of the world into blocs. Once upon a time, the Communist world faced the Capitalist world. Capitalism won. Today, such a sharp ideological, political and economic division no longer exists. China is the most important commercial partner of well over 100 countries. Some of those may fear China's economic clout, but they don't want to detach from it, nor do they feel threatened ideologically or militarily. Few want

---

[191] Kishore Mahbubani expresses this sentiment most eloquently in his remarkable essay *Has the West Lost It?*

[192] The subversion is most clearly described in Murray, Douglas (2022) *The War on the West* London: Harper Collins.

to choose sides, 'democracies' versus 'authoritarianism'. Life is not as simple as the Southern Baptists think. By inventing this dichotomy, the US has alienated many, increasing the fragmentation of the world.[193] We must not go along with it, lest it lead to war.[194]

The *third* principle, which derives from the first two, is that we should reinforce the international rules-based order – a constellation of understandings and rules both written and unwritten - and seek to build bridges to those non-Western powers which have lost faith in Anglo-American moral authority. The order has lost credibility, not just because the non-Western countries had little part in making the rules, but because we showed, by ignoring them, that we didn't take those rules seriously when US interests were involved.[195] By contrast, China can be seen to have attempted to support the order while, like every other country, also seeking to work the system so that it operates in its own interests.[196]

The *fourth* principle must be that which animated our statesmen in past centuries, for it is the only rule to which a leader should unfailingly adhere: strategic pragmatism.

---

[193] Leonard, Mark, China is ready for the world to disorder, America is not. *Foreign Affairs*, July, August 2023, p127.

[194] Allison, Graham (2017) *Destined for War: Can America and China Escape Thucydides's Trap?* London: Scribe

[195] Leonard, Mark, China is ready for the world to disorder, America is not. *Foreign Affairs*, July-August 2023, p118

[196] Robert Zoellick, former US Deputy Secretary of State, has been vocal on this point. https://www.youtube.com/watch?v=TVfZBdx7Rgk

In the wider world in which nations and cultures trade, we are on the trading floor with all the rest: Our capital is the WISE identity; our currency is creativity; our wares are ideas that stimulate, motivate and galvanise.

Our leaders' first duty is the perpetuation and enhancement of WISE, not only because this matters to every other society on earth but also because they are in their positions to represent the interests of the people who made, make and will make up these nations: past, present and future.

Section 7

WISE in the World: The Invention of Liberty

'Global Britain' only gradually became our international policy. It was in the 16th century that the resourceful and the desperate started *going out* from WISE,[197] first as pirates, then traders and settlers, finally as administrators and educators. How this came about, and its consequences, were covered in Section 6. Now we remind ourselves of the international strategy of WISE from the 16th to 20th centuries, *opposition to tyranny in Europe,* which became the basis of our identity as the liberator.

A China Story

In 1941, as Japanese troops bayonetted, raped and burnt in Hong Kong, a young Welsh corporal, Taffy Whitehead, shimmied down a sewage pipe and swam to the mainland. Eventually, he travelled nearly 1,000 miles to where a British commando unit was working with our Chinese allies

---

[197] I deliberately use the term *going out*, from the Chinese 走出去, the practice of investing money and energy overseas.

to undermine the Japanese.[198] *The Second World War had begun in China in 1937, with a Japanese invasion. It was not until 1941, however, that the Anglo-American countries seriously aided their Chinese allies, two years after the Nazi - Soviet assault on Poland of September 1939. Hard pressed in Europe, our contribution was small, though the alliance with China was possibly what prevented the Japanese from enslaving India.*

Taffy Whitehead was a soldier of an imperial power which, though now its ally, had subjected China to defeat and humiliation for the last 100 years, yet this did not weigh with the Chinese who helped him in his escape from the Japanese. He represented resistance to something much worse.

....

Liberty in Europe

Once the Norman kings had lost their territories on the European mainland, they realised that they were not continental rulers with holiday homes on the offshore islands, but should put all their efforts into the island kingdoms. By the reign of Henry III, there was a faction in government which considered that involvement in continental wars was justifiable only if necessary to subvert

---

[198] Whitehead, John S. et al. (1990) *Escape to Fight On* London: Robert Hale

any attempts at hegemony on the continent.[199] After the Reformation of 1532 in England, 1560 in Scotland, when Roman Catholicism was ousted as the state religion, the differences between us and our continental enemies became ideological as much as political.

In 1585, the English saw off an invasion by Spain with the defeat of the Spanish Armada. The Spanish monarch had planned to establish a religious despotism in the British Isles. This was not just a power grab, but an ideological crusade. Spain's attempts to attack from Ireland, where Roman Catholicism had retained its hold on the peasantry and would manage to associate itself with Celtic grievances,[200] prompted a doubling down of Queen Mary's colonisation of Ireland by her 17th-century successors. In 1690, it was France that invaded, expecting to use Ireland to launch an attack on England, but was repulsed.

The campaigns of Marlborough, from 1701 onwards, prevented domination of Western Europe by France and ended in a treaty of 1713. WISE would come to oppose hostile takeovers of any small countries. By the late 18th century, it protected Holland, Belgium, Greece and Portugal and provided refuge for freedom fighters from Italy to Poland, from Hungary to Russia.

---

[199] See Churchill, Winston (2003) *A History of the English-Speaking Peoples*, pp224-7; Carpenter, D.A. (1990) *The Minority of Henry III* London: Methuen, pp134-145 and elsewhere.

[200] A clever volte-face because the Roman church had earlier undermined and absorbed the Celtic (or Irish-Scottish) church.

In 1805, Admiral Nelson thwarted Napoleon's invasion of Britain at the Battle of Trafalgar. Afterwards, we would grow our Royal Navy into the force that would turn Britain into a global power. In 1815, allied with German states and Holland, Wellington destroyed Napoleon on land, rescuing the small nations from his tyranny.

One hundred years later, we would ally with the French against Germany's would-be Napoleon, Wilhelm II. The World War of 1914-18 was recognised by all reformist people, for example, the suffragettes, as a righteous war to uphold moral values[201] that Germany was determined to extirpate, along with the British Empire, which was diffusing those values. In the 19th century, the Germans had foreshadowed the Holocaust of the 1940s by attempting genocide on several African peoples, inventing death camps and carrying out inhumane 'medical' experiments.[202]

The Second World War (1937-45) was the next effort by WISE to contain or destroy would-be totalitarian powers.

---

[201] The words used included 'civilisation' and 'decency', what we would now term 'democracy', 'human rights' and 'diversity'. On the victory medal issued by all allies is the inscription 'The Great War for Civilisation'.

[202] We should distinguish between 'concentration camps' in which people are herded for political or military reasons as a temporary measure, where murder is not the objective, and 'death camps' where the intention is that the inmates be either worked to death, starved to death or simply liquidated.

World War Two: How WISE Beggared Itself and Saved the World

The story of 'The Few' is rightly celebrated. In 1940, 500 airmen died to see off a German conquest. That much, most Britons know. But why did they do what they did, and why was it necessary?

Following successful invasions of Czechoslovakia and Poland, German armies attacked and overcame France in 1940. These were not just cases of nationalistic opportunism. Hitler had stated his strategic and genocidal intentions in his writings and speeches over many years, and they attracted at least some supporters in every European nation.

Since Hitler had come to power in Germany in 1933, refugees had been fleeing to anywhere that would take them. To the Polish, Czech and German opponents of Nazism, 'the alternative was to acquiesce in world domination by an alliance of genocidal fascist states.'[203] In Latimer House, near London, the MI9 Atrocities File recorded the horrors of Nazi extermination policies and provided the data to our government.

---

[203] Tombs (2021) *This Sovereign Isle: Britain In and Out of Europe*, p17. He is referring to Japan, Communist Russia and Nazi Germany. Germans had carried out genocide in Africa in the 19th century and had been guilty of many atrocities in WWI, so Hitler's plans could be seen as merely an extension of a genocidal programme. Japan's barbarity in China commenced as early as 1931 and intensified following the invasions of 1937.

Thus, WISE was very aware that this was not just a war of nations, but a battle for civilised life for the sake of all humankind.[204] Had they caved in to aggression, Nazism and its then ally, Soviet Russia, would have conquered much of the world. So, the ideological threat was paramount for Britain, though not for France, where most people acquiesced, and many abetted, the Nazi *new order*.

The proximate reason why we were alone was that the Polish Army had been destroyed by the combined invasion of the Nazis and Soviets acting in concert. The challenge to Britain was not only the fact that all its allies in Europe had been defeated but also that Japan, temporarily held down by Chinese resistance, menaced our Asian allies, and Russia was backing Germany with supplies. We faced three mighty enemies, and the USA would not come to our aid.

---

[204] Many have tried to portray the war as nationalist. My parents, both in the army, never had any doubt that this was a multinational war against a barbaric ideology. True, my mother was unusually informed, since she worked on atrocities for MI9, first at Latimer House, then in Combined Services Detailed Interrogation Centre (CISDIC) North Africa and finally at Army HQ Caserta. She then transferred to the Allied Screening Commission and served with Germans, Poles and Italians. Captured in North Africa, my father spent two years in several different prison camps among men of every conceivable background who nevertheless shared the same realisation that they were fighting against an ideological movement as inhumane as communism. On the revelations of Nazi prisoners at Latimer House and elsewhere, see Fry, Helen (2020) *The Walls Have Ears: The Greatest Intelligence Operation of World War II* Yale: YUP

Because The Few saw off multiple air attacks in the Battle of Britain, our islands survived to be the launching pad for the 1944 liberation of the continent[205]. Aside from this extraordinary feat, WISE achieved so much else in WWII that we have a right to see the victory as that of the British Empire. Here are nine more often great feats.

Two: After that air battle, the next significant achievement was bolstering Russian resistance, once the USSR had been obliged, by the vexing attack from its Nazi ally, to change sides. Early in the war, fighting on three continents, WISE suffered many setbacks. Nevertheless, we supplied massive resources to Russia, depriving our own troops. We ran a bombing campaign in Germany designed to help Russia rather than to advance ourselves. We made their counterattacks possible.

Three: WISE was able to supply the Russians because our industry performed miracles, turning out vastly more military equipment than the Germans, sufficient to supply our armies worldwide and our allies.

Four: We took in innumerable refugees from the conquered nations and allowed their governments to operate from Britain.

Five: Our scientists broke the Axis codes at Bletchley, and our psychiatrists prised information out of prisoners

---

[205] Less well known is the Air Battle for Malta, by which that island, at great cost in airmen and machines, was saved as a hub of Allied resistance. See Douglas-Hamilton, James (2006) *The Air Battle for Malta: Diaries of a Spitfire Pilot*, Barnsley: Pen & Sword and many other works.

so that we were able to provide essential intelligence to our own troops as well as to our allies. These were donations of the intellectuals.

Six: Our campaign in the North African desert prevented the Germans from taking over the oilfields of the Middle East; this was the strategic significance of the Battle of El Alamein in 1942. The victorious commander was from Donegal, Bernard Montgomery.

Seven: The invasion of Italy, led by another Irishman, Alexander, was undertaken both to relieve pressure on Russia and further to divide Nazi forces, by this time multinational,[206] in preparation for the allied landings in France.

Eight: Some films imply that US soldiers ran the largest invasion ever mounted in world history, Operation Overlord, which started on D-Day 1944. In fact, the brunt of the Normandy fighting was by WISE troops, and all land forces were commanded by Montgomery.

Nine: The anti-fascist alliance was 'indispensable to victory'[207] and was pulled together—could only be pulled together—by Britain.

Finally, ten: The architect of resistance was Winston Churchill. He was the strategist of the free world, not only

---

[206] About a million non-Germans volunteered to serve in the Nazi armies. About a quarter of those fighting with the Nazis at Stalingrad are believed to have been Russians. Later, in 1944, Soviet General Vlasov recruited the ill-fated Russian Liberation Army to fight against communism.

[207] Tombs (2021) *This Sovereign Isle: Britain In and Out of Europe*, p20

uniting the Anglophone countries and the British Empire but also pulling the USA and USSR together and inspiring the conquered nations of Europe to resist.[208]

With these, along with many other contributions, WISE was the moral victor of WWII, yet our economy and international business were wrecked.[209] Incidentally, we further indebted ourselves and tightened our own rationing to get food to starving Germany after its defeat.

Three centuries before, it had been the persecuted Protestant communities of Europe which were grateful to us. In the 19th century, we rescued the emerging small nations from absorption by Napoleon; in the 20th century, much of the world was saved, thanks to WISE, from the second most vicious form of totalitarianism yet devised, Nazism.[210]

We had once again shown that WISE had unique responsibilities which its people were still able to meet.

---

[208] Ferguson (2006) *The War of the World: History's Age of Hatred* makes the point that Britain's war was managed by committee, avoiding the mistakes that might have been made had Churchill wielded the power of a Hitler. Nevertheless, as a symbol and figurehead, Churchill's influence was immense.

[209] John Keegan summarises this succinctly in Keegan, John (1995) *The Battle for History* London: Hutchinson, p97.

[210] Yet is often forgotten that Lenin and his heirs conquered the nations which became the USSR, slaughtering many millions in the 30-year process of empire-building and carrying out genocide, the techniques of which the Nazis studied and systematised. (See Evans, Richard J. (2012) *The Third Reich in Power* London: Penguin.

Our mission in Europe was to save the French from their philosophers, the Italians from their politicians, and the Germans from their perverts.

From the Frying Pan into the Fire

In recent years, it has often been noted that the British political class, after the dissolution of their Empire, felt that their own country was not enough to hold their interest and that their own people were decidedly unattractive.[211] Many became desperate to join the project for a United States of Europe. The commoners generally saw our entering (what became) the EU as joining a common market: a purely business proposition. Yet, for many members of the European political classes, the European project, like Mussolini's *Mare Nostrum,* comes from nostalgia for the Roman Empire, if not from the simple urge to hoard power that is common to the administrative and political classes everywhere, often excused as 'economies of scale'.

It was also justified with the myth that WWII was a nationalist war and that we would only abolish war if we abolished nations. In truth, WWII was yet another religious or ideological war, and the fascist Axis was opposed by patriots defying a transnational ideology: Scandinavians, Dutch, Greeks, Czechs, Poles, and the Offshore Islanders

---

[211] Paul Embery, in *Despised: Why the Modern Left Loathes the Working Class* (2021) Cambridge: Polity, describes the latest iteration of a revulsion that George Orwell first noted.

themselves. Germans and Austrians—refugees from Nazism or Communism—served in the British and US forces. Both Stalin and Hitler sold their schemes as patriotic but deployed ideology to use and abuse their nations.[212]

European integration has long been marketed as a project for keeping peace by phasing nations out, but NATO is more apt for such peacekeeping. We were told that European integration would keep Germany down, yet Germany is in charge. Over the years, it was the predominance of Germany that made the British position in the EU untenable. At the European Commission, German interests come first. As the pro-German former UK Ambassador to Germany, Paul Lever, writes, 'No decision can be taken that goes counter to the German government.'[213] Germany cannot be outvoted in the European Parliament, and the president must always be a person acceptable to Germany.

It is the German economy that has benefitted above all: the EU is its large, tariff-free market in which German industry is shielded from competition – by tariffs! Germany uses the EU agenda to reduce the competitiveness of other firms and countries. It can do this because of the

---

[212] To get absolute power for themselves, greedy men have to persuade people to believe in nonsense, of which the greedy men are the keeper and interpreter. They then need to implicate the masses in their crimes (e.g. genocide in Communist Russia and Nazi Germany). Unfortunately, in the monotheistic world, this has not proved difficult.

[213] Lever, Paul (2017) *Berlin Rules* London: IB Tauris

powerful network of German officials in the Commission and because of the German members of the European Parliament and their dependents.[214]

Much of this was foreseen by the prescient Labour politician Peter Shore at the time of our accession.[215] However, it was not even raised at the time of the referendum, when the key issue for the British people was the restoration of democracy here, rather than who ran Europe. For the Dutch, Danes and Irish, who had all voted against membership of the EU at some point, it was the EU's damage to their economies that figured first.

Expansion of the EU and NATO to include Eastern Europe was a German project, as was policy towards Ukraine in 2014-15,[216] both of which have had dreadful consequences.

Brexit and Our Identity

As the wartime exploits of Taffy Whitehead show, WISE has not, for a long time, been only a European entity. It took the French leader, Charles de Gaulle, who detested Britain, to summarise this best. '[Britain] is an island, seagoing, bound up by its trade, its markets, its food supplies, with

---

[214] Lever (2017) *Berlin Rules,* p187
[215] Hickson, Kevin et al. (2020) *Peter Shore: Labour's Forgotten Patriot* London: Biteback, Section 3
[216] Lever (2017) *Berlin Rules,* p25, p219

the most varied and often the most distant countries.'[217] He foresaw that Britain, no matter how hard its then-political class might try to chop off its global relationships, would be an uneasy and perhaps disruptive element in the new Roman Empire that was under construction.

I have tended to emphasise the differences between WISE and the rest of the world, but this should not be taken as a denial of the *Europeanness* of WISE. Although WISE provided much thought leadership and effected revolutions of the mind faster and more thoroughly than the neighbours, WISE had been fertilised by Greek, Roman, Italian, French, Dutch and German ideas. The advance of continental European countries in so many spheres came about in great measure because of the competition and variety between the states. WISE played a big part in ensuring that Europe's many nations were not subordinated to any one authority.

---

[217] https://www.historyextra.com/period/20th-century/the-reluctant-europeans/, accessed 221222. Like Chinese and Italians, the French rarely bring themselves to utter the word 'Britain' but conflate all WISE into 'England'. Thanks to the English Channel and WISE's sense of otherness, during WWII, WISE was able to save France, not to speak of the rest of Europe, from a fate worse than death. During the war, General de Gaulle, in opposition to the collaborationist French government, took refuge in Hampstead. He involved himself in the schemes of the Anglo-American allies and planned the resurrection of France from London's Connaught Hotel. He was allowed to pretend that he and his kind were representative, when they were not, and, finally, to posture that he had liberated France, which he had not.

Other points can be made about our relationship with the 44 states that make up Europe, and particularly with the EU, which comprises 27 of them. Both those who regret Brexit[218] and those who celebrate it, surely agree that, in the years ahead, we will nevertheless find ourselves allied with European countries and the EU in innumerable ways.

We have seen what happened to China when an open society was closed by political fiat, when the possibilities inherent in the remarkable scientific and technological advances of pre-modern China were repressed. Some see the EU today as aping the repressive regime of Ming Dynasty China or the European Counter-Reformation, suppressing free thought and enterprise. For them, Brexit is an assertion, not just of sovereignty or of our political difference from countries where the commoners have never been the architects of the state, but of our tradition of preserving the variety and competitiveness of Europe. Yesterday, we challenged, on behalf of ethnic and religious minorities, kings in periwigs and pickelhaubes; today, we are protecting difference from the haughty mandarins of Brussels and the bankers of Berlin.

In the 20th century, it was because we had not been subsumed into the continent that we could rally the conquered. It was because of Britain's global connections—the empire but also the Anglosphere—that Europe was

---

[218] Sayers, Fred (2023) notes that many regret Brexit, see 'Introducing UnHerd Britain 2023' What does your constituency think about today's political issues? https://unherd.com/2023/01/introducing-unherd-britain-2023/, accessed 201023.

saved. Conditions are different now. The sea is not such a barrier; our trusty allies are limited to the Aukus, with which, however, our interests have diverged. The USA and Australasia feel challenged in Asia. We are challenged by the Islamic world nearby and by Putin's Russia. If WISE is to continue to stand for freedom and justice in the world, it cannot do so alone, yet must not be dependent on any one global power but waltz with all: the USA, EU, China, India and Russia. To manage this requires a higher order of skill than that displayed by our present political leaders. They would do well to study Disraeli and Pitt, if not Machiavelli and Sun Tzu, if they are to lead the inventors of liberty successfully into the future.

SECTION **8**

WISE and the USA: Poor Relations

Notions common in the political class—that we should glory in our deference to the USA because it has taken over the burden of running the world from us, and that we can count on generosity from our closest ally—are romantic. They diminish us. Subservience to the USA has seen us forfeit what moral authority we had. In return, we have been patronised and exploited. We need to take off our rose-tinted glasses and face reality.

....

A China Story

Pearl Buck (1892-1973) was an American missionary, the daughter of missionaries, who spent much of her youth in China and was a most profound observer of Chinese society, world famous writer and Nobel laureate. Her experiences in China made her a stern critic of her country's attitudes and behaviour towards others.

Pearl Buck accused the USA of insular absurdity. She described it as 'attempting to superimpose 19th-century biblical orthodoxy on an ancient, highly civilized culture, naturally tolerant, non-evangelical, and mellowed by long human experience into a philosophy of humanism. Militant Christianity, backed up by armed force and gunboats, subverted deep-rooted systems of ethical belief, judicial practice and administrative organization in favour of a simplistic morality that denounced any but the most basic education as elitist claptrap, regarded tolerance as a vice, and prized 'aggressive evangelistic work' as a self-evident good. [] The effrontery of all this still makes my soul shrink' [Pearl Buck] *wrote.*[219]

What Pearl Buck saw in China years ago is on the cards elsewhere: communities caving in to the US notion of the world, becoming cultural satrapies and political dependents. We have been warned.

Anglo-America: 'One Country, Two Systems?'

Modern historians have been revising the old view, commonplace in the mid-20th century, that Britain and the USA are distinct countries and competitors. Instead, they have started to look at Anglo-America as one entity divided by geography: one country, two systems. They emphasise the continuity of political and cultural traditions from the Offshore Islanders in what became the USA,[220] and the

---

[219] Spurling, Hilary (2010) *Burying the Bones: Pearl Buck in China* London: Profile, p54.

[220] Freedland, Jonathan (1998) *Bring Home the Revolution* argues that US democracy today is the logical extension of 18th-century British traditions, stymied here.

adoption of WISE agricultural and industrial IP in the 'new world'. Lawrence Mead puts it this way: '…America was never a new nation….The British gave it the rule of law and government by consent on a plate. The Americans never had to develop these things on their own.'[221]

The American 'War of Independence' (1775-1783) is now seen as a WISE civil war and, indeed, a continuation of the Civil War of 1640-1649.[222] These two conflicts pitted against each other predominantly dissenting[223] communities, both commercial and relatively democratic, with those who tended to be Anglo-Catholic, agricultural and hierarchical. Dissenters were at the forefront of what, in Section 12, I term the *Respect* movement and were more likely to be concerned with what we now call 'human rights and democracy' than their opponents.

Victory in each of these wars, as in the negotiations around the British Glorious Revolution of 1688, went to the rising business class, usually dissenters, although landowners remained powerful. The politics of 17th-century Britain influenced the USA because, at that time, Americans considered themselves part of the British political world.

---

[221] Mead, Lawrence M. (2019) *Burdens of Freedom: Cultural Difference and American Power,* p174

[222] Phillips, Kevin (1999) *The Cousins' Wars* New York: Basic; Fischer, David Hackett (1989) *Albion's Seed: Four British Folkways in America* Oxford: OUP

[223] In the UK, dissenters also included Roman Catholics, but as is common, when I use the term here, I am indicating Protestants, Quakers and Unitarians.

The shared ideology was Protestantism, and it has animated the USA ever since.

Britain was, in turn, also affected by the defeat of the Crown and patriots in the US War of Independence. Our political class grasped that it should not hold out against calls for political liberties by the ever more prosperous commercial classes, or it might find a revolution on its hands.

Victory in the Civil War of 1861-65 is thought to have reflected and reinforced democratic tendencies in Britain. It has been claimed that our Great Reform Bill came about as much because of the US Civil War as of agitation at home.[224]

Civil Wars of Anglo-America

The myth of the founding of the United States in rebellion against an overweening Crown is thus only partly true. It was long used to paint the USA as an underdog, struggling against exploitative imperialists.

The rebellion probably had little, if anything, to do with taxes.[225] Some rebels, a tiny minority at the outset, were concerned about representation in Parliament, using the old English slogan 'No taxation without representation'. What really infuriated George Washington and his fellow rebels about the Crown, though, was not so much the taxes—lower than in the UK, anyway—but that the British

---

[224] Phillips, *The Cousins' Wars* (1999), passim
[225] Ferguson (2012) *The Great Degeneration*, p85 and onwards

government wanted to protect the rights of the indigenous peoples and prevent slavery.[226]

Wealthy settlers could not abide that the British wanted to shield the natives from their rapacity. Under British administration, natives were treated with consideration. There was a flourishing British Indian Society with a Mohican cleric. Parliament was introducing an Indian Bill of Rights. In 1763, the Native American tribes joined together with the Crown, in order to defend themselves against genocide by the settlers.[227]

These contrasting approaches continued after the founding of the USA. In the War of 1812, the British were allied with Native Americans and African-American slaves against the colonists. The British advocated setting up a Native American state in Ohio, Indiana and Michigan, but the USA defeated the Native American defence. In 1812-14, Britain successfully protected Canada, to which many patriots had fled, from attempted conquest by the US.

---

[226] Tombs (2015) *The English and their History*, p353. In citing these facts, I have no desire to give support to the USA's 1619 Movement to tear down the US founding myth. No matter that there are blemishes in the story and that its heroes were not perfect, the founding of the USA is the greatest story ever told, the first and greatest attempt to create a polity from scratch, or, rather, based on the principles and institutions devised in WISE.

[227] Ferguson, Niall (2011) *Civilization: The West and the Rest* London: Penguin, pp85 and 115-17

Strange Alliances – The USA and the UK in the 20th Century

By the latter half of the 19th century, many Britons had begun to regret the enlargement of Empire and to see it as a responsibility and a burden. Not so the USA, which expanded immensely through its seizure of 55% of Mexico's territory (1846) to create the US states of California, Nevada, Utah, New Mexico, Arizona and Colorado. Bits of Mexico were given to Oklahoma, Kansas, and Wyoming. The US attacked Spain in the Philippine-American War of 1898 and netted itself the colonies of Philippines, Guam and Puerto Rico.[228]

During the First World War, the USA did not ally with the UK until it was threatened by the possibility of a German-Mexican alliance in 1917. Similarly, in the Second World War, the USA allied with us only after war had been declared on it by Japan and Germany. Before doing so, the USA had sold supplies to WISE, but on commercial terms, even though the collapse of France made Britain's situation desperate. The US approach was, as described by Churchill, that of 'a sheriff collecting the last assets of a

---

[228] The story of US imperialism is too vast to deal with here. See these websites, all accessed 151222:

https://www.brookings.edu/articles/american-empire-not-if-but-what-kind/

https://en.wikipedia.org/wiki/Foreign_interventions_by_the_United_States

https://en.wikipedia.org/wiki/American_imperialism

helpless debtor.'[229] The USA privileged the USSR among its allies, preferring to donate to Stalin, murderous heir of the murderous Lenin.

The story of how the USA took advantage of Britain's plight, taking over resources of the British Empire or undermining its rule during and after the Second World War, has been told in great detail elsewhere,[230] as has the story of how British generosity—or naivety—built the US intelligence services.[231]

After Britain had supplied the USA with nuclear know-how, the USA stopped dealing with us until an agreement was made by which the UK became dependent upon the USA for its defence.[232] As bad, Britain succumbed to the extraordinary arrangement by which there are up to 103 US bases on UK soil that are extraterritorial (i.e. we have no power over or in them). Even the Philippines, a former US colony, does not have such an arrangement.

George Orwell complained about extraterritoriality in 1943. Not only does WISE have no influence over US bases' deployment of weapons, but their personnel are not subject to British law. When, in 2019, the wife of a diplomat killed a local boy while driving near a US base in

---

[229] Hitchens, Christopher (2004) *Blood, Class and Empire: The Enduring Anglo-American Relationship* London: Atlantic, p209

[230] Hitchens (2004) *Blood, Class and Empire*, chapters 7 & 8

[231] Littell, Robert, (2002) *The Company* London: MacMillan and Kerbaj, Richard (2022) *The Secret History of the Five Eyes* London: John Blake

[232] Hitchens, (2004) *Blook, Class and Empire*, Section 13

Northamptonshire, she fled to the USA. The USA refuses to extradite her to face trial.

On the plus side, the US government gave us reluctant support when Britain sent a task force to liberate the Falkland Islands in 1982. Public opinion in the USA was much more supportive than that of the political class, suggesting that a WISE politician might find it possible to make common cause with US commoners to pressure their politicians. Since the Falklands War, our relationship with the USA has been less helpful. It was cleverly summarised by Boris Johnson, in a novel written long before he became Prime Minister. One of his characters thinks about that relationship:

Britain slavishly followed America in the war on terror. She helped her take out the Taliban. British taxpayers coughed up more than 5 billion pounds to gratify the neocons of Washington and remove Saddam Hussein. [] When the war on terror yielded its first spoils and British subjects were arrested in Afghanistan on suspicion of being members of Al-Qaeda, Britain dutifully assented to their incarceration without trial, without due process, without any regard to the ancient principle of *habeas corpus* in a mysterious camp in Cuba. []

British citizens were being held without charge or access to lawyers in the illegal extraterritorial fourth dimension of an American army camp on a communist island on suspicion of being on the slightly more anti-western side of a war between two sets of bearded Islamists somewhere in Central Asia. [] Soon the British public had forgotten about the infamies of Camp X-Ray, eclipsed as they were by the scandals of Abu Ghraib.

And how had the Americans behaved [] when Britain was fighting her own war on terror? Irish Republicans [IRA] blew up pubs, fish and chip shops, cars and rubbish bins. They tried to blow up the stock exchange in Canary Wharf in plots that could have been as calamitous as the bombing of the Twin Towers. They murdered and maimed hundreds of civilians, and yet Americans moronically passed around a hat for them in Boston and New York. American presidents invited IRA leaders to the White House and shook hands with them on the lawn in defiance of the wishes of Downing Street.[233]

They didn't care whether they gave legitimacy to these cruel and bitter men; they cared about the Irish vote [in the USA]. And when Britain wanted to extradite Irish terrorist suspects to the UK to face the due process of the law, Washington did not want to know.[234]

---

[233] Johnson could have made a more positive point: that US politicians played a valuable part in the Northern Ireland Peace Process, possibly influencing the terrorist leaders to abjure violence and embrace politics.

[234] Johnson, Boris (2005) *Seventy-Two Virgins* London: Harper Collins, pp184-185

The above omits the contribution that US President Clinton and Senator George Mitchell (whose biography is an affirmation of the American Dream) made to the Irish Peace Process. Nevertheless, it reminds us that WISE should not be sentimental about our relationship with the US state, even if the people are our cousins and colleagues. We can recognise the positive contributions of the USA to humanity: Millions have emigrated to the USA and been able to create a better life for themselves and their descendants than at home. The USA admitted refugees from Russia and Eastern Europe who fled pogroms and Soviet imperialism. The USA invented the Marshall Plan after the Second World War and provided aid to the wrecked nations of Europe and East Asia so that they could buy US products and be knitted into the anti-Communist bloc. This was made easier by the fact that the war had galvanised the previously depressed US economy, and the whole country had boomed. Without US power, atrocities in Yugoslavia in the 1990s would never have been stopped;[235] the Europeans showed themselves to be pitiful. Over the war in Ukraine and the 2023 Hamas assault on Israel, the USA showed the way. Its open society, modelled on WISE, has spawned innumerable innovations, great universities, prodigious scientific advances and world-changing enterprise.

Nevertheless, the two contrasting notions of the world that we initially came across in the first Anglo-American

---

[235] Ferguson Niall (2006) *The War of the World: History's Age of Hatred* London: Penguin, Section 24

Civil War of the 1640s have exchanged locations. By contrast with the aftermath of the Second World War, the USA has since been notable for the aggressive pursuit of its own interests, while *Respect* is more associated with WISE.[236] As a result, the USA is seen by many Asians, among others, as a violent and corrupt hooligan, the media of which promote greed and selfish individualism, poisoning as much of the world as they can gain access to. They are cynical about the humanitarian interventions, the peace process in the Middle East, the contributions to international organisations aiming at peace and prosperity for all, and the championing of democracy. To them, these are all just attempts to continue Western domination by other means.[237]

The British Political Class and US Hegemony

With their myth of liberation from British colonialism, Americans presented themselves as more democratic and egalitarian than we. In the early 20th century, they ignored the shared cultural origins, even as we made much of them. By the time of the Second World War, to US leaders, Britain was just another importuning country; after it, many in WISE came to see the USA as imperial and even tyrannical. They pointed out its corrupt politics, endemic violence and shocking poverty. They demonstrated against USAF bases and nuclear facilities in the UK. It is as if the dissenting

---

[236] There are minorities in both countries advocating the opposite.
[237] Mahbubani, *Has the West Lost It?* (2019), p50

tradition that created the USA had come back to life in Britain to counterbalance the belligerence of today's USA.

The British relationship with the USA needed and still needs to be pragmatic and flexible. Yet, aside from Harold Wilson, who refused to commit to the disastrous war on Vietnam, and Margaret Thatcher, who had a dignified relationship of equals with Ronald Reagan, British political leaders have allowed us to become dependent upon the United States, even servile.

The 21st Century

By the time Blair resigned as Prime Minister to take a job as an international spokesman for President Bush in 2007,[238] the UK was so integrated into the USA, militarily and commercially, that even if his successors understood the dangers, they couldn't decouple. Under Johnson, we cringingly joined its gambit to derail China's advance by ruining Chinese high-tech companies. Democrats shelved the free trade deal, that was planned with the Trump administration for after we left the EU, and made explicit their hatred for Britain in noising it around that Brexit would reignite terrorism in Ireland.

When we are posing as on the side of reason and light, or at least democracy, it is galling to know that our partner

---

[238] Technically, he was a UN Envoy, but the post was created for him. He was the only applicant and was interviewed for the job by President Bush.

is doing the same wicked things for which it condemns other countries. On many different dimensions, such as maintenance of the rule of law and freedom from corruption, for example, 'its reputation is shockingly bad.'[239]

Edward Snowden, whistle blower at the National Security Agency, revealed the mass acquisition of telecommunications data, and bulk interception of internet traffic by the US, in 2013. He showed that we too took part in a global surveillance apparatus, jointly run by the Five Eyes Network, which ignores laws or accountability. We learnt that the agencies have secretly negotiated for 'backdoors' in the security of computer programs, social networking sites, websites and smartphones. This gives them an 'extraordinary capability to hoover up and store personal emails, voice contact, social networking activity and even internet searches.'[240]

Snowden's revelations, and those of other whistle-blowers, remind us that the USA considers itself to be above the global rules-based order which the Anglosphere initiated. This was obvious with the Iraq invasion of 2003. Torture was used on detainees during the war on terror, hostility was shown to the International Criminal Court and the US walked away from an international treaty with

---

[239] Ferguson (2012) p101 quotes the World Economic Forum's *Global Competitiveness Index* and the Heritage Foundation's *Freedom Index*.

[240] The preceding paragraph is a truncated version of a section of my Introduction to de Burgh, H. and Lashmar, P. (2021) *Investigative Journalism*, 3rd edition.

Iran on nuclear issues, 'even though Iran was complying with that treaty.'[241]

Should the inventors of freedom be implicated in these actions? Should our politicians not make it clear that we are with the USA when it upholds the civilised order we have together created, but not when it reverts to chauvinism? The circumstances that allowed 20th-century UK politicians to fantasise about a 'special relationship' with the USA have changed. The USA today is oriented towards the countries bordering the Pacific, not Europe. Influences on the US outlook are increasingly Hispanic and Asian. It is tied to China commercially and financially yet likes to position China as its nemesis. It is possible that elements in the USA wish to provoke a war with China out of pique. It is truly dangerous for the whole world that, according to Mahbubani, 'There is a significant group of thinkers, policymakers and activists in Washington DC, who are quietly plotting and planning various ways of derailing China.'[242]

China is not WISE's enemy, or rival, yet much of the WISE political class has thoughtlessly adopted US attitudes, attempting to rupture relationships with China for Britons. In the meantime, German, French and US business increase their commercial connections heedless of politicians' warlike drumbeats.

---

[241] Snell, Arthur (2022) *How Britain Broke the World* London: Simon & Schuster, p334.

[242] Mahbubani, *Has the West Lost It?* (2019), p81

Meanwhile Europeans, surely, feel profound gratitude for what the USA has done to reinforce Ukrainian resistance. Russian aggression may have revived the NATO alliance – it has certainly expanded it - and former President Trump's censures have awoken us to the urgent need for the European countries to be able to defend themselves. They now know that we may not, for long, rely upon the USA to distract itself from Asia on their behalf. WISE defence policy should follow suit, otherwise the promised resuscitation of the German military looks to put the UK, with its faltering economy and diminishing armed forces, in the shade. If the UK continue to undermine its ability to defend itself locally[243], the USA's European ally in the future, if there is to be one, will be Germany. With WISE so weak, that will mean German military leadership of the continent, as much a can of worms for WISE as for Europeans of both East and West.

Back to WISE and the USA. We already find it hard to get the attention of US policymakers, although we need to do so as the US is such an important trading partner and owns large chunks of our industries. Following the Brexit referendum, foreign investment into the UK has surged by 44%, more than Germany and France combined.[244] The cost is that we lose IP, patents and skills, usually to the USA. Angus Hanton writes that US companies have taken

---

[243] Vast resources have been put into operations far from Europe, while local-oriented resources have been cut.

[244] Brummer, Alex (2020) *The Great British Reboot* Yale: Yale University Press, p316

over our most profitable businesses, usually in high-growth sectors and often with monopoly power. They asset strip and pay low taxes in the UK. Through their control of internet platforms, US companies charge UK consumers simply to do business with each other, owning the 'bridges' and 'pipes' through which the economy operates.[245]

Our politicians have permitted the transfer of a vast proportion of our economy to unaccountable US owners, diminishing our governments' tax take, making WISE very vulnerable if US and UK interests diverge. I write more about our failure to defend our industries in the final section, so here I will simply suggest that one aspect of getting our own house in order will be to place our relationship with the USA on a more mutually respectful footing. The Hua Wei issue is a shocking example of how WISE politicians caved in to bullying. The UK government had exhaustively examined whether we should work with Hua Wei and decided that we should. Then US politicians demanded that we change our minds and help them try to destroy one of the world's most successful companies. President Trump was within his rights to *demand*; our politicians were not within theirs, to *submit*. Recollecting many such acts of cowardice and treachery, Hanton calls Britain the *Vassal State*. He likens our relationship to the USA with that of Belarus with Russia.[246]

[245] Hanton, Angus (2024) *Vassal State*, London: Swift Press, p185
[246] Hanton, Angus (2024) *Vassal State*, p7. Hanton also points out that The UK government surrendered to US demands by abandoning

We should be independent enough and principled enough to refuse the USA when it is doing wrong, or what is against our interests. When it is right to do so and in our peoples' interests, we should make common cause with the US, and our European neighbours, without being managed by either.[247] We have (we hope) escaped from being managed by the EU, we now need to recalibrate our relationship with the USA. Our cultural affinities and economic relationships with both are undeniable; the need for subservience is not.

Finally, I want to stress that, advocating a self-respecting approach to the USA does not amount to a rejection of the USA. That idea is ludicrous. The world will be a much worse place if totalitarian countries replace the USA as arbitrator and as policeman of such international norms and rules as we have. Although the USA has violated its own rules it has also done many things that have helped other nations rise to 'greater wealth, confidence and dignity'. It is not completely selfish[248]. WISE must try to work with the USA so that its power is used for good. The USA is not in decline, whatever its political shenanigans may suggest or

---

the digital tax on tech giants and supporting a 15% global tax rate, p225.

[247] The Continental and Anglo-American polities are contrasted as the *vanguard tradition* (active authority, passive democracy) versus the *Magna Carta* tradition. See Tombs (2021) *This Sovereign Isle: Britain In and Out of Europe,* p70

[248] Zakaria, Fareed (2024) 'The Self-Doubting Superpower', puts this very well and at much greater length.

hostile powers want us to believe, and, could be resurgent. China may be a superpower, but it is our offspring that still has the most powerful economy, dominates technology development and has armed forces that outclass all others. Its internal problems are nothing like as intractable as those of China, Iran or Russia, and an Anglophone society is much more capable of self-renewal than are they.

Summary

In their relations with the USA, successive Prime Ministers have been biddable when they should have been admonishing. In part, this is because Britain has been becoming weaker economically over the past 20 years. It is also because our politicians have no vision of Britain in the 21st century, with little grasp of our nation's achievements, but only either wilting nostalgia for an imperial past or embarrassment at our 'crimes'. Political careerists can neither inspire nor unify WISE. Nor can they deal with the USA with moral authority, be a critical friend and disentangle us from servitude.

The foundation of US greatness is the *Respect* that the founding fathers transplanted from the offshore islands, which is articulated in the Declaration of Independence and the Gettysburg Address.

Yet the settlers, and we at home in WISE, have drifted apart culturally and psychologically. This, and our subservience to our former colony, constitute contradictions in our own identity that have to be resolved.

Rudyard Kipling famously reminded us that it is difficult to understand your own country when you know about no other.[249] Pearl Buck, an astute thinker about the relationship between the USA and China, saw the limitations of the USA's evangelising of the world just as US missionaries were converting many Chinese to adopting our strange religions as routes to wealth and power. Her's is a salutary warning for WISE people who have lost a clear sense of what we are, how we should relate to our American cousins, and to what values we should hold fast.

---

[249] "What do they know of England, who only England know?" is the lament often attributed to Rudyard Kipling.

Section 9

The Empire Was WISE

As the British Empire has come in for stick, and as that stick has been used to beat the Offshore Islanders for their supposedly perpetual perversity, some Welsh, Irish and Scots have skedaddled, modestly declining the honour of having been complicit. In reality, the English could not have done it on their own: the diverse cultures of these islands were all essential to the project.

....

A China Story

Before we realised his lifelong dream of visiting Scotland, a member of the CCP Central Committee talked up Kew Gardens to me, which he described as a wonder of the world. He admired our explorers, botanists and naturalists for helping other peoples to understand and appreciate the natural world. Strolling by the plants, flowers and trees, he and I read how some WISE visitor to Asia, Africa or Latin America had identified this or that species. The country in question now had its own botanic gardens and staff with which Kew specialists worked. When reading, I also came across the name William Roxburgh. Roxburgh was a surgeon from Edinburgh who joined the Madras Medical Service in 1776. He became the East India Company botanist in Madras in 1879 and, over the following years, published many illustrated books on Indian botany. He is known as the 'Father of Indian botany'.

Roxburgh's life reminded us not only of the innumerable positive achievements of the British Empire, even while it was under commercial, rather than state, control, but also of how all four of our nations can share the glory.

The Chinese Politician and the Scots Botanist

Roxburgh was a late product of the most fecund period of Scots history and the only time that the tiny country has been so significant: the Scottish Enlightenment. From 1707, its fame spread well beyond Scotland across the British Empire and Continental Europe. Its political ideas influenced the founding fathers of the USA. The Scottish *School of Common Sense*—opposing French theorising—swept North America in the 18th and 19th centuries.

My Chinese guest, a professor of philosophy earlier in his life, had specified that he wanted to go to Scotland for two reasons. To see the birthplace of Adam Smith and the tomb of David Hume, 'who are still among the most widely cited thinkers in the world'[250] and 'because, through

---

[250] These are the words of the then Director of the Party Literature Research Office of the Central Committee of the CCP, ideological adviser to China's leader, whom I accompanied in 2014 on a visit to 'the land of Adam Smith and David Hume'.

your Empire, Scotland was so important in the diffusion of modern ideas.'

The spirit of inquiry, enterprise and observation that the Enlightenment fostered, infused Scots with zeal to understand the world better and spread reason. David Livingstone (1813-73), the explorer and opponent of slavery, initiated modern education and healthcare in Africa. Andrew Carnegie (1835-1919) used the wealth earned from his creation of the US steel industry in philanthropy throughout the Empire. They were just two of the several million Scots who 'went out'. In the 18th century, the British presence in India was overwhelmingly Scots. Their influence was particularly in medicine, environmental sciences, education and evangelism. In my twenties, I went to Tennessee to visit my grandmother's second cousins, whose forebears had emigrated from rural Aberdeenshire in the 19th century. I found that they were chemists, physicists and physicians.

Glasgow developed as the second city of the Empire thanks to imperial free trade. Its exports helped to turn Scotland from one of the very poorest countries in Europe to one of the wealthiest. Scotland not only took, but it also gave. It has a long history of investing and providing credit abroad, in gold and silver mining, sheep and cattle farming, and land reclamation and development.

Competition with Wales

Until they started to acquiesce in the hostile views of the British Empire that became fashionable with Marxist histography in the 1960s, Scots scholars claimed that 'it was the specific character of the Scots that helped to build the Empire, as well as the fact that far greater numbers of them were involved in the Empire than were the other three nations.'[251] The other three nations might demur. For its size and population, Wales was a disproportionate participant in the Empire, perhaps even the first, if you count the Welsh-Norman colonies in 12th century Ireland as imperialism.

From 1650, thousands of Welsh emigrated to the Americas and the Caribbean. Missionaries left for India, Syria and North Africa. It is likely that the primary motivation for Welsh involvement in the empire was moral and religious. Of the tens of thousands of district officers, missionaries, health workers and engineers, many were Welsh.[252] 'They dedicated—and often lost—their lives to bringing law and order, education, medicine, sanitation, and railways, among many other benefits, to distant

---

[251] MacKenzie, John M. (ed) (2016) *Scotland and the British Empire* Oxford: OUP is the source for most of the points about Scots. The quotation is from Section 11, Finlay, Richard J: *National Identity, Union and Empire, c.1850-c.1970* (pp280-316). There was even clamour for the British Empire to be known as the 'Anglo Scots Empire'.

[252] Few of their names are widely remembered, but there are three Welshmen whose influence on these islands has been immense: Henry VII, who restored good governance and stability after the Wars of the Roses; Robert Owen, originator of socialism; Aneurin Bevan, who reconstructed the NHS.

peoples who needed them, with little or no hope of personal reward, at least in this life.'[253]

Ireland as Spearhead of Empire

As for Ireland, antagonists of the Empire have called Ireland the Empire's first colony and aligned their country with the subjects of the Empire rather than its pioneers. Yet the Irish contribution to the imperial achievement is so great as to justify calling it the spearhead.

In the 17th century, Ireland was the chief source of migration to the West Indies. Many younger sons of Irish Catholic families migrated there and set up as merchants and planters. Many owned African slaves.[254] In the 18th century, those migrating from Ireland outnumbered the total English and Scottish migrants combined. Irish migration totalled 6 million between 1820 and 1920.[255]

---

[253] Bowen, H. V. (ed) (2016) *Wales and the British Overseas Empire*, Manchester: MUP is the source of most of the points about Wales, but the quotation is from *Wales: History, Myth and Empire*, a lecture by John Winterson Richards, at the Institute of Welsh Affairs on 05/12/15. https://www.iwa.wales/agenda/2015/12/wales-history-myth-and-empire/

[254] 'The Irish in the Empire' p95 in Kenny, Kevin (ed) (2006) *Ireland and the British Empire*, Oxford: OUP

[255] Members of my (southern Irish) family sailed to Australia in 1840; my paternal grandfather went to California in 1890. As with emigration from suffering parts of the world today, for most Irish, going out was driven by necessity rather than by enthusiasm. The penal laws, prohibition of whole-estate inheritance for Catholics

Irish served as soldiers and administrators, policemen, doctors, engineers, lawyers, journalists or businessmen throughout the Empire, but most of all in India. In the mid-19th century, 24% of appointees to the Indian Civil Service were Irish.[256] Irishmen, and I am here conflating some mutually suspicious identities, Gaelic/Catholic Irish, Old English Irish, Anglo-Irish and Ulster Protestant, in the perhaps naïve hope that they each now recognise the other as Irish, have been leading UK statesmen: Shelburne, Wellington, Castlereagh, O'Connell, Palmerston, and I'd include John Hume, among them. Edmund Burke, Irish MP and arguably these islands' greatest political philosopher, campaigned to clean up imperial administration and crusaded against slavery.

Although the romantic Wild Geese who fought for continental kingdoms after 1690 are often eulogised, from the 18th century onwards, Irish Catholic soldiers typically served the British Empire rather than its competitors. Fifty percent of the East India Company soldiers were Irish. In 1830, 42% of all British soldiers were Irish-born. In the First World War, 200,000 Irish served. There is a saying in Gaelic, 'Hunger makes a soldier.'[257]

---

and dissenters, subdivision of farms and its consequences, the absent landlord system, the prohibitions on education until 1831, the banning of the Irish language, and the ineligibility for the vast majority of the population to be members of parliament until catholic emancipation in 1829, these strictures help to account for it.

[256] The principal source on Ireland is Kenny, Kevin (ed) (2006) *Ireland and the British Empire* Oxford: OUP

[257] I am indebted to Mark Logan MP for this, as for many corrections.

Effectively an arm of imperialism, the Roman Catholic Church established itself in all the Irish communities of North America and Australasia. The Irish Christian Brothers became the leading teaching order in India, among many Irish missionary initiatives. 'Catholic Ireland left a lasting impact on African culture, especially healthcare, education, politics and the English Language. The idea of the missionary, characterised by heroic self-sacrifice, helped to reinforce Irish identity as a land of saints and scholars; this was reflected in the tone and mood of the 1916 Easter Rising.'[258]

While missionary work has been rightly criticised as subversive and authoritarian, it could also be egalitarian and anti-racist. There is a paradox. Despite the holy aims, Irishmen participated in the moments of which we are now ashamed: they were actively involved in slavery when it was still permissible. The two generals held responsible for an infamous massacre at Amritsar were both Irish, and a Scotsman and an Irishman were guilty of the maltreatment of Mau Mau guerrillas in Kenya in the 1950s.

Yet, like the English, Welsh and Scots, the Irish helped populate, organise and raise standards in the Empire. Many died doing so. This was a great contribution to human progress by a small nation on the edge of the known world, made

---

[258] Dudley Edwards, Ruth (2016) *The Seven: The Lives and Legacies of the Leaders of the Irish Republic* London: Oneworld, p364. See also, 'The Irish in the Empire', p112-21 in Kenny, Kevin (ed) (2006) *Ireland and the British Empire.*

possible because of the unity of the offshore islands under the British crown. Recognition of this is occluded by a myth.

Myths and Modernity

From the late 12th century onwards, Ireland saw multiple and regular rebellions in assertion both of its freedom and of its difference. By the 19th century, the Gaelic Revival promoted Gaelic culture and guarded against its absorption into English culture.[259] Scottish nationalism came later, probably because the cultural gulf that marked Ireland, between the ruling class and the majority, was much less pronounced. After starting out as genial cultural patriots,[260] Scottish nationalists have come to promote an adversarial

---

[259] The Irish population is made up of Celts who were in place by 450 BC, Vikings (795 AD), Normans (1200 AD), English (1536), Scots (1605), Asians and black people of various origins (1980s). Norse people may have formed the majority population of Eastern Ireland as early as the 9th century. https://www.siliconrepublic.com/innovation/viking-dna-ireland-genealogy. Many went to Ireland as unwanted colonists, but the Irish also migrated to the mainland, so large numbers of 'English' and 'Scots' have Irish origins. The revival of Gaelic culture in the 19th century was very positive, but not the attempts to play down or marginalise the other equally Irish traditions. See Beckett, J. C. (1976) *The Anglo-Irish Tradition* Newtownards: Blackstaff.

[260] A chance meeting with 'the father of the SNP', Dr Robert McIntyre, when hitchhiking in 1977, persuaded me to vote for devolution in the referendum the following year. McIntyre, the very first SNP MP, had none of the rancour of later SNP activists. He was an admired physician and cultural patriot rather than a professional politician.

history of Scotland and England and celebrate less the world-class achievements which followed the Act of Union of 1707 than the thuggish Middle Ages.[261]

The myth of Ireland as the victim and perpetual enemy of the United Kingdom inspired the seven zealots in what was subsequently extolled as the Easter Rising of 1916. The zealots chose violence in what was 'initially seen as a lunatic gesture by an unrepresentative minority,'[262] to force Ireland out of the UK.[263] The electorate had endorsed Home Rule, but the seven were impatient with democracy. They sought

---

[261] When I served in 2/52 Lowland in the late 1970s, the song *Flower of Scotland* was all the rage among we squaddies but banned from being piped in the officer's mess, correctly, as I now realise, because it is historically inaccurate. However, it is not as inaccurate as the appalling film *Braveheart*. It depicts a simple battle between good (Scots) and evil (English, when the reality was of skirmishes in a long war of Scots and English against Norman overlords, complicated by the interrelationships, by the 13th century, of Scots, Anglo-Saxons, Normans and Gaels. Scotland's greatest King before Robert I was David I, typically part Gael, part Anglo-Saxon, who deployed Norman knights to create the Scottish nation and apply Anglo-Saxon erudition and governance. An illustration of how repudiation of reality has become mainstream is in the fact that the only bilingual school in Edinburgh is not bilingual in English and Scots, the fertile language used by most Scots for over 1,000 years and by all her great thinkers, but in English and Gaelic, admired largely because unconnected with English.

[262] Foster, Roy, the pre-eminent Irish historian of Ireland, quoted in Roberts (2006) *A History of the English-Speaking Peoples Since 1900* p113.

[263] For an overview of the contribution of the (local) Catholic church to the myth and references, see https://www.theguardian.com/

support from Germany[264] at a time when many Irishmen were defending Britain from Germany's stated desire to destroy democracy.

One interpretation is that 'the rising was a catastrophe that poisoned Irish veins with a toxin of political violence.'[265] Much of the responsibility for that falls on British politicians, from Lloyd George downwards, for their dysfunctional and savage response. They authorised the brutal Black and Tans, a repressive militia which achieved what the seven could never have done without them: popular sympathy for the men of violence and, before long, support for Sinn Fein. By the 1930s, the heirs of the Easter Rising had again linked up with Britain's enemies, especially Nazi Germany, although, ironically, Hitler planned to abolish Ireland. Influential members of the Irish political class were sympathetic to Nazism.[266] During the Second World

---

world/2009/nov/28/christian-brothers-ireland-child-abuse, accessed 011222.

[264] Dudley Edwards, Ruth (2016) The Fading Myths of 1916, *Prospect Magazine*, 21st April 2016. See also the New Statesman review of her book, *The Seven*, cited below: https://www.ruthdudleyedwards. co.uk/non-fiction/the-seven-new-statesman-review/, accessed 070523

[265] Dudley Edwards, Ruth (2016) *The Seven: The Lives and Legacies of the Founding Fathers of the Irish Republic*, p371

[266] The Republic's Ambassador to Germany, Bewley, was an admirer of Nazism who rejected applications for visas from Jews trying to flee Germany and, living in Rome after WW2, wrote an admiring biography of Hermann Goering. Father Denis Fahey, a close friend of President de Valera, was a rabid antisemite and involved with several neo-Nazi and ultramontane organisations. Famously,

War, the Irish state remained neutral, gaining popular support for Fianna Fail, the governing party. Nevertheless, although only two Irishmen are known to have joined the Nazi forces, at least 80,000 Irish volunteered to fight for Britain in the Second World War.

Due to circumstances beyond their control, the Nazis could no longer help out after 1945. Arms and money from the USA made up the deficit. These were supplied by Americans who deluded themselves that what was happening in Ireland was an epic struggle between two nations, in which any violence was justified and killing to be celebrated. Recently, antagonism has decreased, violence on the north/south border has been marginalised, and admissions of fault and regret have smoothed relations.

In 2011, Queen Elizabeth II endorsed the orthodox interpretation of the Easter Rising on her state visit, acknowledged the struggle for independence and, in effect, expressed contrition for the past. Today, Ireland is as economically bound to the UK as to the EU, although sentiment in Ireland is very pro-EU, despite the plebiscite of 2008.[267] One day, it may be possible publicly to acknowledge the achievements, as well as the suffering,

President de Valera offered his condolences at the German Embassy on the death of Hitler. By this time, the Führer's crimes against humanity were well known.

[267] The 2008 vote against the EU was on the Treaty of Lisbon. See *The Case for an Irish Brexit is Growing Stronger* at https://www.briefingsforbritain.co.uk/the-case-for-an-irish-brexit-is-growing-stronger/, accessed 011223.

in the collaboration between Ireland and the other three nations. A United States of the Four Nations would be an acknowledgement of cultural reality.

A Global Perspective on WISE Identity

My Chinese visitor saw through the tergiversations of some Scots and Irish in ignoring what WISE has in common and in their sharing of the Empire. Yet, it is not only we who have a tangled attitude toward the Empire. Mahatma Gandhi, often cited as its opponent, was, in WWI, also its staunch advocate. The great anti-colonialist Nigerian writer Chinua Achebe praised British administration,[268] comparing it favourably with both before and after. As with Indians and Nigerians, it is not necessary for the Irish or Scots to deny their part in the Empire or its benefactions in order to prove their patriotism.

The diversity of WISE has been, is, and will be even more enriching, stimulating and inspiring. Their contributions to humanity were made possible by their unity in diversity; yesterday, the Empire was the means by which those contributions were made; today, upholding our shared values.

---

[268] https://web.pdx.edu/~gilleyb/Achebe_Final_AsPublished.pdf, accessed 160123.

Section **10**

WISE Betrayed!

Part 1: Flawed System, Guilty People

Everywhere, political leaders should assure three fundamentals: defence, solidarity, and the conditions that allow for citizens to prosper. Over the last 30 years, the four nations have become less safe, less unified, and have worse economic prospects. Political leaders have been indifferent to our interests and acted in accordance with an outdated view of the world, an insouciance about our existential problems and absorption in their own careers and their parties' prejudices.

....

A China Story

There's a talk show[269] from China presented by Professor Zhang Weiwei, who likes to compare the ignorance and shallowness of Anglo-American political decision-makers with Chinese equivalents. He, enthusiastically, describes the

---

[269] Zhang has had the talk show *This is China* since 2019. He is also an Internet celebrity through Xigua Video, Bilibili, TikTok and YouTube.

high standards of education and the wealth of experience expected of high-level leaders in China and compares them with the crowd-pleasers and voter-getters of Anglo-American politics. Zhang has studied at a Swiss university and debated at the Oxford Union. He knows a thing or two about the West, but only to our detriment. He fails to acknowledge that the high level of education of China's meritocratic officials could not stop the leaders from betraying the people over decades of cruel repression and destructive economic policies. His one-sided analysis reminds us of a great advantage we have: We can influence our leaders, though it is not easy. Even so, it's worth paying attention to his criticisms of our politics, for he's found our weaknesses.

Whatever their long-term consequences, Prime Minister Thatcher's domestic reforms were followed by an economic boom for many in the 1990s. Yet Thatcher and her Labour successors, who endorsed her reforms, failed to address the negative repercussions. The removal of state subsidies, to industries that were deemed parasitic, damaged communities and stymied careers and opportunities. Once she had created the conditions for revival by reforming the infrastructure of the economy, several other actions were needed. They were recognised by the incoming Labour government of 1997:

- Reform of the cripplingly expensive and expansive health and welfare systems,

- reform of education and attitudes to education,
- British investment in British industry and
- conversion of the civil service and local authorities from naysayers into facilitators and development activists.

Although limited moves have been made in these directions since, politicians have never come clean about the seriousness of the situation, or the measures required. They have tinkered with decline. Worst of all, they leapt at distractions: ideological mansplaining and foreign adventures.

My explanation for this is that our political system and social changes since the Second World War enabled the emergence of a political class whose interests, before long, overrode those of the electors. Below the surface declarations of tender loving care for the people, public affairs became more about keeping that class in jobs and magnifying its power.

To build support, governments used the taxpayer's money to favour certain categories; in other words, they bought votes. The conservatives privileged the pensioners, evoking sympathy for those who had 'done their bit', while Labour contrived new categories of supporters, 'the oppressed', from recent immigrants to unmarried mothers to drug addicts.[270] The privileging of those categories came

---

[270] Anglo society always appears—at least since it adopted Christianity— to have divided people into categories, damned or saved, and we are still doing it. For example, whereas in many societies, same-

to be justified by an ideology whose adherents trashed the beliefs and institutions of their predecessors, from flag to family, and encouraged alternative lifestyles beloved of the affluent and irresponsible.

This has alienated the commoners. In my twenties, I took a night shift job in an Ipswich food factory, where most of my colleagues were women, of every generation and colour. It was a shock to me, who planned to be a Community Worker, to find that the people they hated most in the world were not capitalists, gangers or landlords. They were the social workers who interfered with their families and were seen as the executive arm of a dictatorial political class.[271] Working-class women would later dump the Labour Party, recognising it as the party most opposed to their interests. In response, the Labour leadership accumulated new supporters by pandering to lobby groups, noisy minorities and ideological fanatics.[272]

---

sex love was, historically, pretty much assumed to be part of the natural order, an unimportant but acceptable deviation, we created a category 'homosexual' which we once demonised but now eulogise. Black Lives Matter is a very Anglo-American phenomenon because it similarly classifies and judges people as damned or saved according to characteristics such as whiteness or blackness.

[271] Attending meetings of the union, USDAW, I was struck by how the males still believed that everything could be put right by the Labour Party, whereas the females were sceptical of any politician or bureaucrat.

[272] This treachery is normally associated with the Labour Party (see Cobley, Ben (2018) *The Tribe: The Liberal-Left and the System of Diversity* London: Societas), but the Conservatives were equally involved, though, for them, it was less essential because they

The Resistible Rise of Career Politicians

We talk routinely about our politicians as being detached from the rest of us, living in a "bubble kingdom", and speaking a language as artificial as the dialogue in bad soap operas. That many are detached from those who elect them became obvious at the time of the EU Membership Referendum. Four hundred constituencies which voted to leave the EU found that their MPs had disagreed with them: 95% of Labour MPs voted to remain.

Since then, we have often seen what little account many pols take of the people. This is not a new story. The undermining of representative democracy started with the growing dominance of career politicians around 60 years ago. Consolidation took place from 1997, under the Prime Minister, whom his Chancellor dubbed 'Phoney Blur'.

In this section, I briefly remind us of some of the worst betrayals of trust. First, let me explain who the pols are and why. I use the word 'commoners' in preference to 'ordinary people', 'working classes', 'citizens', 'the majority', 'the people', or 'the poor', all of which have patronising and maybe divisive undertones. By 'the commoners', I mean those who are neither members of the political class nor the rich who can afford to be nonchalant about deteriorating conditions at home. Most of us: The betrayed.

---

had held on to their tribal electoral base. They benefitted from Labour's betrayal of the commoners in the 2019 General Election when the famed Red Wall seats abandoned Labour for the hitherto despised Conservatives.

Who Betrayed Whom?

MPs are part of a *political class*.[273] While individual MPs may mean well, the class in general is at odds with the beliefs, interests and lived experience of their constituents. Its members differ from previous ruling classes because they are professionals whose entire careers are devoted to politics, from which they receive status, salary, perks, pensions and privileges.

Since 1971, it has been possible to make a living from politics. Before then, parliamentarians did not go into politics expecting a reliable income or career advancement. They spent relatively short periods in Parliament, and few remained for their entire working lives. Today, the salaries are substantial compared to most fellow citizens, so fewer and fewer MPs have any professional income other than what they can get paid for their political knowledge or contacts. There are many perks, including allowances for research and assistance and a superior pension scheme. This might seem enough for a job that is not very strenuous. Yet many MPs and peers have used means, either grasping or dishonest, to increase their take, so there is a widespread presumption that to be an MP is to be a crook.

---

[273] The following remarks on the pols are from a longer version, to be found in de Burgh, H et al. (2015) *Democracy in England, Possible and Necessary*, London: Civitas. I drew on what is still the best analysis and exposition of this: Oborne, Peter (2008) *The Triumph of the Political Class* London: Pocket. In 2023, Matthew Goodwin elaborated and enriched the analysis in *Values, Voice and Virtue*, London: Penguin.

There are exceptions, yet we can generalise that pols today have no other professional activity, and their lives revolve around politics.[274] As most have achieved little before politics, all their hopes of recognition and achievement are *from* politics. Without practical experience in the operation of, let alone the management of, institutions or companies, it is not surprising that ministers make mistakes. In effect, they gain their experience and learn judgement (if they do), not while in junior jobs in this or that industry or profession, but while playing with vast public budgets. Without the maturity that others develop through dealing with the challenges of life in industry or the professions, they are often incapable of understanding or evaluating advice from experts, scientists, generals, or diplomats. Their callowness also inclines them to be ideological, to impose theories rather than tackle problems empirically, and to be easy targets for lobbyists, propagandists and social media crowds. Is it surprising that recent ministers have wreaked such havoc?[275]

---

[274] Their obsession with themselves and the little world of Westminster politics has often been remarked upon. See, for example, Fletcher, Martin (2022) Why Britain's decline resembles the fall of Rome In *New Statesman* 15/08/2022.

[275] For evidence, see King, Anthony and Crewe, Ivor (2013) *The Blunders of Governments* London: Oneworld; Butler, Eamonn (2009) *The Rotten State of Britain* London: Gibson Square; Craig, David (2006) *Plundering the Public Sector,* London: Constable and the other books of David Craig, for example, David Craig and Matthew Elliot (2009) *Fleeced!: How we've been betrayed*

There is a standard career path. You get involved with the party when at school or university. While trying to progress upwards, you enter a 'brokerage' occupation, which provides time, adequate money and access. In the case of David Cameron, this was as a PR executive for a TV company; for Edward Miliband, it was as a Labour Party researcher. These kinds of jobs make it possible to do all the networking required of the would-be pol. To get *on*, it is essential first to be *in*. Once elected, the overriding objective is to remain. Should (s)he lose his seat, the MP who has proved loyal will be able to find a job in the wider political world until re-entry is possible. If (s)he has upset the gang in charge of the party, (s)he may never work again.

Once upon a time, MPs represented the interests of counties, trade unions, towns, and professions. There was no collective consciousness as MPs. However, the professionalisation, plus similarities in social background, attitude to life and beliefs that transcend party, have come to create a sense of being a distinct class.

This class identifies more with similar careerists at home or abroad than with those who elected them. Their detachment from the mere commoners is shared by other members of the elite. Civil servants nostalgic for imperial jurisdiction, such as a recent cabinet secretary and a director-general of the BBC, pontificate that they are not

---

by the politicians, bureaucrats and bankers - and how much they've cost us London: Constable.

in post to serve the British people who pay their salaries, but the world.[276]

The Wider Political World

Until recently, Parliament used to be the main goal, and being a minister was the height of ambition; but to some it is viewed simply as a step to money or fame elsewhere. After handing over the premiership to Gordon Brown, Blair undertook a lucrative sinecure from the US government. The presidency of the EU eluded him, though other Labour leaders— Kinnock, Mandelson, Miliband—transferred to the EU or other international jobs. George Osborne, Tory former Chancellor of the Exchequer, works for a Russian oligarch who owns British newspapers. Incredible though it may seem, David Cameron, between being Prime Minister and Foreign Secretary, reportedly trousered money from the UAE[277].

These are the higher rungs on the pols' ladder, yet it is not only those in Parliament or trying to get into Parliament who comprise the political class. Shared interests, values

---

[276] Goodhart, David (2017) *The Road to Somewhere* London: Hurst, pp15-16.

[277] Investigations Team (2024) How Cameron rolled out the red carpet for the UAE, in *Daily Telegraph*, 240124, pp10-11. Since writing this, I have learnt, from Hanton's *Vassal State*, that all of the following UK politicians, plenty rich already, slurped up money from foreign companies: Alistair Darling, George Osborne, Philip Hammond, Sajid Javid, Kwasi Kwartung, Theresa May, Rishi Sunak, Nick Clegg and, of course, David Cameron. See Hanton, Angus (2024) *Vassal State*, p41.

and ambitions are also to be found among a much wider group of people, probably numbering several thousand.

They will have settled for different roles in the political system, such as:

- Party employees
- Researchers and Special Advisers (SPAD) to ministers, shadows, MPs, councillors
- Employees of think tanks, the 'Special Adviser academies'
- Members of the House of Lords, increasingly retired or redundant elected politicians
- Political consultants, lobbyists
- Members of policy research institutes, usually receiving public funds
- Local Authority Councillors and policy officials
- Officials of the numerous QUANGOs (quasi-autonomous non-governmental organisations) with many staff,[278] such as the Charity Commission, BBC, Press Complaints Commission (PCC), and the Metropolitan Police Authority
- Officials of NGOs, charities, foundations and trusts, which are increasingly politicised.

All these may be assumed to be members of the class. They are appointed because of their willingness to utter the

---

[278] http://www.parliament.uk/business/publications/research/key-issues-for-the-new-parliament/decentralisation-of-power/quangos/

current mantras, which cascade through the administrative and executive ranks. In the civil service, local government, police and so forth, jobs are secured through conformity rather than competence.[279]

Devolution in 1997 greatly enlarged pols' opportunities to pursue a professional political career when salaried posts were created for members of the Scots, Welsh, Northern Ireland and Greater London assemblies, with attendant gaggles of assistants and advisers.[280] Because the members of these bodies are elected by proportional representation, the party managers have complete control over who may be a candidate.

Parties of Fruitcakes, Loonies and Closet Racists?[281]

The professional party managers make decisions that might once have been made by a mass membership. A party of 2.8 million in the 1950s, the Conservative Party now

---

[279] Douglas Murray has illustrated how politicians rapidly adapt their opinions in his (2021) *The Madness of Crowds* London: Bloomsbury, Section 1

[280] Regional assemblies for England were then proposed. The plan was to start them unelected and then turn them into fully fledged job opportunities for pols by having them elected. However, popular opposition to them has made sure that that plan be put on hold and, instead, unelected Regional Development Agencies were given new powers.

[281] Perhaps the only memorable quote from PM Cameron; this was his designation of UKIP. However, if it applies to anybody, it applies to the memberships of both major parties.

consists of 172,000 who seem not to care what the career politicians do as long as heating allowances, bus passes and free prescriptions remain. Party conferences are not opportunities for debate but rallies. Thus, the Conservative Party is free to serve the interests of the rich donors who want to be allowed to sell their companies to foreign capitalists or to build tower blocks. The Labour Party is supported by ideological zealots and producer cabals, i.e. those seeking to preserve their own privileges rather than represent wider interests. Unless they have their own axes to grind, party activists have to be pretty odd people, choosing to spend their free time eating rubber chicken with career politicians and knocking on doors to convey their nonsense to the longsuffering voters. Thus, in many parliamentary seats, Labour relies upon the collective votes of Muslims, which is curious when you remember that it was a Labour government that teamed up to attack Afghanistan and Iraq.

The upshot is that politicians behaviour is determined by the desire to stay in or get power. The concerns of the electorate feature only as window dressing. The revelations of Dominic Cummings as to how everything in Downing Street is still governed by media appearances, and how policies are adopted or scrapped as they appear to influence ministers' careers, is a horrible confirmation of how the decadence of the Blair years has persisted.[282]

---

[282] Cummings (2023) Dominic Cummings on the dysfunction of the UK government, see an interview with Dwarkesh Patel. https://www.youtube.com/watch?v=3i7ym_Qh7BA, accessed 181123.

In the past, WISE showed other societies how they might become; now, we seem to be regressing towards the typical: a society where the people belong to the state, rather than the state to the people, and the state is the playground of revolving elites.

Conflicting Interests: The Pols Versus the People

It is well known that organisations, regardless of their original purpose, often develop into 'producer cooperatives', i.e., come to exist only to promote their own survival. They also proliferate their branches and employees.[283] It is less well understood *how* this happens.

The executive, now more the gang leaders of the political class than the country's leaders, uses the taxation system to extract a small amount from each member of the population, and then rewards its interest groups to make a voter coalition.[284] This is corruption: bribing some citizens with other people's money.

The advances in wealth since WWII have enriched governments. When not spending the vastly increased tax

---

Trigger warning: both men use squalid language, a current fashion among the rich, presumably in order to persuade us of their proletarian credentials or masculinity.

[283] The classic analysis of the latter is *Parkinson's Law*. Milovan Djilas described the former in his *The New Class*.

[284] Smith, Craig and Miers, Tom (2011) *Democracy and the Fall of the West* p28

revenues on fighting wars, they extended their powers over the economy and society. As Smith and Miers write,[285] they took over important industries (for a few ruinous years, there was a fashion for believing that the Soviet Union provided a good model) and delivered their services for free at the point of delivery. 'All the services are characterized by poor quality, low productivity, lack of innovation, and rationing.' They protected producers, for example, in the NHS and schools, from competition and from consumer choice. Those who see medical and educational services as 'naturally' belonging to the state should reflect that the glory days of both these services were when there was little or no state involvement.[286]

In order to get elected and to remain in office, the pol must show what he has done. This places constant pressure on him or her to act, or create a perception of exertion, leading to a near constant frenzy of activity,[287] including the vast production of new laws and regulations.

The bribing of various sections of the population to pull together a coalition to overcome the commoners' hostility is accompanied by an ideological propaganda war against

---

[285] Ibid, p55
[286] The essential reading on the history of welfare in the UK, and its current problems, is Bartholomew, James (2004) *The Welfare State We're In*, London: Politicos. Bartholomew followed this up with an international comparison which should be on every politician's kindle, (2015) *The Welfare of Nations*, London: Biteback.
[287] Smith, Craig and Miers, Tom (2011*) Democracy and the Fall of the West*, p40

those very commoners. Owen Jones, Paul Embery and others have exposed how the pols have demonised working-class culture.[288] Ferdinand Mount has described the undermining of the family unit, with its grave consequences for the life chances of poorer people.[289] The sabotaging of the cultural and economic institutions which protected the poor and advanced their interests has been noted by writers from different traditions.[290]

It is in both omission and commission that the interests of the British people have been betrayed. The broken promises, the waste of taxpayers' money,[291] and the giving away of our assets to foreign capitalists[292] reflect the indifference of the pols to the commoners as well as their incompetence. Below, I list some of the ways in which the life chances of the commoners have been much diminished.

---

[288] Jones, Owen (2012) Chavs: The Demonization of the Working Class London: Verso and Embury, Paul (2020) *Despised: Why the Modern Left Loathes the Working Class*

[289] Mount, Ferdinand (1998) *The Subversive Family*, New York: The Free Press. See also his (2012) *Mind the Gap* London: Short Books and (2012) *The New Few* London: Simon & Schuster

[290] I summarised some of these in a 2015 pamphlet, de Burgh, H et al. (2015) *Democracy in England: Possible and Necessary* London: Civitas. For more recent expositions, see Field, Frank (2023) *Politics, Poverty and Belief* London: Bloomsbury and Goodwin (2023) *Values, Voice and Virtue.*

[291] King, Anthony and Crewe, Ivor (2013) *The Blunders of Governments,* and Butler, Eamonn (nd) *The Rotten State of Britain* are two records.

[292] Brummer, Alex (2014) *Britain for Sale*, London: Cornerstone/ Random House Business Books

The Elective Dictatorship

There is a much-loved little park in London between Parliament and Lambeth Bridge where, in good weather and bad, children play, pensioners ramble, neighbours greet each other and civil servants take their breaks from government offices nearby. In the dying days of his Prime Ministership, David Cameron decided that Victoria Tower Gardens should be obliterated and have built on it an enormous visitor centre to memorialise the Holocaust that Nazi Germany visited upon ethnic and religious minorities in the 1940s. Residents, the local government, the Historic Parks Trust, prominent members of the Jewish community, and innumerable supporters of the idea of a Holocaust memorial, opposed its being placed in Victoria Tower Gardens.

Judgements of the High Court and Appeal Court upheld opposition to the proposal. The pols are not respecting the will of the people or the findings of the courts. Prime Minister Sunak has instigated a bill in Parliament to change the 1909 law governing all parks, in order to override the wishes of local people. He has aped the despotism of Turkey's President Erdogan, who crushed popular opposition to building over Taksim Square in Istanbul. Sunak's action is a potent illustration of the authoritarianism of our pols, whose contempt for commoners becomes ever more overt. Many other, much graver, examples of politicians' overriding rights or the constitution are to be found in *Overruled*, a 2023 book by barrister Sam Fowles.[293]

But why should the pols care? When the government has a serviceable majority in Parliament, it can rely upon its MPs, around 160 of whom are on the government payroll at any one time, to nod through whatever it wants, often unread and not debated. Few are as financially secure as Sunak and his wife, who have twice as many millions as King Charles III.

Party managers determine who becomes an MP; whips tell them how to vote; ministers make or break their careers; when the obedient ones lose their seats, the party will sort them until they can be re-elected. Is it surprising that parliamentarians have allowed governments to accumulate more and more power for the executive, control the timetable of Parliament, pack committees, force through whatever legislation they want and lie or obfuscate without being held accountable? Is it surprising that they allow Sunak to put the boot in a local community in order to steal its park?

---

[293] Fowles, Sam (2023) *Overruled: Confronting Our Vanishing Democracy in 8 Cases* London: Oneworld. Douglas Carswell and Daniel Hannan also identified the problem of theft of power from the people, but explained it differently. See their (2008) *The Plan: Twelve Months to RENEW BRITAIN* Milton Keynes: Lightening Source. For a global perspective on the accretion of power by corporations, see Hertz, Noreena (2001) *The Silent Takeover: Global Capitalism and the Death of Democracy*, London: Heinemann.

The executive does not give time for proper scrutiny of the mass of legislation it introduces or indeed, does not bother to let MPs know what they are voting for at all. As Fowles points out, skeleton laws—laws which merely outline the general area in which ministers will make laws themselves—executive orders and Henry VIII clauses, allowing ministers to change laws out of sight, are commonplace.[294] When asked to disclose information, the executive claims that national security prevents it from complying, and when caught out lying, ministers do not resign.[295]

Local authorities are largely administrators of government policies rather than initiators, let alone developers. Policing, hospitals, and education have been taken away from local communities, diminishing involvement and commitment, completing a process begun in the 1940s. But local officials can block and frustrate. As I discovered, when trying successively in two authorities to get planning permission for a socially valuable enterprise, the influence of elected *local* politicians is minimal; officials decide. In the case of the Grenfell Tower disaster, it was extraordinary to see elected politicians nobly taking the rap since everybody knew that the kind of decisions which led to the tragedy never involved politicians but only officials.

---

[294] Fowles (2023) *Overruled: Confronting Our Vanishing Democracy in 8 Cases*, p61

[295] Peter Oborne, in (2005) *The Rise of Political Lying* London: Simon and Schuster, pointed to a 'catastrophic decline in trust'; Fowles (2023) *Overruled: Confronting Our Vanishing Democracy in 8 Cases* underlines this nearly 20 years later.

And who makes the decisions once made in Hull or Portsmouth, Ipswich or Hereford? Party leaders, yes, but party leaders who listen to rich donors, media bosses, lobbyists, SPADS and zealots before they pay attention to their electors.[296]

Along with centralising power, the executive has undermined our civil liberties.[297] Reducing legal aid, and increasing the costs of judicial review, limit access to the law for the commoners. The complexity and sloppiness of law, as politicians seek to make rules for every aspect of life, in effect reduces respect for law and the likelihood that people will be law-abiding. The incorporation of much continental European law and the imposition of the European Convention on Human Rights (ECHR) have diminished our system. Measures ostensibly undertaken for national security are among the many examples of a creeping authoritarianism out of kilter with WISE values. These include the growing militarisation of the police and their being deployed to uncover political 'crimes', the protracted detention of terrorism suspects, proposed limitations on demonstrations and the onerous requirements to reveal private information to banks and lawyers (with the excuse that anybody might be money laundering).

---

[296] See Geoghegan, Peter (2020) *Democracy for Sale: Dark Money and Dirty Politics* London: Head of Zeus.

[297] See, *inter alia*, Ferguson (2012) *The Great Degeneration*, p97 and Fowles (2023) *Overruled, passim.*

Part 2: The Offences

The political class that emerged in the latter half of the 20th century, and was well consolidated in the general election of 1997, took charge of a country with great international prestige. WISE had started to adapt successfully to globalisation and, having identified its weaknesses, especially in the economy and education, appeared to be facing up to them.

Unfortunately, from then on, our political leaders were, by and large, indifferent to the fundamentals. They preferred to strut the international stage or distract themselves with virtue signalling over issues of marginal relevance to the commoners.

Today, following Labour, Conservative/Liberal and Conservative governments, we are poorer (and not merely relatively), more divided and less well-governed. Among dispassionate observers, there is widespread agreement on the following:

- Our debt is overwhelming; politicians have spent the security of future generations in buying votes.[298] State debt differs from personal debt, but there is one key difference. Those who will pay off the state

---

[298] The most lucid and empirical report of the negligence of our political class is contained in Johnson, Paul (2023) *Follow the Money* New York: Little, Brown. The dangerous state of debt can be understood from the 2023 OBR report https://obr.uk/frs/fiscal-risks-and-sustainability-july-2023/#Section-1, accessed 051023.

debt did not incur it, or enjoy the spending. Future generations can expect higher taxes, vast spending cuts and social turmoil.

- We are de-developing, in that we have de-skilled much of our economy by losing the great industries that made us the workshop of the world, and selling off the new enterprises that might have grown to replace them.

- Given the two points above, we can predict massive unemployment and few opportunities for the coming generations.

- The society that, more than any other modern community, was built from the bottom up, has seen the commoners ousted and replaced by those answerable to a party centre, denying agency to local communities and demoralising them.

- As more and more of the jobs of the commoners (not only the blue-collar jobs but also those of the professionals and middle classes) are taken over by people abroad, they will struggle to survive; the social polarisation between rich and poor will become ever greater. Polarisation matters because the poor lose hope and become alienated from society, so the potential for revolution grows.

- We export too little and import too much, which means we will eventually go bankrupt unless we carry out cuts in public expenditure so severe that they would ignite that revolution.

- Our economy relies on two service industries, financial services and creative industries, neither of whose products are essential to their overseas customers.

- The differences between economically declined areas and the rich are gross. The former industrial areas, coastal resorts and fishing towns have been abandoned and kept breathing only with taxpayers' largesse.
- De-industrialisation continues: We are undermining such industries in our response to climate change. Other countries are more circumspect in their climate policies.
- We have a population which has expanded beyond the capacity of our institutions to provide for them (housing, healthcare, education) at the level they expect.
- Politicians have deliberately increased the costs of energy for ideological reasons, rendering exports uncompetitive and commoners impoverished. We are dependent on potentially hostile powers[299] for too much of our energy.
- Our politicians have engineered poor relations with our three most important business partners, the USA, the EU and China.

---

[299] 'The combination of having to buy more expensive natural gas from Qatar and the United States losing access to China's lucrative market for European cars, machinery, and luxury goods could cause Europe to deindustrialize.' Sikorsky, Radek: Europe's real test is yet to come. *Foreign Affairs*, July-August 2023.

- The social problems of broken families, drug addiction and inherited dependency are not being tackled at the root[300] and, apart from the toll on human suffering, affect the economy.
- In many areas, we still have an underperforming education system, which is not capable of recharging a modern economy.
- The children of the professional and middle classes cannot afford housing, avoid marriage and abjure raising children out of fear for the future. They are thus becoming proletarianized, miserable for them and dangerous for society.

Above, we noted the trends, and what the political system has morphed into. Here is a *situation report* pointing out some of the betrayals of the political class.

Financial Irresponsibility

In the summer of 2023, the UK's debt mountain climbed to over 100% of GDP for the first time. The Office of Budget Responsibility (OBR) stated that this denoted the highest borrowing since the Second World War, when our leaders had survival on their minds. Borrowing costs are so high that a vast proportion of government earnings goes on interest payments. This is following the Covid pandemic:

---

[300] See Field, Frank (2023) *Politics, Poverty and Belief* London: Bloomsbury and Goodwin (2023) *Values, Voice and Virtue.*

the sharpest rise in energy prices for 50 years and the deepest recession in three centuries.[301] This is happening just when the ageing society, climate change policies and growing geopolitical tensions all impose additional costs.

To cope with these perils, any government will have to slash spending massively and raise taxes hugely unless it finally does what has needed doing for 30 years: Rebuild the economy so that it deliver jobs, replaces imports and secures our nations' future.

Paul Johnson, director of the Institute for Fiscal Studies, writes of feeble economic growth and NHS waiting lists: 'The squeeze on the living standards and the prospects of the young and the disastrous social care system facing the elderly.' He warns, 'Hard choices are everywhere, and it is the failure of our leaders and our failure to face up to them which is largely responsible for landing us in some of the problems which now beset us.'[302]

Attack on the Young

Those perils are only the start. The government is struggling to pay the interest on gargantuan debts, 22% of the working age population are unemployed, productivity is low and sliding and trades unions are clamouring for money. Businesses and government prefer to import cheap

---

[301] https://obr.uk/frs/fiscal-risks-and-sustainability-july-2023/#Section-1, accessed 051023.

[302] Johnson, Paul (2023) *Follow the Money* New York: Little, Brown. Audible edition, Introduction

labour rather than train and redeploy British people. Government borrowing is paying for welfare now, but the price will be paid by Generation Z and tomorrow's youth. They will find that there is no money to pay for their welfare when their ever-higher taxes go to pay interest on debts that funded the cossetting of their grandparents.

A former Treasury official and government minister writes: 'There are other countries where the younger generation are doing badly but nowhere else has the reversal of generation-on-generation progress been so precipitate as in the UK. It is not just a matter of some uncomfortable changes in the world economy affecting everyone.'[303]

The enormous intergenerational transfers implied by current fiscal policies amount to a betrayal by the political class of young people. Voters today are living at the expense of the young or those unborn. Do young people realise that the political class is taking away their futures?

Indifference to Economic De-Development and Inequality

Economists, business leaders and financial journalists[304] have been warning for decades: Britain is economically

---

[303] Willetts, David (2019) *The Pinch: How the Baby Boomers Took Their Children's Future - And Why They Should Give It Back.* Kindle Edition, p24

[304] The most telling, because they predicted the downward spiral of the economy ten or more years ago, are those of Larry Elliott and Dan Atkinson, *The Gods that Failed, Going South* and *Fantasy Island,* cited above.

de-developing, meaning that our future is precarious if we cannot sell enough to buy what we no longer produce but need in order to supply our burgeoning population. Because we are dependent for our exports on services located in the south and have failed to redevelop industry in former industrial heartlands, much of the UK can look forward to a future without opportunities for the next generations, even as the rich nooks and minorities of Britain bask in ever-increasing wealth.

In the south, including much of London, they think abundance is everlasting, because politicians and some media delude them. One of the few economists who has been a minister in recent years, Vince Cable, remarks, 'I find it annoying to hear commentators going on about being the "5th richest economy in the world". Nonsense. We are around 28th in terms of level of income (20th if you cut out the minnows like Monaco) and 9th in economic size, having just been bypassed by Indonesia.'[305]

Furthermore, fifty years ago, we had one of the most egalitarian of societies. Inequality is now stark, with immense wealth in the London area but 22% of the population living in poverty.[306] According to Hanton, a higher percentage of Britons live below the poverty line

---

[305] Correspondence with Vince Cable, October 2023

[306] https://www.jrf.org.uk/uk-poverty-2024-the-essential-guide-to-understanding-poverty-in-the uk#:~:text=Poverty%202024%20report.-,Poverty%20has%20increased%2C%20close%20to%20pre%2Dpandemic%20levels,nearly%203%20in%2010)%20children accessed 270224.

than in Poland, with much of the population 'driven into a precarious existence'. Things can only get worse as government debt gets higher, we sell off more companies and lose their tax revenues which are needed here to reduce – ha! – 'the hidden iceberg of unfunded liabilities.' [307]

The failure to put development at the top of our national agenda is a betrayal of all of us.

The Destruction of the Communities

We saw how, historically, WISE managed to combine efficient central administration of justice and taxation with devolution of power, and how this made the enterprise and industrial revolutions possible. But efforts to make health and welfare more comprehensive, de-industrialisation and the seizure of political and economic power from the localities by Westminster politicians, have had effects well summarised by Matt Ridley:

'In Britain, the welfare state and the mixed economy "corporacy" replaced thousands of effective community institutions – friendly societies, mutuals, hospital trusts and more, all based on reciprocity and gradually-nurtured virtuous circles of trust – with giant, centralized leviathans, like the National Health Service, nationalized industries, and government Quangos, all based on condescension. Because more money was made available through higher taxes, something was gained at first. But soon the

---

[307] Hanton, Angus (2024) *Vassal State* p224-228.

destruction wrought to Britain's sense of community was palpable. Because of its mandatory nature, the welfare state encouraged in its donors a reluctance and resentment, and in its clients, not gratitude, but apathy, anger, or an entrepreneurial drive to exploit the system. Heavy government makes people more selfish, not less.' [308] The citizens of today's China say 'amen' to that.

WISE pioneered a society in which local, often self-made, inventors and thinkers created enterprises, participated in the running of their communities and enriched the culture. Now, those communities are managed by executives in the capital or abroad, mobilised by ideologies which justify their power grabs. It will take a revolution in thought to re-democratise our nations.

Selling Off Our Future

Conservative governments, in particular, have been happy to see sold off British companies and infrastructure, resulting in the loss of many thousands of jobs, tax revenues and skilled personnel. The beneficiaries have been the rich. The USA would simply not allow important companies to be lost to foreigners. As long ago as 2012, Alex Brummer, then at *The Guardian*, tabulated the haemorrhaging of our research, employment and tax capacities in the sales of our companies great and small.[309] Hanton has provided

---

[308] Ridley, Matt (1996) *The Origins of Virtue* London: Penguin
[309] Brummer, Alex (2012) *Britain for Sale*

an updated list of the companies we have lost, as of the journalists who have been raising this vital matter. As to those companies in foreign ownership that have remained in the UK, he tells us that the government doesn't even know who owns what. He had to use US sources to find out the extent of US ownership of UK assets. He did discover, though, that in 1981 only 3.6% of UK shares were owned overseas. By 2020 that number was more than 56%. [310]

Recently, how was it possible we let ARM (Acorn RISC Machines), a micro-processing company of global importance, fundamental to our technological security, be sold abroad in 2016 or listed on the NASDAQ in 2023? Other countries do not permit the destruction of their economies in this manner; their political classes are patriotic.

Failure to Reach Out on Emigration

I buy my fruit and vegetables in Walworth's East Street market. A Farsi-speaking trader has lived here for 37 years, and an Uzbek lad, who always greets me in Turkish, for three. I often find myself chatting to an old gentleman from Guiana who complains that his family didn't allow him to marry when he came to the UK, because they needed his

---

[310] Angus Hanton (*Vassal State,* pp222-223) On p4, Hanton lists those journalists to whom we are all indebted for raising this issue: Alex Brummer and Stephen Glover (the *Daily Mail*), Ben Marlow (the *Daily Telegraph*), Phillip Inman (*The Guardian*), Daniel Thomas, Peggy Hollinger, Harriet Agnew and Kaye Wiggins. (the *Financial Times*).

salary to support 12 people back home. After the market, I can get a good meal for very little in a Uyghur restaurant or a curry in Brick Lane. The NHS consultant who looked after my mother is Italian. The best cake shops are either Arab or Jewish. Every pub and coffee shop seems to have its Romanian barista. How wonderful all this is! Immigration has enriched our culture and may possibly have benefitted our economy. But *mass* immigration has had deleterious effects on education, housing, health and social services for many of those who don't use private schools or medical services and don't inherit a house.

The impact of unemployed or low-paid mass immigration is going to be catastrophic, if it is not already. In London nearly half of social housing has gone to recent immigrants. They get school places, benefits, health services and eventually the state pension. Some immigrants receive more in child benefit and tax credits, than they pay income tax and National insurance. Employers like low paid foreigners and the government avoids training and paying some of the 9.25 million economically inactive British workers to undertake, for example, health care. In 2023, there were 144,000 health and care visas issued; the recipients brought in 174,000 dependents[311].

Since Labour's 1997 policy of encouraging EU immigration into the UK, just under 10 million *legal* immigrants have arrived. We do not know the number

---

[311] Timothy, Nick (2024) Low-paid migration is a subsidy costing the whole country dear in *Daily Telegraph* 280124

of illegal immigrants. The Conservative government has made it possible for 5 million Hong Kongers to come aboard the sinking ship. Even if those don't, over 10 million more (from elsewhere) are expected before long if the pols don't get a grip.[312] Neither major party has proved capable of controlling immigration; in fact, Labour politicians demand that anybody be welcomed in. They have used the, now discredited, arguments that high rates of immigration will solve the 'demographic deficit' or that benefits outweigh costs. They have also made the false allegation that, since the success of the offshore islands derives from the exploitation of others (it doesn't), we should see immigration as some kind of reparation. What idiots.

The logic of letting in more and more people is that we might have 300 million living here by the end of the century. This would bring severe consequences, not for the rich, who will decamp, but for the commoners, among whom are, of course, recent immigrants[313]. Politicians have

---

[312] For recent figures, see Goodwin (2023) *Values, Voice and Virtue*, pp57-63.

[313] We got a glimpse of how immigration may influence our politics from 2014, when Labour activists were seen to be anti-semitic, apparently to curry favour with Muslim voters (around 300,000 Jews live in the UK, over 4 million Muslims). Hamza Yousaf, Scotland's first minister, has advanced a pro Islamist foreign Policy, although the devolved Scots government has no remit in foreign affairs. Meanwhile, in Germany, a new political party has been set up by the Islamist Turkish President, Recep Tayyip Erdoğan, the Democratic Alliance for Diversity (DAVA), to represent Muslims in German elections.

never admitted that we could be overwhelmed by hundreds of millions of people fleeing poverty, war or chaos, hoping to get into societies that most closely resemble WISE. Our politicians have failed to make common cause with other countries over the international emigration crisis. The only long-term way of stopping refugees is for their homelands to develop. Fortunately, their development and stability matter very much to Asian countries, too, who are in need of customers and partners, if not immigrants. But where are the UK politicians with the imagination to work with them?

Substandard Education

State schools which were good enough to enable poor children to compete with those in private schools were abolished in the 1960s by Labour politicians whose own children attended independent, i.e., private, schools or the few remaining selective state schools. *The Guardian's* Nick Cohen puts it that 'selection by ability was replaced with selection by wealth.'[314] To get into those state schools of a reasonable standard, you have to get a home in the catchment area, the prices of which then rise. Why have so few state schools been of acceptable standard? For the same reason that public providers of anything must be suspect. Lack of competition, the accumulating power of vested interests and the failure to respond to the needs of those they are supposed to serve lead

---

[314] https://www.theguardian.com/politics/2005/jul/31/schools. grammarschools, accessed 020823.

to a decline in aspiration and quality. Independent schools fight hard to maintain high standards and make invaluable contributions to their local communities; paying parents keep them on their toes. Wealthy foreigners spend fortunes on wangling their children into them. We need many more, and we need them to be cheaper so that they do not price out local children and see themselves as commercial operations whose most important customers are the rich outsiders aiming for our universities.[315]

Efforts have been made to raise the standards in state schools, including the Free Schools and Academies programmes, with mixed results. The sole cause of low standards and wretched outcomes was thought, by reformers, to be ideological perversion by local authorities. However, other factors, such as the lack of selection, unwillingness to acknowledge that different kinds of intelligence require different kinds of schooling[316] and dysfunctional teaching ideology, were at least as important. The UK still lags

---

[315] James Tooley has been setting up low-cost independent schools in Africa and India; he has now started in the UK. See https://www.jamestooley.org/schools/

[316] Continental European countries distinguish middle or secondary schools as classical (academic), scientific and technical (or vocational). Orthodoxy in UK state school teaching was challenged by Katherine Birbalsingh at Michaela Community School, demonstrating that pupils from disadvantaged backgrounds could have their opportunities enhanced by traditional teaching. See https://en.wikipedia.org/wiki/Katharine_Birbalsingh, accessed 291023.

behind, for example, China, in the PISA tables,[317] despite the fact that China's education system had to be rebuilt from scratch, 35 years ago.

It was back in the year of its founding, 1982, that Channel 4 broadcast a TV series decrying the limitations of our further (technical and vocational) education system. This was something that I, too, then a Scottish Television Reporter specialising in education and employment, was also constantly pointing out. We have progressed very little: Today, our inability to grow our economy is attributed to the failures of this sector.

As if that were not enough, politicians cap the numbers of UK medical and engineering students whom the universities can train. Foreign students are welcomed because they pay, meanwhile the NHS and other industries cream off physicians and engineers from poorer countries, denying healthcare to the needy there. Second and third tier universities have evolved into businesses dependent upon foreign students who pay four or five times more than British applicants. What they buy can be poor quality qualifications, devised to bring in as many customers as possible or to be back door work visas.

For 50 years, we have known what needs to be done to get the intellectual infrastructure of our society right, but it has not been done. Our future prosperity and civility are at risk.

---

[317] The Programme for International Student Assessment (PISA) is a worldwide study by the Organisation for Economic Co-operation and Development (OECD)

Foreign Adventures

In 2011, Prime Minister David Cameron stood in Tahrir Square, Cairo, claiming his part in a great victory, presumably over Britain's ally, President Mubarak. The new rulers of Egypt, with whom Cameron wished to curry favour, were overthrown by popular protests two years later. Cameron's showmanship was as damaging to Britain's reputation as those aggressions in the Middle East and Afghanistan that sucked up money which should have been used for investment in the UK. Those adventures have increased the number of our enemies and made our country less secure. Nearly 1,000 British service personnel have been killed. The senior civil servant at the Foreign Office under three Prime Ministers has bewailed the ignorance and lack of experience of politicians more concerned about their image in the home media than international relations, let alone peoples' lives.[318] The shocking story of the games our pols have played in international affairs is told in Section 6: WISE *in the World: Going Out.*

The appointment of former Prime Minister David Cameron as Foreign Secretary in November 2023 is an almost unimaginable – comic - demonstration of Sunak's estrangement from the electors, to whom Cameron was an appalling failure.

---

[318] Simon McDonald, quoted in Lambert, Harry (2023) 'Britain should not make an enemy of China' in *The New Statesman*, 19-25 May 2023.

Taking Money from the Poor to Give to the Rich

To reduce the impact of the financial crisis of 2008, our political leaders, while excoriating welfare scroungers, poured vast amounts of taxpayers' money into the gaping mouths of another kind of scrounger: bankers.[319] When the bubble burst in 2008, house prices fell. It became impossible to get a loan. Retail sales, especially of household goods, collapsed, and well-established retailers failed. Many people were made unemployed. Tax revenues plummeted, so the government had to cut public spending. Those who were blamed for the crisis remained rich. Very rich. In reality, however, they were not the ultimate villains, any more than were generals who failed in Afghanistan and Iraq. It was politicians who created the incentives for the banks to act as they did. The details on this can be found in Smith (2011) and Elliott (2009).[320]

The ever-widening gap between rich and poor has continued to startle. Managers of protected, market-dominating companies, especially in financial services, always seem at ease to stuff their colleagues' mouths with gold, regardless of their contribution to the company,

---

[319] For the full story, see Brummer, Alex (2015) *Bad Banks*, London: Random House. John Kay has reviewed the entire financial services system in Kay, John (2016) *Other People's Money* London: Profile Books.

[320] Elliott, L. and Atkinson, D. (2009) *The Gods that Failed*. Smith, C. and Miers, T. (2011) *Democracy and the Fall of the West*.

let alone society. Shortly before this book went to press, it was reported that a CEO would be rewarded with remuneration of over £11m upon leaving her post at Nat West Bank, despite having been publicly condemned for moral turpitude. The CEO of the Post Office, during much of the period when it was cheating its employees, driving them to bankruptcy, destitution and, in at least four cases, suicide, received £2.2m in bonuses while this was going on, and a payoff of £4.2m.

Undermining Family, Betraying Children

Social policies introduced to benefit the wealthy or the eccentric have undermined family solidarity and childcare, resulting in broken families, drug addiction and inherited dependence.[321] The family of male and female parents caring for children and grandparents was denigrated and undermined by individualising taxation and benefits policies even before gender ideology became fashionable. Far from being an imposition of 'capitalism', that kind of family evolved from primitive woman-sharing into an institution which protects child bearers and rearers, contains and retrains naturally polygamous males and

---

[321] A racy summary of this can be found in Liddle, Rod (2014) *Selfish Whining Monkeys: How we Ended Up Greedy, Narcissistic and Unhappy* London: Viking. An earlier review of social breakdown and its effects on the poor, which is still only too relevant, is Davies, Nick (1997) *Dark Heart: The Shocking Truth about Hidden Britain* London: Vintage.

rewards reciprocity with mutual dependence. It matters most for the poor and insecure; the rich can be feckless and survive.

Frank Field has long pointed out the destructive effects on family life of the de-industrialisation of much of the UK, working-class unemployment, low wages requiring both parents to try to have jobs and welfare dependency.[322] Matthew Goodwin provides an updated account of how political decisions have resulted in the subversion of family life, the breakdown of communities and the desolation of individuals.[323]

As if that were not enough, children in many schools are now subjected to indoctrination disguised as relationship education, indoctrination in the fantasy beliefs of a small, noisy minority, a kind of institutional grooming. In failing to resist the tentacles of New Fascism, analysed in section 11, the political class has committed yet another betrayal.[324]

---

[322] Field (2023) *Politics, Poverty and Belief.* See also, Bloodworth, James (2019) *Hired: Undercover in Law Wage Britain* London: Atlantic Books. Ben Judah gives us a view of London from the perspective of the marginal in his (2016) *This is London* London: Picador.

[323] Goodwin, Matthew (2023) *Values, Voice and Virtue*, London: Penguin, pp34-45

[324] Lord MacDonald of River Glaven is eloquent on this topic. See https://www.lbc.co.uk/news/parents-school-sex-education-denies-biologic-sex/, accessed 301023 For a journalistic angle, see Cates, Miriam (2023). Parents aren't being told the awful truth about sex education in schools in *The Daily Telegraph* 17/10/2023.

The misery of welfare

Those of us who are detached from the world of agriculture, industry, resource extraction, defence, conservation – the fundamentals – live in an ethereal realm in which it is easy to imagine that books don't have to balance, that virtual reality is real life and that, somehow, smartphones, salaries and electric power will always be there for us. Otherwise, how could successive governments have allowed the welfare state to dominate everything? We cut essential functions, tax businesses and swell debt in order to keep millions on benefits, support millions of immigrants, buy the votes of wealthy pensioners and subsidise childcare for the prosperous.

If we don't resurrect our economy there won't be any welfare or health in the future, just feral children throwing rubbish at wrinklies, on rundown estates. The money spent on welfare should be used for investments, education and training, defence and creating a culture of independence and enterprise. We need good, family-friendly wages, rewarding jobs, an educated and skilled workforce. Having the working population slaving away to pay taxes, so that millions are better off on benefits than their working neighbours, is wrong.

Indefensible Decisions on Defence

The first duty of government is defence. For at least 20 years defence specialists and senior officers have been warning that politicians have so undermined our armed forces as to have abandoned this duty. Decades of cost cutting (the Cameron government implemented an astonishing 20% across the board cut) has had 'a profoundly deleterious impact on our defence capabilities'. Momentous decisions, such as the building of massive aircraft carriers, have partly been made for domestic political reasons – to preserve jobs in certain constituencies, partly for questionable strategic priorities such as 'expeditionary warfare (ie military intervention) and have further weakened more urgent and relevant defence capabilities. They cost around £3.5bn each (plus another few billion for the aircraft), yet we do not have enough warplanes to make these aircraft carriers useful, nor enough of a surface fleet to make them viable or indeed secure. Attacked by Russia – not very likely for Britain, but very possible for our NATO allies in the Baltic – we'd not be able to mobilise a single army division. It will take us 10 years to prepare one. We do not have a functioning reserve. Our nuclear warheads come from an arsenal in the US state of Georgia. We are the only nuclear power whose deterrent is dependent upon another country, utterly bereft of the ability to fight, should a US president decide as much. [325]

The Middle East is in flames, war in Eastern Europe grows more bloody, there are men in Washington and Beijing who would like an invasion of Taiwan to deflect attention from their failings. President Putin has drummed

---

[325] Ledwidge, Frank (2024) 'First duty; the decline of the British Armed Forces' Athenaeum Club Salon Event, 070224

up a Russian orthodox evangelism, a mission against the decadent West, while the Iranian holy men plot a crusade and there are several minor, but deadly, wars in Africa. And WISE can't even defend our borders, let alone our lives, thanks to the pols.

So, Is Professor Zhang Right?

It's mortifying to think that Zhang Weiwei may be right to point out how much better educated and competent Chinese leaders are than many of ours. However, he did not admit that, instead of engaging with people and their needs, Chinese politicians—except in the years when they were forced to let the people have their heads[326]—imposed upon them theories that brought misery to the people (and death to some 70 million). These derived not from a rational analysis of China's needs, but from the musings of a 19th-century pedant from London's Soho, the example of a Russian sadist, and a psychopath's hunger for power.[327]

Although the Chinese example seems, in its violence and scale, too far away from WISE to be relevant, there is a lesson for us there. It is that ideologues—full-time political

---

[326] From the Communist conquest of 1949 to the death of Mao Zedong, CCP rule was a disaster, plunging China backwards politically, economically and culturally. From approximately 1980 to 2012, the CCP had to stand aside as the people rebuilt the economy the CCP had destroyed. In this period, China achieved the industrial and information revolutions simultaneously.

[327] Karl Marx, Vladimir Lenin and Mao Zedong.

activists detached from the means of production and exchange—are a social bacillus. Our universities today are producing many more, 'surplus elites', and the political class is proliferating their parasitic jobs. When our legislature was made up of businessmen and trades unionists, self-employed professionals and dockers, fishermen and engineers, it was not only more representative. It was also much more competent at understanding the societies for which it legislated and provided a higher standard of executive from among its ranks.

We need to devise a way of raising the standard of our legislators while ensuring that they are responsive to the commoners. We need to have more experienced and competent people as ministers while ensuring that they are accountable. All those in the public service, elected or not, need to be imbued with a clear concept of our nations' identity and history, plus a sense of purpose to drive forward their service to the rest of us.

If we do not carry out reforms that put us back on track as the world's most humane and progressive polity, we will be subjected forever to the callow whims of a political class mindful first and foremost of its own survival and comfort.

We, too, have been betrayed.

Section 11

Is WISE Immune to New Fascism?

'Fascist' has become a catch-all term of abuse and, so, is notoriously difficult to define. Nevertheless, many 20th-century movements, including Communism and Nazism, share several characteristics which are widely agreed to be fascist[328].

First, they get their political strength from people who can be inspired to believe that they are victims.

Second, they blame their victimhood on other groups, rather than international trends or market forces: Tutsis, Jews, capitalists, peasant farmers or liberals become scapegoats. For some fascists, 'race' defines the enemy; for others, 'class', or 'faith'.

Third, they propagate an ideology with a strict moral code, often contrasting with traditional ethics; their propagandists come from the credulous young, from Savonarola's Proud Boys to the Hitler Youth or Red Guards[329].

---

[328] I have drawn on the definition of fascism in https://www. britannica.com/topic/fascism, accessed 241023.

[329] Savonarola, the 15th century Florentine preacher, fired up his Proud Boys to beat up the 'immoral' and burn books and 'sinful' art, providing a model of how to channel testosterone fuelled ignoramuses into savagery, while claiming moral duty.

Fourth, they predict a 'utopia' ahead. Once the Messiah comes down to earth, once capitalism is overthrown or once an evil population is eliminated, there will be utopia, known by many names, including 'socialism' and 'The Rapture'.

Fifth, while fascist movements may initially use democratic institutions for political legitimacy, they resort to totalitarianism in practice. The impulse derives from monotheism, the notion that there exists but one god, the invention of Middle Eastern tribal leaders of the sixth century BC. Monotheists believe that there is only one source of truth, that their faith is universal, and, often, that dissent is intolerable. When enforced, that's totalitarianism.

....

A China Story

Mrs Gao told me with cheerful pride that she is a Christian. She bundled me into her little house, saying she would give me proof. There, on a high shelf below which was another shelf of tin cans with sweet-smelling joss sticks, sat a giggling, cross-legged Buddha, a bust of some modern scholar with a complacent smile, a fierce deity who was probably General Guan Yu[330] and a plaster statue of Jesus Christ, standing in a blue robe with his palms turned outward. 'I am Christian and Buddhist and Chinese,' Mrs Gao told me

---

[330] Guan Yu or Guan Di was a general of the Han Dynasty who died in 200 AD and a 'god' in Chinese pantheist folk religion.

with great pride, placing an offering of tangerines and something gooey, like a brown marshmallow, on saucers beneath her gods.

Monotheism

In Mrs Gao's home, I was startled to find Jesus seen as just one among several (potentially hundreds) of man-made gods because, like most of my fellow Brits, deist or atheist, I had a monotheist mindset.

Once Christian bishops drove out the Roman and Greek gods in the 4th century,[331] Europeans were obliged to declare a belief in one exclusive god, outside our world, from whom stem strict moral codes. Way back in history, those tribal leaders persuaded their followers that these codes had been revealed to them tête-à-tête by God.[332]

These codes were the source of moral authority which would outlive individual leaders or witch doctors. They were divine and could be interpreted only by expert humans, known as priests or imams.

Abraham is usually thought of as the inventor of monotheism, which spawned the many versions of Judaism, Christianity, Islam and Sikhism. His objectives in 'discovering'

---

[331] Authorised by the Roman Emperor Theodosius 1st in 391-2 AD.
[332] In the 7th century, Islam developed similarly. The 19th-century founder of Mormonism and that of the 20th-century Unification Church have also succeeded in founding versions of Christianity, which have outlasted them.

a god exclusive to his particular Arab tribe[333] and reporting a deal with him called the 'Covenant', were to make the tribe feel different, united, and confident that their leader had a helpline to a master of the universe.[334]

Once adopted as the state religion of the Roman Empire, Christian leaders evolved mighty institutions with a de facto ideology, only remotely connected with the teachings of the Jewish charismatic, Jesus Christ.

Those leaders insisted that people should believe in several marvels, such as the 'virgin birth', the resurrection, transubstantiation and that God intervenes in human affairs ('miracles'). They insisted that humans are superior to nature (the environment) and that there is a meaning or purpose to our lives, ordained by God, such as preparation for the afterlife or the inauguration of heaven on earth. One's life is supposed to be lived in every aspect according to the church's strictures; in other words, the religion ordains your life *totally*. If your faith wavers or your actions are incompatible, you must confess and seek forgiveness. Such a system is also the template for modern fascism, which has many more tools of surveillance and control at

---

[333] Jews and Arabs were genetically identical. https://www.sciencedaily.com/releases/2000/05/000509003653.htm Before Mohammed, those Arabs who were not Jews or Christians were mostly polytheists.

[334] The Covenant: In return for Abraham promising that all his male descendants would have a bit of their penises chopped off, God offered protection and exclusivity.

its disposal than medieval popes, who relied on terror to get people to self-censor.

Monotheism contrasted with Pluralism

Today, the mainstream Christian churches – the Orthodox, Catholic and Anglican - are moderate or tolerant in the ways that they practice their faiths[335]. Yet for their followers, as well as for their fellow citizens who no longer belong to the local faith, their sense of purpose and their moral code are both universal and exclusive. This is why secular Americans rarely see that trying to impose their values on others can be seen as cultural imperialism.

Someone from a non-monotheist culture sees life differently. Before Communism, Chinese peasants revelled in many gods or saints, who were really just great men and women who had been converted into archetypes, their statues adorning temples,[336] just as Mrs Gao enjoys on a titchy scale at home. Their legends provided tips on how to live, but they gave no *ethical* guidance, and they jostled for affection against numerous competitors. You didn't have

---

[335] There are apparently over 33,000 Christian churches (denominations), of which the oldest is the Ethiopian Church. https://www.wesleyan. edu/christianitystudies/pathways/world.html#:~:text=A%20recent %20compilation%20lists%2033%2C089,with%20fewer%20than %20100%20members. Accessed 080424

[336] We put our heroes in public squares, on plinths and so forth. Those images found in Chinese temples are really the equivalent of our public statues, not 'gods' in any Judaeo-Christian sense.

faith in them in the way that is expected in Christianity or Islam, and you certainly would not be martyred for them like crusaders or ISIS. You could be relaxed about gods, picking up new ones and mixing them. Educated Chinese did not take them very seriously.

As for society's moral tenets, they were those sentiments and rules of conduct passed on by Grandma. China has been like this since at least the Chinese Enlightenment (770 to 481 BC) of which Confucius, Laozi and Mencius are the main exponents. From the reign of Elizabeth I, British society slowly gravitated towards such liberality, or at least wriggled away from dogmatism.

Thus, in WISE, by the 20th century, nobody cared what you believed, as long as you behaved. A Scots landowner, a disciple of David Hume, might be an atheist in private, but he would attend the Kirk with all his family, conforming to cultural practice. So in China, where literate people had long been sceptical about religion's claims, yet continued to take part in temple rituals and supported the nuns and monks.

Oddly enough, while WISE was becoming ever more tolerant and open, thanks to the dragons' teeth sown way back in the days of Alfred,[337] to the European Enlightenment (1687-1789)[338] and to the theory of natural selection (1859), we were exporting to China ways of thinking, out of which

---

[337] Described in Section 3: *Revolutionary Nations*

[338] The dates are disputed, but it is conventional to start with Newton's *Principia Mathematica* and end with the return to barbarism of the French Revolution. The date of the publication of Darwin's *On the Origin of Species* is 1859.

we ourselves were growing: Monotheist ways, introduced to China by missionaries, at first Christian and, later, Marxist. One consequence was the novel (to China) phenomenon of the religious conflict, waged bloodily in 19th-century[339] China by both Muslims and proto-Christians and, in the 20th century, among different denominations of communists. Power seekers no longer simply grabbed at power. They claimed to have doctrinal differences with those they wanted to overthrow and to oppose 'deviation' from a 'truth' derived from Marxist texts.

Monotheism and Modernity

Already in the late 19th century, many Europeans lived in relatively open societies. The educated had abandoned belief in a transcendental god, yet, finding it difficult to kick the habit that there is an authority which gives meaning and purpose to our lives, were susceptible to secularised versions of monotheism. Building on the works of Comte and others, Karl Marx offered a solution: There is meaning to our lives, but it is to be found not in the bible but in history. Active Marxists interpret history as the story of how humanity reaches utopia, the classless, communitarian society with which we began and before

---

[339] The most destructive war of the 19th century, which may have killed more people than the two World Wars, was the Taiping Rebellion, inspired by Christianity. See Platt, Stephen (2012) *Autumn in the Heavenly Kingdom* London: Atlantic Books.

wicked people (aka the capitalists) ruined things. As in the earlier Abrahamic religions, people are divided into the good ('saved', the proletariat, the victims) and the bad ('former people', bourgeoisie, unbelievers). The good people are to spread the gospel of communism, as revealed by Marxist theoreticians, and to eliminate those who cannot be converted and 'saved'. In the communist mentality, as in other monotheist religions, your identity is not your own business. You are damned or saved according to how the priests/commissars classify you, and that is all that need be known about you.

Thus, communism was, in its practices, a throwback to the closed societies of the past, in which people had prescribed identities that determined their different fates. Just as militant Islam rejects the open society, or pluralism, so does communism, and so do its variants, such as National Socialism (Nazism). Yet these were much worse than regimes of the past, because they sought not only to enforce conformity through terror and expropriation but also to obliterate forms of living that had evolved over thousands of years. Brutality in the pursuit of power was excused as being necessary to bring about utopia.

In Russia, Lenin and his heirs seized control of all industry and all property[340]. They expelled thousands

---

[340] Nobody was to be allowed to survive independently of the state. Like the communists, when the Nazis came to power in Germany, they planned to expropriate capitalist enterprises and land. However, recognising that state servants were less competent and more corrupt than independent managers, they generally left the

of communities from their homelands, slaughtered those who resisted their livelihoods being confiscated and created a slave state more barbarous than those of the ancient Egyptians or the Aztecs.[341] Nazi and subordinate communist parties copied these practices from Lenin.

Whereas pre-modern tyrants had made shift to accommodate the family because they had neither the means nor the theory to assault it, 20th-century totalitarians sought to rupture relations between the generations.

To survive, you had to reject any loyalty to other people, your family or friends, colleagues or traditional associations.[342] Your only significant relationship was to the party-state and its leader. Individuals were sundered from alternative sources of values or ideas which might raise questions about the political class or its self-serving ideology.

---

running of businesses and farms to people who knew how. The communists murdered those people, and made mayhem, famine and misery.

[341] Much of this was revealed by Robert Conquest in a series of books published from the 1960s to 1990s. For more recent scholarship, see, for example, Ferguson, Niall (2006) *The War of the World: History's Age of Hatred*, chapters 9 and 10.

[342] It is sometimes argued that 'pro-family' policies are a hallmark of Nazi/Fascist regimes, whereas Communists and left idealists (of the kibbutzim, for example) wanted to eliminate family. In fact, the objectives were the same, but the method was different. For both, reproduction was for the state. Mothers were producers; copulation was, as far as possible, to be shorn of emotional meaning, and males were provided with impersonal opportunities for sexual release wherever feasible.

Communism and Nazism both sought to destroy as well as supplant the faiths which had underpinned the old order. It was not only Lenin and his successors who killed or incarcerated priests. Heinrich Himmler, the former Roman Catholic who ran extermination programmes almost as big as the USSR's, saw the extirpation of Christianity as a sacred task.[343]

It has often been argued that the sufferings inflicted were deviations and can be blamed on psychopathic leaders. Rubbish. Power hungry politicians conjure up a utopian purpose to which people become emotionally attached, so that they can be manipulated into seeing the politician's demands as necessary to build the bright future. The 'mission' justifies destruction of what is called 'old', to contrast with the politician's 'new'. John Gray has explained how mass murder was always part of Lenin's programme, as it was of his students, Mao Zedong and Pol Pot. 'The destruction of historic forms of communal life was integral to the soviet project.' 'The emergence of a new human type required the systematic severing of human beings from their cultural roots.' Violence was used 'to liquidate social groups that had no space in the new world they were building'.[344]

This is the logical outcome of a monotheist crusade. It starts with optimistic ideas. It ends in a wasteland.

---

[343] https://ghdi.ghi-dc.org/sub_document.cfm?document_id=1573, accessed 220723.

[344] Gray, John (2023) *The New Leviathan*, p33. New to me, was the use of Mongolia as an experiment. One third of the population was liquidated by Russian communists when eradicating ideas and collectivizing the economy. Gray, John (2023) *The New Leviathans* p35.

How Did the Chinese Contract the Virus of Monotheism?

Traditional China was a relatively inclusive society, tolerant of religious diversity because people conformed to a set of norms which were not attributed to a god. They were associated with the very pragmatic teachings of philosophers whose main concern was to maintain a harmonious society, complementary with nature, not to pretend that something or someone outside the universe had revealed a special connection with our unusual species of ape. The (Chinese) Enlightenment, when imagined gods were squelched, at least by the educated, took place over 500 years before the Middle East's most famous charismatic, Jesus Christ, was born. Superstitions abounded in China, but rarely were given high status, let alone permitted to monopolise religious discourse. The conventional lore, common to all Chinese, regardless of whether they practised religions, was ritualised respect for forebears.[345] In daily life, this amounted to having memorials to departed forebears at home (rather as eminent European families have ancestral portraits on their walls), visiting their graves to show respect and drawing upon the copious writings of the past to understand the problems of the present.

In the 19th and 20th centuries, when China wilted as it came face to face with the industrial, military and

---

[345] Variously termed 'Confucianism' or 'Ancestor Worship' in the West.

organisational superiority of the 'West', some Chinese intellectuals jumped to the conclusion that this was all the fault of their lore, which had held China back.

Missionaries encouraged the idea that the advances of the Europeans had originated in Christianity; would-be reformers in China blamed their country's weaknesses on her *lack* of such an intransigent ideology. A few, ultimately very influential, educated Chinese turned to Christianity as a means of galvanising their civilisation, or at least of gaining sympathy from Christian powers.[346]

Some patriots, however, opted for the newer, Russian religion of communism and, eventually, forced it on China. From 1949 to 1976, under the psychopathic despot, Mao Zedong, the Chinese were coerced into a monotheist way of thinking that was alien to previous generations.[347] Today, thanks to globalisation and social media, it is more difficult

---

[346] The assault on Chinese civilisation began with the Taiping Rebellion, 1850-1871, inspired by Christian missionaries. The Taipings were precursors of the Communists, i.e. trying to convert China to monotheism. See Platt, Stephen R. (2012) *Autumn in the Heavenly Kingdom: China, The West and the Epic Story of the Taiping Civil War.*

[347] It is ironic that the CCP, while claiming to be patriotic, is today doubling down on the 'westernisation' of China by once again trying to replace traditional ways of thinking with a long discredited hypothesis dreamed up by the racist and pro-slavery Karl Marx. He was wrong about almost everything on which he opined, yet he has provided slogans for malevolent power grabbers for generations. Marx himself is still too often given undeserved respect, despite the misery to which his core ideas gave rise. https://intellectualtakeout. org/2017/02/karl-marx-was-a-pretty-bad-person/

to get people to believe in communist theory, the practice of which has been discredited by the destructive failures of government based on it. What is replacing it today is dogmatic nationalism and, for a reported 100 million, various versions of Christianity.

Why Do People Believe? Why Didn't We?

Thanks to Queen Elizabeth I (1558-1603),[348] WISE was not seduced by Nazism and communism. Here, we ought to distinguish fascism from authoritarianism. Elizabeth I was an authoritarian insofar as English monarchs could be. Authoritarian rulers usually allow civil society and private enterprise to continue unmolested. Under totalitarian rule, what I have dubbed 'fascism', you are only a citizen ('saved') if you exhibit no desire to be different or to have interests other than those of the totality. The Poetry Society or Stoat Fancier's Club is as suspect as the buccaneer businessman. As I write, thought control is being reimposed on the long-suffering Chinese. Elizabeth I went in the opposite direction.

Nevertheless, during our Civil War(s) and republic (The Protectorate 1642-1660), and notwithstanding the democratically minded sects fighting for Parliament,

---

[348] Todd would argue (*Explanation*, p102) that the Anglo family system is 'incapable of producing totalitarian ideologies or political forms which seek and achieve the total absorption of civil society by the state.' He states: 'The proletariat of the individualist world is not easily controlled.' I hope he is right.

Cromwell and the Puritans were, in some ways, also throwbacks to an intolerant past. They, and the pilgrims who left for New England to uphold a religion at least as totalist as that of the Roman Catholics, were as suspect to Anglicans as to the Catholic James II and VII.

Over succeeding centuries, a pragmatic consensus developed that open argument, compromise and piecemeal reform are better than faith. The return of Charles II was stage 1. The replacement of James II by the relatively hamstrung William III and Mary II reinforced it. The Georgian aristocracy was willing to accede to demands for political change.[349] It became generally agreed that revolutions always lead to killings, military dictators and suffering greater than under the old regime. The United Kingdom of Great Britain and Ireland (as it was from 1801)[350] would improve its institutions and revive its ancient principles and rights through debate and legal changes. Moderation was the watchword of progressives and conservatives alike. Class hatred was irrelevant and pernicious.

Religion didn't matter politically. Whether Protestant or Catholic, dissenters learned to live together with the established Church of England. By the time a Sephardi Jew, Benjamin Disraeli, became Prime Minister in 1868, it was

---

[349] See Foreman, Amanda (2022) *The Georgians: Restraint, Revolution and Reform*, BBC Radio 4.

[350] Castlereagh engineered the abolition of the Irish Parliament in order to try to bring Britain and Ireland together. However, his failure to achieve Catholic emancipation doomed that and caused much bitterness and Irish separatism.

enough that he had been baptised; he did not need to *believe* in church tenets, though he should practise its (ostensible) values. The Anglican church (and its equivalents in the three other nations and overseas) became, by the late 20th century, a rather woolly but well-meaning ministry, trying very hard to express the teachings of that great Jewish charismatic rather than emphasise rules and rituals derived from ancient Rome.[351]

This was our story: We were the free peoples who had toppled the despots, put the priests in their place and liberated men and women to make their own fate. WISE self-satisfaction was bolstered by the admiration for our politics, expressed by liberals and radicals from all over the world who hoped to emulate us, from countries as different as Hungary and China, Italy, Egypt and India.

Maltese and Argentinians proudly called themselves British, rather in the manner of Middle Easterners who were Roman Citizens, two thousand years earlier. Bolivar, Mazzini and Sun Yatsen came to London to study our constitution. Gandhi recruited Indians to fight for Britain in the First World War. We had an identity which was vicariously hankered after by many people who believed in WISE values, despite imperialism.

---

[351] As a child, I enjoyed singing *Vicar of Bray* without appreciating that it was a satire on Anglican flexibility. For the words of this quintessentially English song, see https://www.poetrynook.com/poem/vicar-bray-0, accessed 210723.

So, it is not surprising that, in WISE in the 20th century, neither the Nazi nor communist versions of fascism appealed to any but a few oddballs.[352] By contrast, in Continental Europe, especially where the churches were authoritarian, if not totalitarian, ambitious men worked up movements galvanised by secular religions, with disastrous consequences known to all. After the destruction of Nazi Europe and the disintegration of the Soviet Empire, German and East European survivors did their best to adopt our ways, abjuring the monotheism that had justified so many religious wars.

Through a Scientific Lens

From a natural history perspective, intergroup violence takes place in times of stress. Populations turn on those distinct from them and conveniently located, hence the pogroms against Armenians in Turkey, Jews in Eastern Europe, Tutsis in Rwanda and Rohingya in Myanmar. When politicians make violent bids for power, they channel jealousy and hatred to help them; we term this a revolution. Ideologies are merely the stories told by leaders to excuse and unite. We shouldn't think too much about the content of the ideology, because what matters is the function it

---

[352] The Blueshirts in Ireland and the Red Clydesiders, both extremists, were exceptions. Both originated among people with backgrounds in a totalitarian version of Christianity.

performs and the techniques (brainwashing, faith, ritual, charismatic leadership, persecution) deployed.

Intergroup violence also comes about when political leaders already in power cannot solve problems which threaten their own survival. If they do not have the resources to attack an external enemy, then they find a domestic enemy, usually an ethnic or religious minority. Genocide can rarely, if ever, be explained by racial differences or even geopolitical purposes.[353] As with our cousins, the apes, they are products of male power struggles.

So, when we see a new ideology taking hold, we should ask ourselves whether its practices reflect the characteristics of fascist movements identified above. If they do, we should be very afraid.

A Variant of the Virus

Let's look at the recent manifestations of identity politics,[354] which appear to derive from the monotheist tradition. Its tenets are that:

---

[353] Ferguson (2006) concludes as much in his remarkable *The War of the World*.

[354] Douglas Murray's *The Madness of Crowds* (London: Bloomsbury 2019) is the most thorough investigation of the emergence of this ideology, particularly in the USA, and of its proponents' fascistic practices. The best exposition of the phenomenon in the UK that I have come across is Williams, Joanna (2022) *How Woke Won* London: Spiked. Valuable contributions to our understanding of this new religion have been provided by Pluckrose, Helen and

(1) Racial and sexual minorities are being victimised 'institutionally' and must be championed, even privileged.

(2) Our identities are determined by the supposed recent history of our 'race', such that all black people are victims, and all white people are exploiters, at least until they have admitted their crimes and washed their brains.

(3) Gender is not determined by biology; we can transcend biology and nature; not believing in this delusion is immoral.

(4) European civilisation and capitalism are synonymous, wicked and should be replaced.

(5) The expression of any views conflicting with the above constitutes aggression and should not be tolerated.[355].

Whether any of these contentions stand up to serious analysis is irrelevant. [356] If people want to believe them,

---

Lindsay, James (2020) *Cynical Theories*, Durham: Pitchstone and Cobley, Ben (2018) *The Tribe.*

[355] It is not only in their ideas that the proponents of identity politics are similar to the fascists. Douglas Murray reports on the bullying and humiliation of liberal university academics at Yale and other US universities by thugs behaving exactly like Nazi brownshirts in 1930s Germany. Murray, (2019) *The Madness of Crowds,* Section 3. From p51-53 Murray traces the various manifestations of identity politics to their roots in Marxism and shows how they constitute a political ideology.

[356] Goodwin (2023) *Values, Voice and Virtue* debunks them effectively.

they won't analyse them. The emergence of such religions is a naturally occurring social phenomenon brought about by economic and social changes which destabilise populations and reorder their relationships. And the emergence of 'superfluous elites' or too many people who cannot be integrated into the political order. To explain them as political phenomena, there is no need to pay much attention to their claims, their ideas, nor even to the personalities of the leaders or the psychology of their adherents, but to examine the environment in which they have come about. This takes us into deep waters, so let's move to the rituals associated with the modern versions.

In 20th-century fascist societies, especially the USSR, affirmative action was undertaken so that students and job applicants were selected, not according to their strengths and weaknesses, but because their parents were members of the supposed victim classes[357] or the enlightened elite. In industry, competence was less important than social category. This is, apparently, becoming the case in the UK. Organisations such as the NHS, the BBC, local authorities and even commercial businesses put effort into ideological activities that have nothing to do with what the taxpayers or their customers expect from them. Instead, they devote themselves to imposing religious norms and demanding

---

[357] Canadian Jan Wong (*Red China Blues*, 1994) was the first 'foreign' student in China in 1972. She found that her fellow students at China's Oxford, Peking University, were peasant illiterates, beneficiaries of affirmative action in favour of those who were 'red' rather than 'expert'.

adherence to them from employees and contractors. Not that all the norms ('diversity') are necessarily reprehensible. It is the bigotry that should be questioned.

If you interrogate an orthodoxy—for example, suggest that the jury is still out on whether two males make for satisfactory parenting—you are at risk of losing your job.[358] A remark suggesting that a particular religion justifies violence may be investigated by the police as a hate crime (please note that I do not name a religion). People are favoured for jobs or university places because they are from 'preferred categories'.[359] Art, especially fiction, is to reflect the ruling ideology and publishers and agents are scared of heterodoxy. Even past theatre, films and children's books (such as those of Roald Dahl in 2023) must, reportedly, be purged of 'oldthink'. The patriotic, those who resist

---

[358] For the phenomenon in two different areas of national life, banking and sport, see Young, Toby (2023) 'Let's protect free speech for all not just the Left' in *Express*. https://www.express.co.uk/comment/expresscomment/1796615/free-speech-farage-coutts-trans-rights-left-comment, accessed 301023, and Hume, Mick (2023) English football's new blasphemy laws. https://www.spiked-online.com/2023/08/11/english-footballs-new-blasphemy-laws/, accessed 301023.

[359] Extensively discussed in Cobley, Ben (2018) *The Tribe,* Section 3. Goodwin (2023) *Values, Voice and Virtue* demonstrates that much higher proportions of ethnic minorities classed as victims take up elite university places or have elite jobs than the supposed 'privileged'. How ideological conformity is imposed in the UK is discussed in McConalogue, Jim, et al (2021) *Is the curbing of free speech in universities most prevalent in those with inflated diversity grievance bureaucracies?* London : Civitas

having either exploiter or victim identity foisted on them, or (Muslim and Christian) mothers who resist proposals for the indoctrination of their children, are patronised as in need of re-education.

Commoners may see through the racism that is embraced by many teachers, public servants and lawyers, the 'administrative elite', but are shouted down if they demur. Most dare not, they practise *inner emigration*, hiding any deviancy from their associates. 90 years ago, in Germany, it was the 'administrative elite' of teachers, lawyers, personnel managers and so on, which made up the largest phalanx of Nazi party members, being the speediest to conform to the new religion.[360] Resistance came from the working class, what we now call 'populism'.

You will immediately notice such similarity, in the doctrine and techniques of the various monotheist movements, as to suggest that they are all manifestations of the same social phenomenon.[361] Power seekers, who hope to overthrow the existing order, start by promoting a validating ideology, which becomes the orthodoxy which will lead to the suppression of the alternatives. This is fascism.

It works like this: The *advanced (*aka the *chosen)* present a picture of the world that is unjust, in that all the resources

---

[360] How this worked in Nazi Germany is described in detail in Evans, Richard J. (2012) *The Third Reich in Power* Section 11.

[361] A rich source of examples of how Puritan fascism held sway in 18th-century America and laid down the foundations for many US attitudes today, is contained in Hackett, David (1989) *Albion's Seed: Four British Folkways in America.*

are controlled by *exploiters*, the wicked people, who have kept down the good people, the *victims*. On the side of the victims are their leaders, the *advanced ones*, who help us see our situation as it really is. A kind landlord in China might have been thought by his fellow villagers to be just and good, but the *advanced* will show us that he is, in fact, a member of an identity group that must be exterminated.[362] In the 2020s, a liberal professor at a US university may think that he treats all equally. However, he will soon be shown up as a racist and homophobe because equality is exactly what he should *not* be practising.

When the *advanced* have the power, they seek to force a new morality on the people to replace the traditional.[363] For example, in communist countries, love towards parents and spouse was to be replaced by loyalty to the party; under Nazism, having children was not for family reasons but to

---

[362] The process, in 1950s China, is grippingly shown up by Eileen Chang in her great novel (2015) *Naked Earth* New York: NYRB Classics. During the 'Cultural Revolution', known to Chinese victims as 'the ten-year horror', just being old made you a target. In Red August, in 1966, young activists went on a rampage through Peking, slaughtering (often with appalling cruelty) anybody 'old'. The leader, whose name is well known, has never been indicted, although her alleged savagery was no less than Nazi concentration camp guards. For the consequences of ideological rectification, see Johnson, Ian (2023) *Sparks: China's Underground Historians and Their Battle for the Future*, London: Penguin.

[363] The similarities with Nazi Germany are illuminating. The processes through which German society went, and the opposition it encountered from the old religions, are detailed in Evans, Richard J. (2012) *The Third Reich in Power*

provide soldiers for the cause. You should not show respect or concern for others because they are old, young, wise or weak, but only if they belong to an approved identity group.[364]

In Lenin's Russia, there were two main categories: the bourgeois ('former people') and victims ('proletariat'). Those classified as bourgeois, if they were allowed to live, would find that their children and grandchildren would suffer persecution. If you had any instinct for survival, you tried to identify with the victims pretty fast.[365]

For communists, people were (in theory) classified according to social class; for other movements, it is race or gender which determines our fate. Today, in the USA, black people are perpetually victims because of the way in which slaves from Africa were treated in the past [366]. White people are 'permanently trapped in the legacy of their founding crimes',[367] no matter that none of the white people alive today participated in those crimes.

---

[364] Branigan, Tania (2023) *Red Memory: Living, Remembering and Forgetting China's Cultural Revolution*, London: Faber and Faber

[365] In China, persecuted members of the 'black' classes tried to marry poor peasants or proletarians. This did not save them from punishment but they might avoid the worst excesses of persecution, such as life imprisonment or being beaten to death during a rectification campaign, in which the descendants of the *black elements* would be brought out for ritual chastisement.

[366] This is not to deny that racism has been prevalent in the USA for many years since the formal abolition of slavery.

[367] Williams, Joanna (2022) *How Woke Won* London, p166.

Any movement which shares key characteristics of fascism as I have defined them, is a modern iteration of an old-fashioned, illiberal bid for domination, which disguises itself, as did communism, as a movement for justice or, as Nazism did, as a righting of old wrongs.

The Sea of Faith

It is obvious why political activists propagate these religions. They are invaluable in bringing people together and under control. They are, after violence, the most potent weapon in the armoury of the would-be despot, from Moses to Moon Sun Myung, Louis XIV to Lenin. He exploits the human impulse to conform, and to follow those with supernatural insight.[368]

A testosterone-fuelled urge for power may be a prime motivator in politics and corporate life. Successful societies have tempered and institutionalised these urges, for example (in Imperial China), by making literacy and cultural orthodoxy the principal criteria for joining the bureaucracy. A young official was more admired for his calligraphy than for any muscle flexing. The Victorians channelled aggression into self sacrifice and created an

---

[368] Lenin consciously set himself up as an icon, a messiah-like figure. Leading Nazis sought to copy the USSR in creating a substitute church with sacred texts, rituals and holy places, see Evans, Richard J. (2012) *The Third Reich in Power.*

ideal of manliness that delimited violence, expressed most idealistically in Kipling's poem *If*.

It is less obvious why the followers fall for fascism, unless it be out of fear of exclusion. Perhaps a latent desire for belonging, regardless of the price paid in adopting those beliefs, is just part of being human.[369] Most of us like to conform to a peer group. When we passionately advocate something, we don't even realise that we are distilling our frenzy 'from some academic scribbler of a few years back'[370] and contradicting what we believed five years ago. Not many of us have the time or energy to question what is in the ether or fashionable, let alone the shibboleths of a pullulating faith.

This makes us vulnerable to faith viruses, of which identity politics is a recent one. As the virus spreads, we adapt to the new consensus, modifying our language, dress and habits. We agree that women can have penises or that consecrated wine turns into real blood. We start dividing people into the damned and the saved.[371]

---

[369] Richard Dawkins has other ideas about why humans expend so much time, energy and resources on religions. He thinks of genetic and psychological reasons, but to me, the most persuasive is that of bonding.

[370] The original quotation from JM Keynes is, 'Practical men who believe themselves to be quite exempt from any intellectual influence, are usually the slaves of some defunct economist. Madmen in authority, who hear voices in the air, are distilling their frenzy from some academic scribbler of a few years back.'

[371] This can lead to the condemnation of whole categories of people. Protestants, Jews, Herreros and the bourgeoisie have featured as

Those with a strong immune system can resist. Since 1949, Chinese loyalty to family and the intensity of identification with Enlightenment principles, plus the well-honed skills of pretending conformity, have made it possible for at least some to conserve their identity throughout savage attacks intended to brainwash them into becoming what the tyrants think of as modern. In the 1930s, the British were confident of the efficacy of their traditions and the success of their institutions. That gave them immunity.

What has happened to our immune system that many of us are susceptible to the identity politics virus?[372] Is it that our political leaders and opinion-formers have lost confidence in our story, or simply don't know it at all? Parents and teachers have been shy of imparting it, lest they seem triumphalist and snobbish. Globalisation and social media have given rise to the illusion that we all belong to a global (aka American) culture. Netizens have had their manners corrupted and brains stewed, thanks to Silicon Valley entrepreneurs who facilitate the debasement of language and incivility, even as they open up

---

targets. For Islamic fundamentalists, anyone who deviates from their version of Islam is fair game. In the US today, even a minor deviation, for example, from the assertions of Black Lives Matter, can ruin a career, even a life. See Murray, Douglas (2022) *The War on the West* London, p191, but also throughout.

[372] How it manifests itself in daily life is amusingly recounted by Piers Morgan in his (2021) *Wake Up* London: Harper Collins, pp301 onwards. A more sober and detailed analysis is in Goodwin (2023) *Values, Voice and Virtue.*

global conversation. Identity politics, emanating from the parochial politics of the USA, has seized the imagination of those seeking meaning in their lives as tumultuous changes appear to render all old religions and theories irrelevant.

We avoided fascism in the 20th century because we had our own faith, based on empirical facts rather than supernatural fantasies. We shared a belief in our identity as a group of nations whose peoples had made their own society and, because they had had contact with many less fortunate peoples, that theirs was more humane than any other. More and more countries now define themselves as democracies,[373] yet the default position of many nations looks authoritarian. Everywhere, people are cleaving to religions, old and new, and even in Anglo-American societies, open society is denigrated.

No violent revolution has ever shown how a society can be made better by replacing it with a faith-based totalitarian order. We should build on the incremental achievements of the past,[374] not abolish them; in other words, revivify our

---

[373] https://ourworldindata.org/democracies-age, accessed 030423.

[374] The communist claim that their revolutions replaced irredeemably flawed polities does not bear scrutiny. We have long known that about Russia and Eastern Europe, flung back into prehistoric misery by communism. The advances swept away by Mao's barbarism are summarised in Dikötter, Frank (2008) *The Age of Openness, China before Mao*, Los Angeles: U of California Press. Communist revolutions everywhere made life much worse for the majority and empowered only the elite.

own identity and not let it dissolve in another reductivist, universalist ideology.

The powers of surveillance and misinformation in the hands of the wicked or depraved are greater than ever before. [375] The difference between open and fascist societies needs to be more marked than ever. We must resist exclusive and divisive ideologies if the open society is to survive. Mrs Gao knows that.

---

[375] A thorough and chilling account of how fascism may have penetrated and perverted minds in China today can be found in Strittmatter, Kai (2019) *We Have Been Harmonized: Life in China's Surveillance State* Exeter: Old Street. I write 'may have' because, since the Covid lockdown, discussion about public affairs and criticism of politicians has become less constrained than for many years.

Section **12**

Key WISE: *Respect*

We, who live in a country in which we take for granted *Respect* of one human being for another, need to have it explained to us how unusual this is. As I mention elsewhere, the use of *Respect* as a political term was introduced to me by refugees from China in the 1970s. It was the lack of *Respect* that, they believe, distinguished the Peoples' Republic of China (PRC)[376] from Hong Kong under British rule. When people have wanted to name the benign gift of the Anglosphere, they have talked of 'liberalism' or 'democracy'. Like those refugees, I prefer to call it '*Respect*'.

....

A China Story

Upon their release from prison, the two Chinese teachers discovered they could never work in schools again. Classified

---

[376] British people sometimes need reminding that Chinese civilisation is not contained in one country, though the PRC is the biggest Chinese community. The Republic of China, usually referred to as Taiwan, has a distinct political culture, as have Singapore and the large Chinese communities in Malaysia, Indonesia and North America.

as dissidents, they had to live off friends and family until they could find parents courageous enough to employ them as private tutors. Neighbours and former colleagues cold shouldered, or cursed, them. Regularly, the local police would rampage through their home, looking for forbidden books or other proofs of heresy, breaking drawers and cupboards, ripping apart possible hiding places, causing Grandma and the boy to hold each other tight, weeping from fear.

Applying for asylum in Britain, those teachers, Mr and Mrs Hou, looked exhausted by life. Mrs Hou, her son told me, had been a quite different person after prison. From a tender mother of few words and many smiles, she had emerged hysterical, intransigent, filled with an obsessive hatred for the ruling class and all who might compromise with it. She was harsh and bitter with her family and those who tried to console her. Had she been tortured, raped or had an organ removed? She would not say. However they had done it, the perpetrators had succeeded in abolishing her old self.

The Rarity of Respect

What do I mean by *Respect*? Usually, the word connotes good manners, consideration for the other, and treating him or her as a distinct person whose way of life may be different from our own. It means all that, but it also implies concern for others, tolerance of difference and willingness to compromise rather than confront. These attitudes first became institutionalised in WISE. It may be true, as Frank Field has written,[377] that they are in rapid decline, but they remain hallmarks of WISE society.

Visitors mock our queues, our naïve belief in 'fairness', concern for losers with whom we have little in common, our willingness to admit wrongdoing, obsessive adherence to rules and polite drivers who stop at crossings. Yet they value these demonstrations of neighbourliness and equality. Our fixations on consumer protection and health and safety are also manifestations of *Respect*. More significant is the consideration we give to minorities previously hidden or subdued: disabled, transgender, and ethnic.

Where Does *Respect* Come From?

It is often assumed that these behaviours are derived from religion, whereas it is more plausible that religion has been adapted to legitimate our customs. The Reformation changed the Christian church in WISE, and had it make more of those moral teachings that were closest to WISE values.[378] After all, the admonitions of Jesus Christ are very similar to those of the oracles of other religions. They can be adapted to cultures other than the Mediterranean, which is what happened at the Reformation, when Scots,

---

[377] Field, Frank (2023) *Politics, Poverty and Belief: A Political Memoir,* Section 9

[378] Those values emerged first in Anglo-Saxon England, as I describe in 'Why WISE?' The Abrahamic religions have a kernel of *Respect*, which the moderates in those religions have tried to emphasise.

German, Scandinavian, Anglican and other versions of the religion, more suited to their social environment, came into their own.

In the Middle Ages, when the Muslim world was more magnanimous, our society was brutal and intolerant, almost as cruel as continental European countries. The Latin Church[379] extirpated the old pre-Christian religions of the Roman Empire, and later hounded Muslims out of Europe. We, too, set about burning and breaking heretics. So, how was it that WISE came to *Respect* others' freedom of expression and their liberty earlier than anyone else?

Respect as a social habit is not exclusive to WISE, but it developed in a particular way in WISE society.[380] Here's my hypothesis: Economic security and the rule of law are the essential conditions for *Respect* to emerge as a driving force in human communities. Not until people's struggle for

---

[379] Well before the Protestant Reformation, there were many Christian churches, of which the Latin Church (now referred to as the Roman Catholic Church) was but one. The first Christian countries were Armenia and Ethiopia.

[380] Oliver Letwin has pointed out to me (in an email dated 310523) that 'other Europeans can lay claim to much of what we now regard as the creation of the liberal international order in the 20th Century. The Geneva Conventions, the ECHR, the legal protection of rights within the EU... all of these are part of a tradition that can be traced back to Kant and the thinkers of the Enlightenment, in which Hume and the Lockeans certainly played a part, but not as great a part as the Germans or the French.' What he is rightly noting is a parallel development of the concept of *Respect*, preceded by that of WISE.

survival is less acute, do they have a notion that 'others' have human rights. When WISE forebears were ground down by necessity and informed only by an illiberal religion,[381] they cared, at most, for their own people. Before the 18th century, Britain was a harsh society, even though it was less harsh than elsewhere. The brigands, slavers and colonists who initiated what became the Empire could be barbaric.[382]

In the 18th century, occluded quirks of WISE society emerged, which I have collectively termed *'Respect'*. They became part of our public discourse earlier than elsewhere, not only because WISE was wealthier and more stable, but also because of its relative egalitarianism: the security of a trusted legal system and the freedom to which people had believed they had a right since early times. These were dealt with in Section 5.

Emergence of Respect in WISE

As early as the reign of Henry II (1133-89), the Inquisition, that agency of the Roman Church which used torture

---

[381] It is difficult for modern WISE people to understand the hold that the church had on pre-modern minds. Arthur Miller's play, *The Crucible*, is an exposition of the power of religion to pervert and atomise. A detailed description of pre-modern totalitarianism in Massachusetts in the 18th century is found in *Albion's Seed*.

[382] The cruelty of the slave trade, the ruthlessness of the subjugation and genocide of indigenous peoples is nowhere more graphically described than in Ferguson, Niall (2012) *Empire, How Britain Made the Modern World* London: Penguin

and terror to root out diversity, had been forbidden from operating in England; this was an outlier in Europe.

Common Law had always prohibited torture,[383] which has been mainstream in much of the world well into our times. It could be undertaken only with special permission of the monarch's advisory body, which issued its last permit in 1628. In Scotland, torture was prohibited in 1708. This was earlier than any other country.

Another indication of evolving *Respect* was the (first in the world) emergence of a welfare state.[384] Our welfare state has its origins in the 1536 Poor Laws, which codified ancient legislation to provide help for the sick, old and unemployed. The tradition of providing alms-houses for them had started in the 10th century under King Athelstan and a supplementary arm of poor relief was provided by the monasteries, before their dissolution under Henry VIII. From 1536, a tax was collected at parish level, that relief might be provided locally.

Over the centuries, many welfare institutions and associations were founded independently of the state. They

---

[383] Friedman, Danny (2009) *Torture and the Common Law* London: Matrix Law https://www.matrixlaw.co.uk/wp-content/upl oads/2016/03/25_11_2009_04_52_16_Torture-and-the-Common-Law-2006-2-EHRLR-180.pdf

[384] The essential reading on the history of welfare in the UK, and its current problems, is Bartholomew, James (2004) *The Welfare State We're In*, London: Politicos. Bartholomew followed this up with an international comparison which should be in every politician's knapsack, (2015) *The Welfare of Nations*, London: Biteback.

came to make up the most substantial civil society of any country anywhere. In the town of Woodbridge, Suffolk, for example, alms-houses, a library, schools and parks were provided from the donations of one 16th-century family and are in operation to this day. A 20-minute bicycle ride in London, from Lambeth Bridge to Tower Bridge, can pass by at least six groups of alms-houses, many other voluntary organisations and the library founded by John Harvard, who established Harvard University in 1636.

The emergence of these institutions of *Respect* was followed, in time, by the championing of equality and rights. The man who thought most about these things was the 3rd Earl of Shaftesbury (1671-1713), whose philosophy was influential throughout Europe for two centuries following his death. His descendant, the 7th Earl, was our most eminent social reformer, campaigning for better working conditions, limiting child labour and providing schools for the poor.

Earlier than other Christian societies, we tolerated diversity in religion. (Catholics were treated with suspicion because continental politicians sought to use them as saboteurs). Today, there are 2,000 mosques in Britain, benefitting from freedoms won by Christian dissenters centuries earlier.[385] The Reformation removed the restrictions on Jews imposed

---

[385] Khan, Sara (2016) *The Battle for British Islam* London Saqi, p192. The first mosque was established in 1889 by a Jewish academic. It is Woking's Shah Jahan Mosque. The first synagogue in the UK dates from 1701.

by the Catholic church, enabling them to practise their faith from the 1650s, under the republic.

I'm not suggesting that WISE had a monopoly on *Respect* for human life. Imperial China mandated its officials to make the relief of famine and flood a high priority, maintaining huge grain stores for emergencies. Buddhism commands attention to the needs of those less fortunate, and its monasteries provide the same kind of services to the indigent as those of the Christian world. Charitableness towards our neighbour is part of our biological makeup.[386] Only in Britain did *Respect* so come to permeate the social unconscious that, in time, it was institutionalised.

The contrast between WISE and other European countries in the 20th century is indicative. In the Spanish Civil War, both sides promoted appalling cruelty, as Ernest Hemingway exposed in *For Whom the Bell Tolls*. The barbarity of Italian forces in North Africa and of fascist and communist rivals in their homeland was worse than anything we experienced even as far back as our civil war. Then, there was the enthusiasm with which French society joined in the Nazi-instigated abuse and murder of ethnic minorities. We do not need to remind anyone of the persecutions in Germany, Russia, the Balkans and the Middle East.

---

[386] This is best analysed in Ridley, Matt (1997) *The Origins of Virtue*. See also Richard Dawkins in (2016) *The God Delusion*, London: Black Swan.

Politics and Respect

Politics is the word we give to the practices of power struggle, how men establish status and accumulate and distribute resources. Communities of apes practise politics through social manipulation or violence. Successful apes grab for themselves all the females, food and authority over the other apes. What humans can seize is checked by the traditions of the community in which they operate and the ability of others to uphold those traditions. Thus, in WISE, a would-be dictator would have to eliminate defenders of constitutional politics such as the monarch, law lords and those army generals and police commissioners who understand their roles as loyalty to WISE custom, rather than to the politician of the moment.

Understanding this, the first acts of Lenin, Hitler and Mao, like smaller despots, were to destroy the moral inhibitions and customary courtesies that would impede the subjection of all to their will. They deployed ideology to convince people; ideology, as we have seen, is the means to unite followers. Followers can also be united by being made complicit in the persecution of the scapegoat, for the problems which the leader will solve. The scapegoat might be the nobility, shopkeepers, Romanies or whoever is convenient. From current trends in the USA, we might deduce that a future power grab there might identify WASPs as scapegoats.

Some polities have not progressed very far from the apes—Chad, Venezuela and Belarus spring to mind—and some have regressed after achieving more sophisticated arrangements, i.e. those through which there was some emerging *Respect* for others. In the 20th century, Germany astonished admirers of its intellectual and cultural advances when its politics went into reverse. Other examples of regression in modern times are Cambodia under the Khmer Rouge and China under Mao. In both those countries, institutions which might have tamed megalomania were swept away, and the majority enslaved.

Respect and Equality

Respect bundles not merely empathy, but that sense of equality that has deep roots in WISE. This contrasts very remarkably with the sense of inequality found among citizens of communist China, in a very distinct way in India and probably in other cultures too.[387] It is virtually impossible for a person from a hierarchical culture to conceive of a relationship of equality, whether as an employee, lover or associate. No sooner does she join an entity than she will seek to figure out the ranking so that she can take the part of subordinate or tyrant (sometimes both).

As Frank Field notes, 'our commoner institutions— trades unions, friendly societies, working men's clubs— were egalitarian, insisted upon cooperative behaviour and

---

[387] Although generations born into social media may think differently. Methods of suppression used on ethnic and religious minorities may not be efficacious for those who have absorbed the egalitarian and individualistic culture of social media.

mutual help; they originated and were organised without government interference.'[388] A secular philosophy closely connected to Christianity, English Idealism, became an alternative theorisation of these attitudes and behaviours. Field tells us that the Idealists extended the idea of freedom, beyond freedom from restrictions, to *freedom to do things*.[389]

That the obligation of *Respect* should come to permeate a society so completely as to influence its politics was unique to WISE. Even 'hawks'—we might now refer to them as exemplars of 'toxic masculinity'—could evolve under the influence of *Respect*'s doves. By the 19th century, in WISE, the male thug was turning into the sportsman – football, horse- or whippet-racing fan, cricketer or shot. The colonial master was being elided into the fatherly district officer, exhausting himself in the nurture of 'sullen peoples'. The warrior became the upstanding Tommy who abjured looting, rape or gratuitous violence. Instead of being ashamed of showing sympathy, he became ashamed to show a lack of it.[390] By the world wars of the 20th century, the difference between the brutality of German and Russian

---

[388] Field, Frank (2023) *Politics, Poverty and Belief: A Political Memoir* London: Bloomsbury, Section 9. He builds on the historical work of EP Thompson (1963), *The Making of the English Working Class*.

[389] Field (2023) *Politics, Poverty and Belief: A Political Memoir,* Section 6

[390] Thanks to Hackett (1989), we can contrast this with how settlers in the Americas encouraged aggression and brutishness. Francis Hsu's *Chinese and Americans* describes how the socialisation of Chinese children traditionally discouraged self-assertiveness and aggression, in marked contrast to the socialisation of American children.

troops on the one hand, and the restraint of the British on the other, was very marked.[391] In WISE, those ambitious for political power, for good or ill, have to play an elaborate game which curtails their aggression. *Respect* took root in WISE long before elsewhere.[392]

Our Glorious Record on Slavery

Of all the achievements of the British Empire, the epitome is our record on slavery. Of my forebears, I am particularly proud of the Kildare man who was active in the campaign against slavery.[393] He was a committed Anglican. The leading figures in the anti-slavery movement were mostly Anglicans, though the current head of that church, Archbishop Welby, appears not to know this.[394] Agnostics or atheists,

---

[391] Elkins has exposed a terrible exception. Under the command of a Colonel Robin Stephens, CISDIC subjected both SS prisoners and Soviet defectors to sadistic, Communist-style tortures at Bad Nenndorf in 1945-6. There was an investigation and court martial, documented in Elkins, Caroline (2022) *Legacy of Violence: A History of the British Empire,* Section 8 Pt 2.

[392] Norbert Elias (1939), in *The Civilising Process,* described how he thought changes in human behaviour came about in Europe. However, what he thinks of as civilised behaviour is not quite the same as what I identify as *Respect.*

[393] William de Burgh MP (1741-1808) see *Dictionary of National Biography.* Ferguson attributes the anti-slavery movement to the Clapham Sect in Ferguson, Niall (2012) *Empire, How Britain Made the Modern World* pp116-17.

[394] https://catholicherald.co.uk/the-ideological-error-of-welbys-100-million-fund-to-compensate-descendants-of-slavery/, accessed

prominent thought leaders such as David Hume and John Stuart Mill, also excoriated slavery. Once the argument had been won in Parliament, we not only outlawed slavery at home but sought to close down a barbarous international industry which had been conducted by Arabs and Africans for thousands of years.

As soon as African rulers had enticed them into this lucrative business, unscrupulous Britons, as well as many other Europeans, joined in. From 1525 to 1866, 12.5m were transported to the Americas, and rather more went to Arab countries.[395] Why are the heirs of those enslaved in the Arab world not calling for reparations, as are those of the USA? Because there were no descendants. African slaves taken to Arab countries were all castrated so that they would leave no trace.[396] That slave trade was genocidal.

Today's polemicists talk of slaves as if they were exclusively black, but for centuries, there were probably at least as many

---

060823. Two heroes of identity politics have curious résumés: Karl Marx's writings reveal him as a racist who approved of slavery. Michel Foucault purchased and raped young children in poor countries. https://www.aljazeera.com/opinions/2021/4/16/reckoning-with-foucaults-sexual-abuse-of-boys-in-tunisia accessed 280224

[395] Different scholars give different figures, sometimes as high as 17 million before the 20th century. The Wikipedia entry suggests 11.5–15 million. Also see Thomas, Gordon (1990) *Enslaved: Investigation into Modern-Day Slavery* London: Bantam Press.

[396] https://www.fairplanet.org/dossier/beyond-slavery/forgotten-slavery-the-arab-muslim-slave-trade/, accessed 010523

white slaves as black.[397] If reparations are to be paid to descendants of slaves transported to the USA, they should also be paid to those communities whose youths were seized in Europe and the Caucasus. More just would be to invest such resources in helping modern slaves. It is said that there are 200 million of them. Slavery is particularly prevalent in much of Africa, India and Russia.[398] It is managed mainly by Arab and African traders.[399]

After legal abolition in 1791, British authorities inaugurated an operation to suppress the trade worldwide, which lasted 150 years. Royal Navy patrols prevented shipments and rescued captives; taxpayers' money was used to buy off British slave owners, Arab traders and African rulers alike, once they committed to ending the practice. They resisted, and so did the United States.

It has been claimed that the wealth of WISE was founded on slavery.[400] The reality is that it was insignificant to the

---

[397] For an account of white slavery in the 18th century, see Milton, Giles (2005) *White Gold: The Extraordinary Story of Thomas Pellow and North Africa's One Million European Slaves London*: Hodder & Stoughton

[398] https://www.ijmuk.org/modern-slavery-and-trafficking?gclid= EAIaIQobChMIleSJ45z0-gIVEu7tCh0vKAmoEAAYBCAAEgISKvD_ BwE, accessed 221022. Also see Thomas, Gordon (1990) *Enslaved: Investigation into Modern-Day Slavery.*

[399] https://time.com/longform/african-slave-trade/, accessed 060823

[400] On this, see https://historyreclaimed.co.uk/did-slavery-make-britain-rich-decolonisation-and-progressive-masochism/, accessed 191122.

development of the British economy.[401] Some families and places became rich from it, especially those which were compensated for lost business when forbidden to trade. However, the industrial revolution was not fuelled by the slave trade, nor even by exports. It came about because, long before the participation of a few Britons in the slave trade, WISE was wealthier and more welcoming to ingenuity and enterprise than anywhere else.[402]

The Empire of Liberation

It was *Respect* that motivated public opinion to condemn the East India Company in the 18th century and to call for the government to take responsibility for India. *Respect* was behind the British Parliament seeking to protect the indigenous peoples of Australia and North America from colonists. One reason Washington and others sought independence from Britain in the 18th century was that Parliament intended to protect the land rights of indigenous peoples. By contrast, aggressive settlers wanted to wipe them out.[403]

Free trade was advocated in WISE in the interests of the colonies and dominions. Some suggest that free trade was the first 'universalistic ideology'. It was certainly championed by liberals and religious groups who believed

---

[401] Landes (1998) *The Wealth and Poverty of Nations*, pp119-20
[402] Dispassionately conveyed evidence is to be found in Biggar (2021) *Colonialism: A Moral Reckoning*, pp342 and 348.
[403] Ferguson (2012) *The Great Degeneration,* p85 et seq.

it would bring both economic development and political freedom. For this, they were willing that Britain should be poorer.[404]

The policy of free trade, far from harming Indian industry, ensured that it modernised and eventually challenged ours. Thanks to free trade, throughout the latter half of the 19th century, the American and European economies filched what we would now call our IP, eventually overtaking us.

The British inclination to *Respect* was widely recognised abroad as giving a unique character to British rule. Why else did elites in the colonies seek to emulate the British and cooperate with them? Had they not done so, the Empire could not have been maintained. The number of WISE personnel running the colonies was tiny and became smaller and smaller because of the policy of 'indigenisation, or letting the locals run themselves.' By 1946, there were only 600 WISE officials in India, for a population of 400 million. There had never been many more than 1,000.

Up until the late 20th century, British rule was seen as desirable, especially when compared with that of the Japanese, Germans or Russians. Everywhere, the oppressed looked to WISE for help. New Zealand Māori and Fijians asked to be incorporated into the Empire for protection against ruthless settlers. Those in Britain who pushed for the annexation of Natal and the Gold Coast in Africa[405] did

---

[404] Tombs (2015) *The English and their History,* p552. See also Tombs (2021) *This Sovereign Isle: Britain In and Out of Europe,* p30

[405] Tombs (2015) *The English and their History,* p547

so to protect the inhabitants. Corsica requested membership of the Empire and was rejected, as were Ethiopia, Mexico, Sarawak, Uruguay, Katanga and Morocco.[406]

We must acknowledge that there were lapses after 1945, when the government was trying to shore up the remaining Empire. Elkins has recorded the foul behaviour of uniformed personnel in Palestine, Kenya and Malaya and the attempts at cover-up by their leaders. Had wartime rendered them insensitive to misery, contemptuous of life? The perpetrators and facilitators of unspeakable cruelties died unpunished, despite efforts of whistle-blowers such as the valiant MP, Barbara Castle; the exposures came too late.[407]

Crimes were committed in the British Empire, but we have long had legal processes to correct abuses and the idea of *Respect* to propel their application. There were 'commissions of inquiry, parliamentary debates, metropolitan blue books, and similar records which formed part of a self-correcting mechanism. They played an important part in putting a stop to imperial abuses.'[408] It is this which distinguishes the British Empire from others. Critics have pointed to a discrepancy between our expectations at home and practices abroad. However, awareness of the principles on which WISE prided themselves at home gave ammunition to defenders of liberties in the Empire. This was unique in the histories of empires, as noted in Section 6.

[406] Tombs (2015) ibid, p541
[407] Elkins (2022) *Legacy of Violence*, especially Chapters 13 and 14
[408] Biggar (2021) *Colonialism: A Moral Reckoning*, p351

The moralists and investigative journalists, whistle-blowers and lawyers of our open society make it hard for the wicked to escape discovery, whereas, in most other societies, nobody dares to hold them to account or even to notice that crimes have been committed. Kitchener's treatment of Boer families in the Boer War was exposed by Emily Hobhouse; the 1945 handing over of refugees to extermination by the USSR was castigated by Nicholas Bethell and Nikolai Tolstoy,[409] and cruelties in Kenya have been documented by Caroline Elkins.[410] Bungling reactions to a famine or a demonstration have been investigated and charged. Japanese or German imperialists got away with slavery, sadism and genocide. Who has been called to account for savagery under Lenin or Mao?

Today, *Respect* is manifested in the sympathy for asylum seekers, which has allowed us to admit vast numbers of people here—many of whom are economic migrants rather than refugees—precisely because they are refused admission by contiguous or culturally similar nations. Arab countries have mostly rejected refugees from Syria and

---

[409] For an overview of the Bethell-Tolstoy exposure, see 'Gravedigging' The case of the Cossacks', Section 14 in de Burgh, Hugo (2000) *Investigative Journalism: Context and Practice,* London: Routledge, pp256-267

[410] Elkins, Caroline (2005) *Imperial Reckoning: The Untold Story of Britain's Gulag in Kenya* New York: Henry Holt. Caveat: Since I referenced this book, it has been described as inaccurate and defamatory by Elstein, David (2024) 'How Kenyan History is Being Rewritten' in *The Critic*, January 2024.

other war zones. They feel no guilt for their part in creating the refugee crises, any more than they take responsibility for slavery.

Respect is also manifested in the relaxed attitude to independence movements. Whereas Chechens, Tibetans, Tuaregs, Mapuche or Catalans risk their freedom and often their lives when they claim autonomy, the demands for independence for Scotland have been met with understanding and reason. The contrast between those nations that *Respect* other human beings and their cultures, and those that do not, is instructive.

Summary

Before the British Empire demonstrated *Respect* through its administration and institutions, most people in most societies were fatalistic about themselves and vicious towards those different from them. Practices that we in WISE already considered barbaric were normal.

Respect emerged as a mobilising force in WISE for a variety of reasons, and its advocates always struggled against the power drive and instinctive harshness, what we now talk of as toxic masculinity. By the 20th century, thoughtful people in many countries sought to emulate us. There were lapses. From 1917 to 1989, Russia, and from 1949 to 1979, China, returned to primitiveness and denied *Respect* to their citizens.

Even today, the countries contributing to humanitarian aid and the people running aid programmes, or negotiating and conciliating in conflicts, are overwhelmingly European and very likely to be Anglo-American. In such circumstances, it matters that WISE be aware of its own distinctness and be vigilant in upholding the values of *Respect*. In a world in which despots and religious fanatics are brazen in persecuting even powerless people like those two teachers, Mr and Mrs Hou, WISE is needed as much as ever as a 'light unto the nations,' 'yearning to breathe free',[411].

---

[411] Four words from the poem by Emma Lazarus on the Statue of Liberty.

Section 13

So, What Is WISE?

In this book, so far, I have explained why we are still relevant, how WISE came about and why its extraordinary achievement is in danger. Now I address how we can re-imagine WISE in the Age of Asia.

....

A China Story

In China in September 1976, Mrs Zhu, a teacher who had been born a poor peasant,[412] heard that Chairman Mao, dictator since 1949, had died. She promptly strangled her only chicken and roasted it for a family celebration. The family partied privately because most of their neighbours, as required, were out on the street, weeping. Soon after, millions of people who had been turned into slaves by the

---

[412] 'Poor peasant' is a communist-created social category. As opposed to 'rich peasants' or 'middle peasants', these were supposed to be the main supporters of the CCP, whereas they became, at least by the time of collectivisation, equally victims. The only supporters of party policies in the countryside, by the 1970s, were the thugs and hooligans who had been licensed to prey upon everybody else. Anybody who questioned the ideology was a 'class enemy'.

Communist seizure of their land and means of livelihood clandestinely started up businesses, opened markets and resisted the party officials who tried to drive them back into pens – the 'communes'. They also became less surreptitious about schooling children, celebrating the turning points in life, reclaiming religious traditions and asserting their right to love and live as they want. Little by little, they reclaimed their culture.

....

China's Road to Rediscovery

In the 1980s, following Mrs Zhu's celebration, party ideologists slunk into the background, let people do their own thing, and goggled at the most spectacular economic transformation ever. In what we can call the 'Great Leap Backwards' of 1949-1979, the population had been traumatised by incompetence and barbarity and had seen whatever progress had been achieved under the Republic of China (1912-1949)[413] smashed. Nevertheless, they undertook the industrial revolution and the information revolution in 30 years – one-tenth of the time that it took Anglo-America.[414]

---

[413] The best summary is: Dikötter, Frank (2008) *The Age of Openness: China before Mao*

[414] Until recently, the paragraph above would have expressed what thinking Chinese agreed about recent history. It was reflected in screen dramas such as *Like a Flowing River* (2018) and *A Wenzhou Family* (2015). The courageous and enterprising are

Underpinning this were the values that had driven Chinese civilisation and not been obliterated, although greatly damaged. Recovery from communism, as in Russia, will take generations. In Russia, perhaps it will never happen.

What lessons am I trying to draw for us from this Chinese experience? First, that when politicians are impediments to progress, there can come a time when the commoners take matters into their own hands, as they have done so often in WISE history. When politicians put ideology or personal and party interests first, they forfeit their authority. It took much more courage for the Chinese, after Mao's death, to resist politicians than it would for us, but, then, they did so in desperation.[415] Second, that the 'unlettered', as Burke termed the commoners, draw upon inherited principles and instinctive morality to challenge the fantasies of politicians. These are incorporated into stories.

Our Story

WISE comprises four small nations on the edge of Europe which have had an influence on the rest of humanity out of

---

seen surviving party officials' obstruction to restoring their livelihoods and rebuilding their communities. The revulsion against communist ideology was publicly acceptable. After all, the leader who authorised the rejection of communist economics, Deng Xiaoping, had told people not to 'talk theory' and to eschew 'modern superstition'.

[415] In the anti-lockdown demonstrations that erupted all over China in November 2022, we saw resistance once again.

all proportion to their size; our nations are the revolutionary nations. WISE has learnt much from the rest of the world, especially continental Europe. Our particular contribution has been the humanitarian idea put into practice through institutions of *Respect*.

We subjected our rulers to the same laws as the powerless. We invented and created as no other civilisation had done, and then we shared our ideas with others, giving them words and weapons to use against us and in competition with us. We curbed our hawks and made them turn their swords into ploughshares, their conquests into responsibilities. We studied and admired other civilisations and then showed them how to restore themselves.

We prevented hideous despotisms being imposed on continental Europe. We provided islands of hope amid oceans of insecurity and exploitation: The USA, Canada, Australia and New Zealand. All these countries, and others from among the Empire's former colonies, are grounded on principles that evolved in WISE.[416]

We have good reason to believe that, for all its deficiencies, our system is better and more humane than any other. We must not forget that, although we are living in the best of all times at the best of all places, 'such a life, free of violence and despotism and fear, is far from being the ordinary state

---

[416] India, Singapore and Malaysia immediately spring to mind, but countries as diverse as Nigeria, Israel and South Africa have modelled their institutions on those of the UK.

of affairs in the long history of humankind. It was, and still is, the rather unlikely exception.'[417]

We cannot be complacent. We should understand what we have, so that we can plan how to preserve and improve our progress. This is how we can and should describe ourselves:

- We have had the earliest state successfully to develop the rule of law, the concept of Common Law and equality before it.
- We built the most successful democracy over 1,000 years and allowed self-government to local communities (until we recently put this into reverse);
- We had the first (popular) enterprise revolution, which led to the industrial revolution;
- We invented the joint stock company, international maritime law and innumerable commercial institutions.
- Since the 18th century and until recently, WISE has been the source of most major scientific and technical advances, particularly in health.
- We proscribed the millennia-old practice of slavery and championed human equality and rights; most aid and charitable bodies originate from the Anglosphere.

---

[417] Strittmatter, Kai (2019) *We Have Been Harmonized*, p12. He is writing about Europe more generally, but he expresses the sentiments so well that I have stolen his words. Scandinavia and Switzerland have also achieved model but less influential democracies.

- WISE created the Anglosphere, i.e. the USA, Australia, Canada and New Zealand, generally agreed to be among the best societies in which to live.
- We introduced the rule of law and democracy to India and many other non-European nations.
- WISE was the model and ally for Italian, Greek and other reformers of the 18th and 19th centuries and many others since.
- WISE played the key part in resisting imperialism in Europe, whether Napoleonic, German or Soviet, rescuing France, Poland, Belgium and other European countries from totalitarian conquest.

The Values

As to WISE values, there comes to mind a famous speech by Prime Minister Gordon Brown in 2007.[418] He claimed tolerance, liberty and fair play as quintessentially ours. Subsequently, public statements have proposed that our values consist of three items that are really institutions rather than values—democracy, the rule of law and individual liberty—plus one attribute, 'mutual respect and tolerance of different faiths and beliefs'. That bundled the right to be different, to have a hyphenated identity (Anglo-Irish, Afro-English, British Jew, Coatbridge Catholic, Chinglish or BBC (British Born Chinese)). I boil our values down

---

[418] https://www.theguardian.com/politics/2007/feb/27/immigrationpolicy. race

to *Respect,* which is a fundamental characteristic of our society. It extends to nature, which is why WISE people have been thought leaders over the environment as over so much else.[419] The interpersonal emotion of *Respect* goes hand in hand with political arrangements best described as the 'open society'.

Those who have chosen to come to this open society, or whose parents did, are often better at defining our values than those who think of themselves as natives. The refugees from fascism, with whose grandchildren I played as a child, were ever so clear about what they, members of persecuted minorities in their countries of origin, valued about WISE. And so, today, are the victims of tyranny or simply economic migrants: they value the ability to practise their rites, care for their families and blend into the society which gave them a haven.

In *Beyond Grievance: What the Left Gets Wrong about Ethnic Minorities*, Rakib Ehsan explains eloquently why and how most recent immigrants look upon USA identity politics with horror and seek leaders who will uphold faith, family and flag, yearnings now abhorrent to many

---

[419] Monotheist societies have posited that humans are distinct from other animals and above nature, which exists for our exploitation, the gift of a benevolent god. So, how did the almost Taoist respect for nature appear? To me, the fact that environmentalism emerged in WISE indicates that the hold of Christian church ideology was very weak, certainly after, and perhaps long before, the Reformation. The explanation for this, as for so much else, may be in our family form.

of the elite.[420] The opposition of minority communities to further immigration is based on the fear that the country to which they chose to immigrate may be transformed into something akin to those from which they fled. WISE will no longer be inclusive when it has been so inclusive as to have lost cohesion.

Identity and Cohesion

As noted in Section 5, one of the reasons why WISE has been so successful is because we cooperate. Our society is communitarian. The vigour of civil society is not some universal historical trend but a defining feature of the Anglosphere.[421] Despite the ethnic diversity of Celtic, Norse, Saxon, Danish, Norman, Middle Easterners and occasional Africans, we evolved a consensus about fundamental things. Being British, like being Roman in the days of Empire, has had little or nothing to do with race.[422] In Willetts' words, it is 'a celebration of the institutions that shaped our country and which should be open to everyone. In fact, successive waves of migration brought distinctive ideas and

---

[420] Ehsan, Rakib (2023) *Beyond Grievance: What the Left Gets Wrong about Ethnic Minorities* London: Forum

[421] Willetts, David (2019) *The Pinch: How the Baby Boomers Took Their Children's Future - And Why They Should Give It Back.* Kindle Edition, p59

[422] In the latter years of the Empire, there was a fashion for racism. As with identity politics today, a minority adopted beliefs about people for which there is no scientific evidence.

institutions that, between them, developed into what we now call Britishness.'[423]

We could argue about a thousand issues but cohere over a common story, which, although not everybody subscribed to it in its entirety, kept us together. Shared stories matter because, when people internalise them, they obey the same laws and conventions, making cooperation possible.

Confusion about identity makes people insecure. Its most heinous effect is that it undermines cohesion, pits us against each other and rubbishes the story upon which our self-respect and ability to contribute to the worldwide conversation rests.[424] On a planet in which over half of humankind is under the cosh of retrograde dictators, we need a clear idea of what we stand for and how we distance ourselves from them.[425]

Nations have historically cohered around some combination of race, ethnicity, culture or religion. What about the four nations of WISE?

---

[423] Willetts (2019) *The Pinch*, p57

[424] Interviewed in the NYT, a German Jew observed that 'People crave a strong national identity… and the old West German recipe of deliberately tying it to humility—"being proud of not being proud"—has not satisfied that need'. https://www.nytimes.com/2019/11/08/world/europe/germany-identity.html, accessed 181222. The UK and German cases are very different, since we can be positive about our earlier identity. Yet, we, too, need to recast ours to emphasise the life-enhancing aspects of our tradition and ensure that future generations know them.

[425] Cowley, Jason (2022) *Who Are We Now?* London: Picador

That WISE has not been bound together by blood, religion or ethnicity, as have been the Germans and the Slavic nations, for example, is a great strength. Today, WISE really is a multi-ethnic society in which families can succeed on their own merits regardless of origin[426]. This is an enrichment, and those who think that they are 'pure' Scots must surely be jealous of the multi-dimensional Scots-Pakistanis, Scots-Jews or Anglo-Scots. Religion, meanwhile, is a pastime, irrelevant to society as long as it is not rabid, with almost every kind of superstition cheerfully tolerated under the leaky but protective umbrella of the established church. For a few years, we described our society as multicultural until the head of the Commission for Racial Equality denounced that as a 'racket'[427]. WISE has a distinct culture, albeit an inclusive one, into which people of many races and religions are welcomed[428].

---

[426] By the 19th century, aside from the diversity of the four nations, we had French Protestants, Jews and Poles in substantial numbers, plus smaller groups from many other European countries. In China, the CCP is doing everything it can to promote a narrow, racist version of identity in a land which, until Westernisation came in the forms of Christianity and Communism, embraced diverse religions and races under a tolerant, Confucian umbrella.

[427] https://www.huffingtonpost.co.uk/2015/03/16/multiculturalism-race-trevor-phillips_n_6875826.html accessed 181223

[428] Stig Abell's meditation on this is well worth reading. It can be found in (2019) *How Britain Really Works, Understanding the Ideas and Institutions of a Nation*, London: John Murray, Section 8: Identity

In other respects, we do not cohere as much as we might like. We have already noted the divisiveness of identity politics. Bryan Gould expresses the dismay of many at the polarisation of WISE society from another angle:

'The dominance of neo-liberal thinking and the economic power of business leaders has had a profound impact []. ... values such as loyalty, honesty, duty and patriotism, as well as more progressive values [sic!] such as tolerance, compassion, collective enterprise, social responsibility and generosity – have been increasingly abandoned in favour of a more aggressive sense that the only value by which actions and attitudes are to be judged is the pursuit of individual self-interest.'

'The "free market" has not only determined how we run our economic activity [] but has been allowed to extend itself in every facet of our society, culture and civilisation - and it has done so by replacing the values which are believed to underpin western civilisation as a whole with that much narrower range of values that commend themselves only to a small and self-centred minority.'[429]

Many go further than Gould, seeing liberal democracy as a front for aggressive individualism and an anti-democratic conspiracy. A milder subversion, that of William Clouston and the reviving Social Democratic Party, echoing George Orwell, condemns our political system for 'indifference'.[430]

---

[429] Gould, Bryan (2013) *Myths, Politicians and Money* London: Palgrave Macmillan, p87

[430] https://sdp.org.uk/the-end-of-indifference/, accessed 171023

That our community is being broken into bits, is common ground.

How to Resuscitate Our Identity

At Home

David Edgerton has shown how the Labour government of 1945-51 attempted to replace internationalism with patriotism and community as the underpinning principles of what Edgerton claims to have been a 'distinctly nationalist programme' of economic development. This was more important to its leaders than the social improvements for which it is remembered.[431] Over the succeeding years, however, the political class's international pretensions and missionary impulses grew until we entered (what later became) the European Union, which that class hoped to run. When it failed to do so, an alternative pretension became the fashion, expressed slightly differently in the Conservative and Labour wings. For the former, Britain would once more be great again, and politicians would have important careers, when we would be the USA's sniffer dogs and panders. For the latter, we would promote the nameless

---

[431] Edgerton (2018) *The Rise and Fall of the British Nation: A Twentieth-Century History*, p218. Attlee and his team went so far as to reject the notion that the Empire was their responsibility and sought to exploit the remaining dependencies in Britain's economic interest, even at the cost of jettisoning our reputation for *Respect*. Elkins gives chapter and verse on this.

universal religion masquerading as human rights (which I call 'Westism'), and we would glory in self-flagellating ourselves as the most wicked people on earth, reborn as moralists. Neither wing acknowledged two key truths: that they were dupes of those with business interests in undermining our sovereignty and that, without economic revival, WISE is a mere satrapy.

Whether Brexit was right or wrong, it should have led to a vigorous programme of economic nationalism. It has not. If WISE is to reassert its heroic identity, it needs economic rejuvenation as a condition of independence and of being taken seriously in the world. Even more important, it needs to reinvigorate a sense of community.

Abroad

Internationally, we should declare that we are no longer crusaders and will no longer undermine the rule of law. Our reason for the turnabout is simple: the existential problems facing us all are too great for any country to pursue a selfish path, let alone get embroiled in another criminal disaster such as the Vietnam or Iraq wars.

Our politicians pompously declare our moral superiority, for example, over Hong Kong, while being blind to the vicious abrogation of human rights in which we have participated in the Middle East and Central Asia. This has to be admitted. We should not apologise for slavery or for protecting cultural artefacts, but for Prime Ministers Blair and Cameron. A million people died as a result of the

Blair-Bush crusade into Iraq. We cannot yet quantify the suffering caused by Cameron's adventures.

Show, not Tell

Rather than *assert* that democracy, by which we mean our way of doing things, is superior, we should be able to *show* that balanced economic development, innovation and human happiness are consequences of an open political system. Until China's Covid fiasco, people all over the world were concluding that this was not so and that closed systems such as China's worked better. The financial crises of 2008-9 had damaged Anglo-America's credibility.

Our government is laughable when, despite its economic mismanagement and its political system having been reduced to buffoonery, it takes high moral positions. Human Rights campaigns should be waged by non-governmental bodies. The role of government is to fight for Britain's interests, especially the interests of the commoners, the most vulnerable, including over the environmental issues which are in the interests of everyone. Rather than boast or carp, we should first demonstrate the efficacy of our system by resolving issues at home. Intervention in other countries should be limited to advice and selective aid.

Conclusion

We now know our story. WISE consists of those nations which, working together, incubated the values that have done more to advance human wellbeing than any other and created institutions to realise those values. They are the first polities to have been made from the bottom up, as a result of revolts and claims to rights won in ancient times. WISE is the archetype of Open Society and the world's Thought Leader. To write that is not to believe that WISE is superior, or best, just that in certain aspects that matter a great deal to the lives of human beings, WISE has achieved something incomparable.

Like Mrs Zhu, we should celebrate the start of a new era. We should renew our faith in the WISE story, revive that cohesion which made us strong, revitalise the economy, which is the foundation, reaffirm our culture and restore our position in the world. How we do those things is the subject of the next Section, *Reboot*.

SECTION **14**

WISE Reboot: Development, Democracy, Diplomacy

So far, we have looked at WISE from the perspective of world history and in the context of a century in which Asians may supersede Anglo-Americans and Europeans as the arbiters of the world. We have revisited the history of how WISE, building upon a relatively affluent economy, efficient governance and a sense of national identity, broke free of the limitations of size and geography to recast the destiny of all humanity's civilisations. The book then covered the challenges of the 20th century and our responses to them. Section 13 answered the question of who we are in an Asian-dominated world and whether we are still relevant. I argue that we are, but only if we can (1) regain our moral authority and (2) fortify the foundations of a successful society, its economy and community. This section looks to the future to see how these aspirations might be realised: A reboot. First, how did China tackle similar challenges?

....

A China Story

After five years at sea, a 23-year-old Chinese cadet registered as a student at the Royal Naval College in Greenwich. That was 150 years ago, in 1877, and the cadet, named Yan Fu, was astounded by the wealth and power so suddenly[432] accumulated by the small group of offshore islands whose capital, London, had become the centre of the world.

He realised that China—once as much the apogee of civilisation as the British Empire—had been overtaken in economy, military technology and organisation by foreigners who used their power to wrest concessions from the Chinese empire and, step by step, to weaken and exploit it. A former workshop of the world, China was in debt, spending well beyond its revenues and with a chronic imbalance of payments. Its best assets were being bought up by foreigners, minorities were disaffected, and its identity was undermined by ideologies (especially Christianity) that repudiated the inheritance and eroded self-respect. China could only fight its wars if others bore the brunt.

....

---

[432] Sudden in the Chinese sense, as they at that time knew nothing of the long gestation of British institutions and, anyway, thought of history in terms of dynasties rather than decades.

Sounds familiar? So were the responses. From the late 19th century up to the communist conquest, patriots and think tanks[433] produced reams of proposals. Many studied WISE[434] and devised plans for a constitutional monarchy and other political reforms, a legal system as in England, industrial re-development, reducing foreign involvement in the infrastructure, and rejection of imported ideologies. They wanted to retain the best of the Chinese social system that had been most advanced for several thousand years, yet to learn from us in order to adapt it to modern exigencies and discoveries.

By the 1930s, however, many young patriots, sickened by inequality, lack of opportunity and the relative decline of their country, were impatient at the slowness of change. They felt unable to influence politicians who were obsessed with their own careers or enrichment. As did many Europeans at that time, they allowed themselves to be seduced by totalitarians who called out 'the guilty' and promised utopia.

---

[433] I use the modern expression, 'think tank' but the contemporary term was 'salon'.

[434] The most prominent are Yan Fu and Hu Shih, both intellectual giants and interpreters of Western philosophy. The fact that these names mean nothing, even to most educated Britons, is a measure of our ignorance of China and misunderstanding of its modernisation. I admired Yan Fu in my student days, but I missed that Yan had identified, in a letter to the Chinese ambassador, 'that of the many reasons that make England and other European nations, rich and strong, the most important one is the guarantee of their having justice done.' (Ferguson, 2012, *The Great Degeneration*, p89)

By the 1950s, those totalitarians had, thanks to Russian arms and money, subjugated China and were, initially under Soviet guidance, smashing the civilisation, wrecking its economy and liquidating its educated and enterprising people, consolidating a slave state.[435]

Our Possible Futures

In WISE today, identity politics tunnels away at our story, gains adherence to a fatuous set of supernatural beliefs and imposes a divisive moral hierarchy.[436] Identity politics distracts us from fundamental issues of revival and survival. It seems that, like China a hundred years ago, Britain is at risk of falling for a new iteration of fascism, though so far, less violent. Putting aside that possibility as too terrible to contemplate, here are three possible routes for the nations that have left the EU but not yet found a role.

Rejected

If we simply continue to decline and fail to address our economic problems and imbalances, we may become politically unstable. More and more people in the 'left

---

[435] The recovery of the history of extermination, with all its hideous cruelty, is vividly conveyed in Johnson, Ian (2023) *Sparks: China's Underground Historians and Their Battle for the Future*, London: Penguin For a more systematic, if less emotive, account, see Dikötter, Frank (2013) *The Tragedy of Liberation*.

[436] For the best analysis, see Williams, Joanna (2022) *How Woke Won*.

behind' might resent their impoverishment and compete for the public trough. The impoverished many and the betrayed young will revolt against the incompetence and corruption of the political class; a disruptive ideology gains influence, another symptom of alienation and a predictor of regime change. The great WISE achievement gives way to populist authoritarianism. The revolutionary nations will be seen, by ourselves and by all around the world, to have failed.

In this case, our values and the contribution that we might make to tackling global problems will be ignored in the world's strategic discussions.

Colonised

Second, bereft of ideas on how to generate our own revival, our politicians opt for total servility to one of the great powers in return for benefits that just about allow us to stay afloat, becoming panders on the Blair model. The US or EU may toss us a few concessions in return for our obedience, but we, in essence, turn into an offshore financial centre, outwith the mainstream, our lucky ones employed as concierges to the global elite. Most likely, we double down on our subservience to the USA, our glorious role being to provide a fig leaf of international cooperation for its attempts to beat up competition.

Restored

There is a third possibility. We refuse meekly to accept a subordinate role in US foreign policy, which risks our becoming collateral damage in a US-China war. Instead, we start to stand up for and strengthen our defining qualities. We restore ourselves in our own eyes and that of the world so that we can be seen to have the moral authority of the most beneficent polity. This requires affirmation of our identity as the inventor of freedom, but also that we see ourselves as a developing economy, not a declining one. As Larry Elliott puts it, we should emulate Taiwan.[437]

'The lesson of history is that a country that achieves technological innovation and profitable geopolitical expansion can grow its way out from under a mountain of debt,'[438] though the likelihood of success is not great. It is the only way out of our predicament.

By relaunching our economy, we should ensure that Britain can survive in a perilous world. We will only be able to deal with the other challenges—the funding of the health service or defence, improving education, raising living standards, going green, inequality—if we do so.

---

[437] https://www.briefingsforbritain.co.uk/we-think-of-britain-as-a-world-beating-economy-we-would-be-better-off-thinking-about-taiwan/, accessed 221122. Larry Elliott and Dan Atkinson predicted the downward spiral of the economy ten or more years ago in *The Gods that Failed*, *Going South* and *Fantasy Island*. A few months before completing this book, I asked Larry Elliott whether he stood by his books. He looked very unhappy as he said 'Yes'. In 2010, Elliott and the then Archbishop of Canterbury published *Crisis and Recovery: Ethics, Economics and Justice* London: Palgrave MacMillan, a collection of essays on our economic life with an Anglican perspective.

[438] Ferguson (2012) *The Great Degeneration*, p147

What's needed is *development, democracy* and *diplomacy*. A Sixth Revolution.

Development

What we need are: A development mindset, a strategy for national economic reconstruction, a sense of community and equity between generations and regions.

WISE politicians have been indifferent to the transfer of our industries to foreign countries and allowed the good jobs of the commoners to go elsewhere. They have abandoned the former industrial areas, the coastal resorts and fishing towns. They have been indifferent to our growing reliance on two service industries for our export earnings. They have damaged us immensely by allowing, deliberately, our energy costs to become 52% higher than the average of the advanced economies and three times higher than the USA or Canada[439] . The consequences are not only further

---

[439] Timothy, Nick (2024), citing the International Energy Agency, in High energy costs are a choice – and an act of national self-harm, in *Daily Telegraph*, 190224. Matt Ridley argues that energy–abundance, affordability and reliability of energy–is fundamental to a successful civilisation. 'And I see our climate obsession, and consequent abandonment of reliable and affordable energy, as a symptom of blinkeredness rather than a solution to it.' (email communication 300623) 'The combination of having to buy more expensive natural gas from Qatar and the United States losing access to China's lucrative market for European cars, machinery, and luxury goods could cause Europe to deindustrialize.' Sikorsky, Radek: Europe's real test is yet to come. *Foreign Affairs*, July–August 2023.

relative decline but ever-greater social polarisation between rich and poor.[440]

Our political class has been indifferent to the immense changes in the world, especially to the rise of Asia (and what it means to us) and the damage that globalisation has done to the commoners. While the pols have been playing their silly ideological competitions or helping their friends make good, WISE influence has eroded. Adapting Mahbubani's evocative phrases, in the past, the West drove the growth of the Rest; now, the Rest drive the West. Our leaders should be making a careful appraisal of the new global economic order and working out how we can find opportunities for ourselves.

Development Mindset

We need action. The whole agenda of politics has to change, from trying to please particular lobby groups or special interests, and from making off-the-cuff decisions about important issues for temporary political expediency, to a clear focus on the revival of the economy, reduction of dependence, reducing debt. Political parties should be vying to proclaim better ideas on raising GDP (sustainably) rather than exposing each other's peccadillos. *We need a development mindset.*

---

[440] Milanovich, Branco: the great convergence, global equality, and its discontents. *Foreign Affairs*, July–August 2023.

Policy Directions

- Development cannot be achieved without major changes of attitude: investors must invest in Britain;
- enterprises must not be sold to foreign competitors;
- our infrastructure should be controlled from home.
- Local governments need to be liberated, motivated and empowered to rebuild their local economies.
- Large social organisations should be broken up so that responsibility can be clearly assigned in their units; in human affairs, small is almost always best.
- Central government must provide the framework and incentives for economic revival but not micromanage it.[441]
- Every public policy should be judged by its likely effect on development, whether diversity legislation, immigration, constitutional reform or education.

National Economic Reconstruction

National economic reconstruction has two aspects: *economic nationalism* and *industrial strategy.*

---

[441] I have emphasised the maleficent results of the centralisation of powers in this book, but here, I want to propose beneficent ones. John Micklethwait and Adrian Wooldridge give some good examples of the valuable use of government power in (2020) *The Wake-Up Call* London: Short Books, e.g. p56.

Economic Nationalism

While the term sounds aggressive, economic nationalism, as Attlee and Wilson appear to have conceived it, is no more than putting the interests of the commoners above the fantasies of Mrs Jellybys, the cupidity of investors or (today) the ambitions of politics careerists, who are members of a transnational political class.[442]

Policy Directions

- Identify essential industries, the lack of which renders us dependent on others, for rebuilding and/or renationalisation.
- Implement state-led re-industrialisation of left-behind areas by incentivising and mobilising local governments to see themselves as catalysts for enterprise. We should go well beyond the current Levelling Up Programme.[443]
- Domesticate investment and prevent the selling off of UK companies by introducing rules and restraints that prevail elsewhere (for example Germany and the US).[444]

---

[442] The quintessential transnational pol must surely be Rishi Sunak, not because of his Indian origins but because he had, until recently, a US green card and is married to a multinational business empire which pays very little tax to the UK.

[443] https://www.gov.uk/government/publications/levelling-up-the-united-kingdom, accessed 090523.

[444] David (Viscount) Hanworth, has made proposals to control financial sector, where it is inimical to WISE interests. See

- Reform the taxation system: disincentivise selling enterprises to foreigners and ensure that foreign corporations pay properly, instead of sheltering in tax havens.[445]
- Reduce dependency and ensure food and energy security.
- Enforce a growth mandate for local governments – if they can be mandated to impose diversity, they can be mandated to create sustainable growth.
- Procurement must follow the example of other countries and ensure preference for local supply.
- Reform public servants – incentivised to promote growth rather than implement ideology.[446]
- Provide tax-raising powers to local authorities who should compete with each other to raise the GDP of their area and provide the best environment for the least expense.
- Devolve powers over education, health and welfare to local authorities on the Swedish model, making them responsible for raising most of the funding (yes,

---

Hanton, Angus (2024) *Vassal State*, p39.

[445] Much more on this is at Hanton, Angus (2024) *Vassal State*, p222.

[446] Dominic Cummings, adviser to Prime Minister Boris Johnson, made some telling criticisms of the civil service but, in Leninist style, seemed to want to abolish it rather than re-engineer it. https://www.ippr.org/events/the-hollow-men-whats-wrong-with-westminster-and-whitehall-and-what-to-do-about-it, accessed 230523. As every leader should know, if you want people to improve their performance, you have to work with them, rather than insult and diminish them. Cummings may have been unaware of this principle.

the central government would still redistribute) and introducing competition.

- Complete the reform of state education with reference to the experience of other countries whose outcomes are superior.[447]
- Identify fields for UK specialisation and direction of resources into them.

Industrial Strategy

The urgent need for an industrial strategy has been recognised by a few of our politicians, but ideologists oppose it. They do not see the UK from a global perspective or realise how we have been damaged by a *laissez-faire* attitude.[448]

---

[447] The universities need attention if they are to give priority to resuming the tasks of intellectual inquiry as well as providing vocational and professional training. See Craig, David and Openshaw, Hugh (2018) *The Great University Con* Bournemouth: The Original Book Company. On ideology, see Heffer, Simon (2022) 'Defund woke universities to defeat the new totalitarians' in *The Daily Telegraph* 20/11/2022. Allison Pearson notes that many UK universities have turned into international businesses and marginalised their national role: (2023) 'British universities no longer want British students. They're hooked on Chinese money' in *The Daily Telegraph* 18/05/2023.

[448] Advances were made when Ministers Vince Cable and David Willetts were in office, but Sajid Javid and Kwasi Kwarteng tried to reverse the moves towards an industrial strategy on ideological grounds.

Innovation has long been the main driver of growth and is increasingly also the determinant of geopolitical status.[449] However, with few exceptions, British politicians have rejected the idea that the government should involve itself in promoting innovation, preferring to rely on 'free markets'.

While the US government also trumpets the superiority of free markets, it practises favouritism and subsidy. In the USA, it is widely understood that one of the roles of the government is to lower the risks facing innovators. It provides systematic help to businesses, especially in high-tech, on a scale which is not understood by those who take American free market rhetoric at face value. Elon Musk not only received federal funds to build his business empire but also state funds, totalling about $7bn.[450]

Here, far from promoting innovation, policymakers stymie it. The Competition Commission vetoed the BBC and ITV working together to create a kind of Netflix (Project Kangaroo) in 2009.[451] Eventually, a successor, BritBox, was launched in 2017 after the US had already come to dominate global content streaming services. 5G was to be our opportunity to get ahead through the

---

[449] Schmidt, Eric (2023) Innovation Power: Why Technology Will Define the Future of Geopolitics in *Foreign Affairs,* March April 2023

[450] Elon Musk hates government subsidies, but his companies love them, *Grid News,* 300422

[451] For this section, I am indebted to David Willetts and Andrew Cahn in particular.

Huawei/Vodaphone alliance. When the USA decided to destroy Huawei, we obliged by wrecking our own options, in doing what US politicians commanded. Our government did not help UK industry get into the UK offshore wind sector, so Danish companies succeeded, subsidised by their government. In 2019, our politicians allowed one of Britain's R&D powerhouses, GKN, to be bought by an asset stripper. There are many other examples of how indifference has damaged our prospects.

The recent head of UK Trade & Investment, Andrew Cahn, writes, 'We need to put in the intellectual effort to analyse where Britain can gain an advantage, where we must act to remain competitive, where we are not keeping up with the competition. This means doing planning work over an extended period of time and then facing up to the conclusions.'

'We do not learn from our competitors,' he goes on. 'The most successful, such as Singapore, New Zealand, Canada, now the USA, have higher levels of productivity and innovation than we do. We should be prepared to learn from them how to do industrial strategy.'[452] French, German, Chinese and Scandinavian governments all have well-established modes of protecting and promoting their industries and innovations. We must take lessons.

The National Security and Investment Act 2021 listed 17 areas of vital national interest. We must get moving. Taiwan teaches. In the 1980s, scared of a future without

---

[452] Email communication from Andrew Cahn, 280423.

modern industry, the Prime Minister in Taipei called up a scientist in the USA and asked if he'd come home and start a computer industry from scratch. Today, Taiwan leads the world in the design and manufacture of semiconductors, 60% of all worldwide and 90% of the most advanced. [453]

Alex Brummer can't see why the UK shouldn't do the same. 'With the energy, willpower, imagination and the resources of corporate Britain and the government, anything can be achieved.'[454]

Policy Directions:

Identify key technologies where we have a comparative advantage and which should be backed with public funding.[455]

- Concentrate higher education funding on Science, Technology, Engineering and Mathematics (STEM) areas.
- Re-orientate the FE sector to become an expert and prestigious provider of technical and professional

[453] Conway, Ed (2023) *Material World: A Substantial Story of Our Past and Our Future*, London, ch2
[454] Brummer, Alex (2020) *The Great British Reboot* Yale: Yale University Press, p315
[455] Former Minister for Universities and Science, David Willetts, has pleaded for this over many years. He has all the right ideas, but will any government make a serious attempt to implement them? See Willetts, David (2023) *The Eight Great Technologies 10 years on, An Industrial strategy?* London: Policy Exchange.

education – if necessary, recruiting instructors or curriculum designers from more advanced countries such as Germany or Japan.

- At last, create the technical and professional schools envisaged 60 years ago.
- Re-introduce selection by aptitude into state schools (now, selection is by wealth).
- A world talents programme, to recruit the leaders in those areas of development identified as vital to our future, to come to work in WISE.

Community

Claims made in times of crisis that 'we are all in it together' ring hollow when the pursuits of individual ambition and personal profit have been exalted as the very purposes of life. Paul Collier argues that we must get away from the reductionism implied in the expression 'economic man'.[456] He advances the truism of 'social man', emphasising reciprocity. I will add to that: Once the initiators of businesses have made enough to keep themselves and their families well, it is not the purpose of an enterprise to make individuals filthy rich. Profit is a discipline, not a purpose. The purpose of an enterprise is the contribution of its particular inventions, product or service to society and the community.

---

[456] Collier, Paul (2018) *The Future of Capitalism: Facing the New Anxieties* London: Allen Lane

Collier, on the national level, advocates that richer cities should apply their surpluses to investment in the 'broken cities', worse off due to global competition. There are plenty of candidates, starting with Middlesbrough and its collapsed steel industry. He also advocates heavy taxes on asset management and on those who live off rents rather than enterprise, to nudge the highly skilled towards socially valuable investments.[457]

Colin Mayer not only wants companies to enshrine a higher purpose in their mission statements, but also applauds the foundations that oversee companies such as Tata, Bosch, Ikea and Carlsberg, guaranteeing stable ownership, board accountability and social purpose.[458] He wants to save capitalism from the revulsion felt by many at the global tax arbitrage, executive pay balloons, selfishness and short-termism of some corporations.

Every enterprise, old and new, depends on a hinterland of stakeholders for its survival and success. These include the institutions that educated the founders, the community that provided the employees, the local authority that made available resources, and the nation whose infrastructure of laws and administration made enterprise possible. The idea that, when a company's future is being considered, the only people with skin in the game are financial investors, is anti-social.

---

[457] Collier, ibid, p187
[458] Mayer, Colin (2018) *Prosperity* Oxford: OUP, pp161-163

Guy Standing has a response to James Meek's lament, in *Private Island: Why Britain Now Belongs to Someone Else,* about the privatisation and sale to foreign capitalists of what should be our communal, shared assets. He calls for the restoration of the commons, the taking back of water, energy, landscape, and utilities into WISE ownership.[459] That need not mean management by Whitehall but by bodies answerable to and working in the interests of all stakeholders, the commoners.

And then we have the problem of intergenerational inequity. 'There are other countries where the younger generations are doing badly, but nowhere else has the reversal of generation-on-generation progress been so precipitate as in the UK.'[460] In his radical book, *The Pinch*, David Willetts calls for the older generation to acknowledge that their comfort has been purchased at the expense of their children and grandchildren, who will have much diminished lives thanks to the profligate way in which politicians have borrowed to cosset older voters. This is another type of inequality that came about because of the indifference of the political class; it needs correction.

We need to redefine the relationship between enterprise and society, revitalising the instincts of public service and

[459] Standing, Guy (2017) *The Corruption of Capitalism* London: Biteback, p318 and Meek, James (2014) *Private Island. Why Britain Now Belongs to Someone Else* London: Verso

[460] Willetts, David (2019) *The Pinch: How the baby boomers took their children's future – and why they should give it back*, Kindle edition, p24

collaboration so that the enterprising aim at goals that are more humane than profit-making, or adventure for its own sake. The purpose of getting on with the development that we so badly need if we are to survive, is to recover our ability to sustain ourselves and contribute to other countries once we have revived our own.

Democracy

We need to tackle the UK's trapped transition with a Sixth Revolution in thinking.

After the Second World War, despite many flaws, the UK was perhaps the nearest thing to a democracy that has ever existed. As the protections of consumer society and the welfare state became more established, as discriminatory laws were abolished, we should have continued our historical trajectory, transitioning towards an increasingly participatory society, with politicians ever more representative of articulate electors.

Yet, although society became less hierarchical and much more liberal, in politics two deleterious changes took place. First, parliamentarians representing local and sectional interests began to be replaced by career politicians controlled by their parties. The debilitating effect of this is described in Section 10.

Second, agency has been wrested from the people and their institutions and communities and given to state officials, contrary to our unique tradition. In China, communism smashed local society and imposed the rule of party appointees. Yes, traditional governance needed reform and modernisation, but it was more humane than the slave state which replaced it. That slave state began to unravel once the dictator died, and his rule could be admitted to have been not only unjust but dysfunctional. Rebuilding the institutions of trust is proving much harder than economic development, as in Russia. [461] Something similar, though much less violently, has been happening in WISE. As described in Section 10, there has been a steady erosion of civil society and growing centralisation. We are diverging from our unique tradition.

Changing the Motivations of People in Politics

In WISE, we need responses to the widespread dissatisfaction with the political class and the perception that they are neither democratic in decision nor competent in execution. Many already have lost respect for our institutions. As the situation of the commoners and the 'left behind' areas gets worse, anger may boil over into total rejection. To avoid that, we should rejuvenate the institutions that our

---

[461] The leadership of the PRC is very aware of this. For a period in the 1990s religions and movements of moral regeneration were encouraged. The current leadership, however, has chosen to reinforce communist values, presenting the CCP as the expression of Chinese nationhood: traditional Chinese beliefs are too inclusive and family-centred to those wanting to reconstruct humanity. In Russia, President Putin has revived Orthodox Christianity as inspiration and identity.

forebears built over many centuries. We must make our system work better and show it works.

Let us establish selection criteria for Parliament in order to discourage careerists and recruit commoners to be legislators. Maybe we can abolish political professionals, either by stipulating qualifications for candidature, such as having experience of responsible employment, or simply by reducing their emoluments and obliging legislators to raise funds to support themselves. MPs should serve no more than two terms. The job description can change: Much of what MPs currently say they do in their constituencies can be done either by local councillors or by teams of assistants/ researchers, which we should never begrudge legislators.

Many of those attracted into the present system are not only unrepresentative but also not qualified to be the ministers who spend our taxes and reorganise our lives. We can do better. The experiment in drawing our ministers from among professional, full-time MPs has been a failure. Not only are we condemned to inadequately checked government, but our transition towards the modern realisation of historic WISE principles of devolution of power and democratic decision-making is trapped.

Here's another way, proposed by Anthony King in his *Who Governs Britain?* and by Sam Fowles, the barrister who has fought unaccountable power in the courts and set up the All-Party Parliamentary Group on Democracy: Members of Parliament should not be ministers. We need competent people managing ministries, as in the USA and China (when not hamstrung by their Presidents) but, in accordance with WISE tradition, they should be appointed by Parliament and accountable to it.[462]

Parliament might reserve some powers to itself, such as war and policing; we would need to learn from the US separation of powers how to avoid conflicts.

Activist politics—aiming to show constituents that the proposer is doing something, no matter how inconsequential—has given us too many laws, regulations and codes that nobody can ever fully understand. Many of the policies advanced by politicians are just ideas grabbed from lobbyists and fanatics, in the case of the government, via SPADS.[463] They are dismissively referred to in the policy world as 'luxury legislation'. To control this diarrhoea, laws and regulations should have lifespans; if not renewed, they fall. Legislators should be channelled into reforming, simplifying, the codes, rather than introducing more and more. Financial proposals which affect many

---

[462] For more detail, see Fowles (2023) *Overruled*, Conclusion. This idea was originally trailed by Paul Judge, founder of Jury Team. See Jury Team (2010) *Working Together for the People Politicians Forgot*, London: Jury Team. Ideas on making parliament more representative and powerful are further developed in Sutherland, Keith (2008) *A People's Parliament*, Exeter: Imprint Academic. See also: King, Anthony (2015) *Who governs Britain?* London: Pelican, p92.

[463] SPADS are Special Advisers, ready to change the world in accordance with the latest tweets from fairyland, and employed to defend a minister from the advice of civil servants or other hoary old sages.

people should require greater majorities than those which affect few.[464] And so on.

Then there is the tragedy of local communities, the subversion of which has contributed to social devastation at least as severe as that of the industrial revolution deplored by Dickens.[465] As in the 19th century, if we recognise the malaise, we can tackle it. It's not going to be easy, because the pols have bought the complaisance of vast numbers of people by making them dependent upon the state for their livelihoods. The Revolutionary Nations need a Sixth Revolution, a stride forward which will show that WISE is still the Thought Leader.

Policy Directions

- Eliminate the career ladder which has people enter Parliament aiming to become ministers, such that they put obedience to party managers before their electors.
- Ministers to be outwith, but accountable to, Parliament. They are to be selected by the majority party and approved in public hearings.
- Free MPs to be proper legislators and to hold the executive to account.
- Limit the length of time (to two terms) that an MP may sit in the Commons.

---

[464] Smith, Craig and Tom Miers (2011) *Democracy and the Fall of the West*, p98

[465] Ridley, Matt (1997) *Origins of Virtue,* pp263-4 summarises this in the case of Newcastle.

- Remove the power of the executive to control and timetable Parliament.
- Change the timetable of Parliament to ensure that members with external work can attend and make it unacceptable to be dependent upon politics for a living.
- Reform the remuneration for parliamentarians to encourage recruitment of people who have proven competence in earning their own living, being dependent neither upon inherited wealth nor upon the taxpayer.
- Reform the House of Lords to give representation to no more than 50 historic counties or regions plus a minority of unelected members, to retain the non-political expertise which is the most valuable contribution of the Lords. Upper House membership should not be determined by politicians.
- Today, major reforms are not negotiated painstakingly with stakeholders but handed down from above by governments, like gifts from heaven. We should institutionalise the involvement of all parties and stakeholders in deliberation about major issues and proposed changes. Learn from the Nordic countries how to do this.[466]
- Abolish positions, where dysfunctional, which are boltholes for political careerists, such as the elected mayoralties, police and crime commissioners.

---

[466] King, Anthony (2015) *Who governs Britain?* London: Pelican, p283.

- Require local authorities to develop their economies and own and manage services.
- Empower local authorities by giving them tax-raising powers, such that richer areas support their administration and services themselves, and so that subsidy to poorer areas is used to incentivise initiative and commercial development.
- Reform the public service to be enterprise orientated. Create a national cadre of administrative grade civil servants who would have their careers in local authorities as well as national ministries.
- Curtail 'luxury' legislation; time limit legislation.

The restoration of trust in politics is as fundamental as the restructuring of the economy, yet neither can be done without the other. The commoners are right to be sceptical of politicians' ability to run the reboot. A Sixth Revolution in thinking is called for.[467]

Diplomacy

In international affairs, our political leaders should not parade their ideological prejudices or extol those of their party supporters, but act in the interests of those who elected them. Today, our

---

[467] Cummings is very good on this. See Cummings (2023) Dominic Cummings on the dysfunction of the UK government, an interview with Dwarkesh Patel. https://www.youtube.com/watch?v=3i7ym_Qh7BA, accessed 181123.

overriding interest, as well as that of many others around the world, is that WISE be respected as Thought Leader.[468]

Say No to the Division of the World

Our current politicians have bought into the idea that the world is dividing into two camps: the damned and the saved, or, in polspeak, the democracies and the dictatorships. In such a world, we must choose one side or the other.

Although the Ukraine war appears to bear this out, the positioning of many countries in fact shows the opposite, making it quite clear that this binary view of the world is rejected by most. While the BBC gives the impression that the whole world, bar China, is behind 'Zelensky and democracy' because 141 countries supported UN resolutions condemning the war, only 33 countries have put their money where their mouths are. Some 167 countries have refused to join in attempts to isolate Russia.[469] They please the USA with words and Russia with deeds.

How much more will this be the case if the choice is between China and the USA? China is more important than Russia to most countries. They will not be willing to join a team, for they aspire to self-determination and multi-alignment, playing off one power against another.

---

[468] There is a great deal more to say about our international affairs. A first-rate guide is Ricketts, Peter (2021) *Hard Choices: What Britain Does Next* London: Atlantic Books.

[469] Leonard, Mark, China is ready for a world of disorder in *Foreign Affairs*, July-August 2023, p122.

The world has changed since the Cold War. For a start, neither Russia nor China promote a universal ideology. [470] China is pragmatic, driven by what the rulers see as the material and security needs of their people. That Putin has launched a self-defeating war and Xi might invade Taiwan are anything but indicators of ideological evangelism. They reflect personal vanity but also responses to domestic pressures and, not irrational, fears of the USA.[471]

Attempts by the USA to consolidate an alliance against China are motivated as much by jealousy of China's economic success as by security fears, are alienating countries which want to be on good terms with both. As we saw in Section 6, trust in US impartiality dissipated at the Iraq aggression of 2003, and, despite the efforts of the USA in Eastern Europe and the Middle East today, it is proving difficult to restore.

Contrary to the allegations of some Anglophone politicians, China has taken measures to integrate itself further into the global or regional economies, advocating more globalisation and taking the lead in responding to

---

[470] After reading John Gray (2023) *The New Leviathan*, I should qualify that by saying that Putin would seem to be standard-bearer of an ideology which mixes universalist Christianity with Slavic irredentism. But this has no universal application.

[471] Putin imagined that the USA was too distracted by its internal troubles to confront him in Ukraine. As the USA gets mired in the new conflict in the Middle East (or Western Asia, as Asians refer to it), President Xi may, similarly, think that the USA will not want a third front in Taiwan. The current propaganda barrage in China against Japan may be preparing the ground.

climate change. The USA has never acceded to the Law of the Sea and rejects the authority of judicial bodies such as the International Criminal Court.[472] In remembering this, I do not want to suggest that we should not call out the nefarious activities of China's spies or the threats to other countries' security. We should be clear-eyed about misdemeanours equally, also holding the USA to the standards that it claims are part of its DNA.

So, What Should WISE Do?

In Section 6, I propose 4 principles of a WISE international strategy: Recognition of WISE benefits to humanity; rejection of the division of the world into blocs; reinforcement of the rules based order, building bridges to nations no matter how different; strategic pragmatism with the objective of perpetuating and enhancing WISE.

We are natural partners of the other Anglo-American and northern European nations. This does not mean that we should be their hired guns. Nor, though, should we be China's patsy. We should defend ourselves against Chinese infiltration and cyber activism, and be prepared, through alliances and security at home, against China as

---

[472] Cable, Vince *The Chinese Conundrum* London: Alma Books, pp 230-231, also Zakaria (2023) 'The Self Doubting Superpower', p53. On p51, Zakaria declares that 'China is not a spoiler state like Russia. It has grown rich and powerful within the international system and because of it; it is far more uneasy about overturning that system. '

against any—Iranian, US, Russian, or Saudi—subversion or attempts to exploit our openness.

The human rights issues are grave, but our leaders should not make them the focus of our international policies, still less allow them to be used to create bogeymen of countries with which we need to cooperate. Our politicians have enthusiastically mimicked denunciations of China, which derive more from US domestic politics than from any desire to help the afflicted.[473] Why are we accusing China of genocide in Xinjiang but brown-nosing Indian politicians with track records in this abomination? We gladhand other perpetrators or defenders of genocide, Turkey, Sudan

---

[473] Indefensible things are happening in Xinjiang, but the way to ameliorate the situation of the Uyghurs would have been to accept the Chinese premise that they need to expunge terrorism and work with them to find a better way. Before Xi came to power, delegations of Chinese police and military came to UK to learn how we had coped with Ulster terrorism. Unfortunately, it seems they did not implement what they had learnt. Here, we should recall that Islamist terrorism was conjured into life by the USA when it supported the Mujahideen against the Russian occupation of Afghanistan. The conquest of Iraq then gave it a further fillip. Among the many foul consequences of this has been that Uyghurs were recruited by ISIS to kill Westerners. The PRC government, propelled by popular opinion, reacted decisively, but seemingly brutally and inexpertly. Thereafter, local suppression may have evolved into a national policy of repression of religious and ethnic minorities typical of communist police states. The connection between Western condemnations and China's rapid courting of Islamic countries, especially Saudi Arabia and Iran, deserves further analysis.

and Saudi Arabia among them.[474] In putting their own peoples' interests first, WISE governments are more likely to influence bad polities through positive trading and cultural relations than by confrontations, which rarely benefit the victims. While our leaders practice (let's hope) political realism, our battalions of humanitarians can and will, in the tradition of Cobbett, and Wilberforce, make noises wherever there is persecution or exploitation.

Instead of calling out China as a 'strategic threat and a hostile state' our diplomats should be distinguishing between the oligarchy and the revival of Chinese civility. They should be thinking through how encourage the latter, rather than bolstering those political factions most hostile to us, which are also the most repressive at home. Instead of driving China into alliance with its detested neighbour, Russia, the USA might have built China up as a partner in the resolution of global issues and got it to temper competition simultanously. US politicians' handling China like an impertinent subordinate was only ever going to trigger defiance, which came in the form of 'wolf warrior' diplomacy, an undignified attempt to ape the behaviour of China's critics. We can, and must, do better.

For, it is China that is the country which, above all, the West needs to keep inside the order. Some predict a Cold War to replicate that between the USSR and USA of the last century, but China is much more significant, and its

---

474 https://www.genocidewatch.com/zh/single-post/genocide-emergency-saudi-arabia-and-the-war-in-yemen, accessed 181223.

economy much more integral to the world, than the USSR ever was. To avoid confrontation, the West – led by the USA, egged on by WISE – should engage 'in myriad negotiations: on arms control (urgently needed as China frantically builds up its forces in every domain); on trade; on technology transfers, climate change, and artificial intelligence; and on space. Like SALT, these negotiations would be protracted and tedious – and perhaps even inconclusive. But they would be the "meeting jaw to jaw" that British Prime Minister, Winston Churchill, generally preferred to war.'[475]

The Ukraine war – and President Trump's scepticism at the EU narrative and disenchantment with NATO - should have awoken us to the fact that, sooner or later, Europeans are going to have to defend themselves, rather than stick out their tongues at Russia while hiding behind the USA. [476] Peace on the European mainland matters much more to WISE than the South China Sea, which we can leave to Pacific powers to sort out. It is by no means a betrayal of Brexit for us to inspire all Europe to take defence seriously.

For our own survival, we need cooperative relations with all major powers – and we should work it so that they compete to have our friendship. The USA takes us for

---

[475] Ferguson, Niall (2024) 'Kissinger and the True Meaning of Détente' in *Foreign Affairs*, March/April 2024, p133

[476] Putin has already, in effect, subjugated Belarus; several Baltic and East European states are dependent upon Russian oil; Central Asian countries look to Russia for protection; the burgeoning alliance with Iran means Russia checks the USA throughout the Muslim world.

granted and consequently despises us; China is losing respect for us, and the EU despairs of us. To be taken seriously, we do not need to be a world military power, but we must have an economy and polity that do not put us at the mercy of others. In earlier centuries, as David Reynolds shows,[477] we compensated for our relative weakness by utilising the power of others and by intelligent diplomacy; we should revive this rather than hanker after special relationships.

A Rational and Humane Approach to Population Displacement

The world is witnessing mass movement of peoples, from poor lands and those ravaged by war, into countries perceived as successful. Some rich countries turn away would-be immigrants of any kind: Saudi Arabia, Kuwait, China and Japan. Some neighbours will only grant temporary residence to refugees. Many countries allow immigrants to be treated appallingly. Western Europeans have been the most generous but are now having to close the door as the numbers rise impossibly.

Immigration policy is as much a branch of international policy as of economic affairs. Before devising a policy to curtail immigration, WISE should understand what drives emigrants from other countries to seek a better life in WISE:

---

[477] Reynolds, David (2000) *Britannia Overruled, British Policy and World Power in the 20th Century* London: Pearson

- Longing for an open society in which talent can out
- Failure of home countries to provide opportunities
- Inadequate governance at home, violence and insecurity
- Global warming/environment

Understanding does not mean condoning. We don't want another 10 million people on these islands in the next ten years, as that could transform our society into the kind of place from which the new arrivals are fleeing, and because of the difficulties that another mass expansion will cause to housing, schooling, health and welfare services.

Diplomacy must be used to get agreement with other countries on what can be done about *population displacement* and to evoke an understanding of why we must curtail *immigration*.

Working with Others on Population Displacement

Those who flee from war zones would usually rather stay at home. Before 2011, Syria was, by Middle Eastern standards, for many, a safe and pleasant place to live, with a government that allowed minorities to thrive. Restoration of that may be impossible, but it should be attempted, if the millions of Syrian refugees are ever to be helped to return home.

The majority of would-be emigrants leave their homes because their countries are poor and do not provide work opportunities, let alone healthcare, decent education or security from arbitrary exploitation. In Muslim countries, many young males are unemployed, hanging around ready to be convinced by evil salesmen that they must set off for a Europe paved with gold, whether to seek their fortunes there or to punish it.

In such circumstances, it is in our interests to help the places from which they come, but not out of guilt. British colonialism improved the lot of many of the inhabitants of their colonies, and, in most cases, what came after independence, like what was before, was worse.

No, we have to help the poor countries because we recognise that life is unfair. WISE success was not because we were cleverer, but because our environment and circumstances made it possible for us to deploy such talents as we had. Look at how brilliantly emigrants from many defunct countries do when they leave them and get to an Anglophone environment. It was not the people that were at fault for failing to develop their countries, as much as it was the limitations of the conditions, compared to Europe. Many poor countries are stymied by their climates as much as by their politicians. WISE benefitted from competition with other Europeans. Island status protected us (and would do in North America and Australasia!), and our family form primed us. We developed pragmatic attitudes, curiosity and enterprise, while countries in inhospitable environments remained mired in religious superstition and fatalism.

In other words, the disadvantages of the poor are not of their own making any more than were our advantages. If we do not help them, now that they, thanks to global media, know exactly how much more comfortable we are, they will come to share in our good fortune, whether we like it or not. Landes puts it thus: 'They will seek to take what they cannot make; if they cannot earn by exporting commodities, they will export people. In short, wealth is an irresistible magnet, and poverty is a potentially raging contaminant: it cannot be segregated, and our peace and prosperity depend in the long run on the well-being of others.'[478]

It matters very much to Europeans that we help North African countries develop. If they transform as Malaysia and Indonesia have transformed, their young people will not need to flee to Europe and on to WISE. Those countries will be a bulwark between us and the explosion of the African population. By 2100, there will be 4.5 billion people in Africa.[479]

So, the first step is to work out with the big players—China, Russia, the USA, the EU—what we can do together. Our diplomats should be convincing China and Russia that failed states, the extension of militant religion and vast population movements are dangers to them too. In his *Bottom Billion,* Paul Collier has proposed a strategy for the G-8.[480]

---

[478] Landes (1998) *The Wealth and Poverty of Nations*, pXX

[479] Mahbubani, *Has the West Lost It?* (2019) p64

[480] Collier, Paul (2008) *The Bottom Billion: Why the Poorest Countries are Failing and What Can Be Done About It* Oxford: OUP. Thanks to John Lloyd (email 141023) for this. For more, see https://www.cgdev.org/publication/helping-bottom-billion-there-third-way-development-debate#:~:text=The%20centerpiece%20of%20

Acting on Our Commoners' Fears about Emigration

Alarm at emigration is not confined to any particular WISE group. Racism is not necessarily involved, for mass immigration causes anxiety as much to recent immigrants and asylum seekers as to long-established communities. All honest people can see that no country, especially one that wants to be a welfare state and egalitarian, can easily cope with a 20% increase in population. And now, another 20% is on track.

'Immigration' describes those coming to the UK with the intention of settlement, legally or illegally and includes 'family members' of those already here. It should not include students or people deliberately recruited into sophisticated jobs, as identified in the industrial strategy.

Policy Directions:

- A total moratorium on immigration until we have addressed the problems caused by the failings of the current system of monitoring and control.
- Illegal immigrants must never be accepted. Boats are to be intercepted before docking, and travellers are to be put on ships bound for overseas processing centres to await repatriation. Other holding centres to be created.
- Countries contiguous to those in crisis to be helped to take more migrants/refugees.

Collier's%20argument,politics%2C%20and%20international%20investment)%2C, accessed 171023.

- International collaborations to improve the economies, and therefore the life chances, of the populations from which emigrants are surging.
- Actions against people smugglers stepped up; information about our rejection of illegal immigration to be distributed widely.
- Permanent residence and citizenship to be made difficult to obtain; benefits to those who have not yet contributed to the economy, curtailed.
- Strategy for the rejuvenation of the northern and midland 'left-behind' areas to include incentives to relocate there and to set up businesses.

Summary of Development, Democracy, Diplomacy

WISE needs politicians who think ahead about how future generations will survive in a world in which other nations hold many vital cards. Like Yan Fu, the Greenwich cadet nearly two centuries ago, we can see that the world has changed forever and that we must adapt.

Because of our unique identity as the inventor and disseminator of the ideas which are setting humanity free, how we are matters, even if our economic and military strength is limited. We cannot be a positive influence, if we do not revitalise our economy and restore good governance.

WISE needs leaders who will keep us out of global battles between economic and cultural rivals and muster our resources for the planetary issues; climate change, environmental degradation, terrorism, the proliferation of weapons of mass destruction and mass emigration, and the fallout from failed polities. WISE's role in their solution is to stimulate, inspire and motivate. We should condemn the recent past as aberrations from our history and moral instincts and stand by our identity as the revolutionary nations and Thought Leaders to the world.

Before we can do that, we must sort out our economy, the foundation of our cultural and political life. That may be impossible until we have cleaned up the culture of governance. For this we need leaders who can kick into action those who, supposedly, work for us, leaders who don't care about conformity or convention but will buckle down to getting things done; toss liberal or statist ideology aside in order to move heaven and earth to put WISE to rights. We need those who have vision for humanity and for our place in it, who believe in the *Revolutionary Nations* and know who we are. So will the world, after our Sixth Revolution.

Acknowledgements

I make no claims of originality for this book. All the interpretations of our history derive from the scholarship of recent historians, cited. So, too, do the points about our economies. The proposals for our politics are often those of predecessors. My claim for this book is to have assembled, in a reasonably accessible form, opinions of, and prescriptions for, our nations that have been swirling about the public sphere for a generation. I absorbed them from the media and the ether, and then cogitated. Early versions of some of the sections were published on the *Briefings for Britain* website.

I have found it difficult to be short. I wanted to digress and explain other people's ideas in detail but have instead used the footnotes to advertise books and websites which do. A list of books, courtesy of Julie Helliwell, from which I have drawn inspiration, is on my website, http://hugodeburgh.com/

Conversations have been very helpful, and I list here those interlocutors who were so good as either to talk or to correspond with me, or even to read bits of the emerging manuscript and comment. None necessarily agree with me, but I thank them all.

Maddie Anstruther, Ross Baglin, James Bartholomew, William Beaufoy, Jeremy Black, Liam Byrne, Vince Cable, Andrew Cahn, Ben Cobley, Paul Collier, William Coulson, Mark Davies, Ruth Dudley-Edwards, Clementine Ebel, David Goodhart, Angus Hanton, Hermann Hauser, Kevin Hickson, Isabel Hilton, Mary Hodge, Daniel Hodges, Frank Ledwidge, Alice Leigh, Oliver Letwin, Rod Liddle, John Lloyd, Mark Logan, Alan MacFarlane, Colin Mayer, Alastair Mellon, John Mills, Ferdinand Mount, Patrick O'Flynn, Trevor Phillips, Matt Ridley, Michael Schluter, Arthur Snell, Gareth Stanton, Gisela Stuart, Aleks Szczerbiak, Robert Tombs, David Willetts, Joanna Williams, Christopher Woodhead.

As always, I wish to thank my colleagues at China UK Creative Industries for their support and, in particular, Guo Xu, who has borne many fardels for me during the preparation of my books. The team at Publishing Push has been very helpful to a neophyte in the world of independent publishing and demonstrated that they are at least as effective as the traditional publishers of my previous books.

As I wrote and revised, I always tried to heed the warnings of two great observers of the human condition. Let me share them with you:

O wad some pow'r the giftie gie us
To see oursels as ithers see us!

Rabbie Burns, *To a Louse*

假作真時真亦假， 無為有處有還無
Truth becomes fiction when the fiction's true;
Real becomes unreal where the unreal's real.

Cao Xueqin, *Dream of the Red Chamber*

About the Author

Hugo 'Huge' de Burgh is Director of *China UK Creative Industries @Goldsmiths College*, University of London. He started working life on night shift in an Ipswich food factory, then went on to be a community development worker in impoverished areas of Scotland. Activism led him into broadcast journalism, focussing on poverty, undereducation and employability, and then to teaching journalism in Nottingham, in London and in China. He recently completed a fourth term at Tsinghua University, as Walt Disney Professor of Media and Communications in *Schwarzman,* the US college of international relations.

Huge has founded and run three successful businesses and a charity, and has authored or co-authored 15 books. His *China's Media in the Emerging World Order* (2020) describes and analyses a burgeoning global power of the 21st century. *Investigative Journalism* (2021) tracks the emergence of new tools and techniques for holding power to account and maps emerging models of global cross -border collaboration and exposure. Earlier books have dealt with environment reporting, how China works and the functions of journalists in the globalised, digitised, world. His first novel, *TO THE RIVER, why would you risk your life, and all that you love, for a stranger?* was published in 2024. It is a reflection on altruism, set in warn-torn Italy, 1943.

Milton Keynes UK
Ingram Content Group UK Ltd.
UKHW022013300724
446318UK00010B/198